WANDERLUST INK

300 FINE LINE TATTOO DESIGNS INSPIRED BY NATURE AND LIFE ON THE ROAD

OLLIE SMITHER

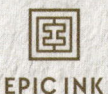

EPIC INK

CONTENTS

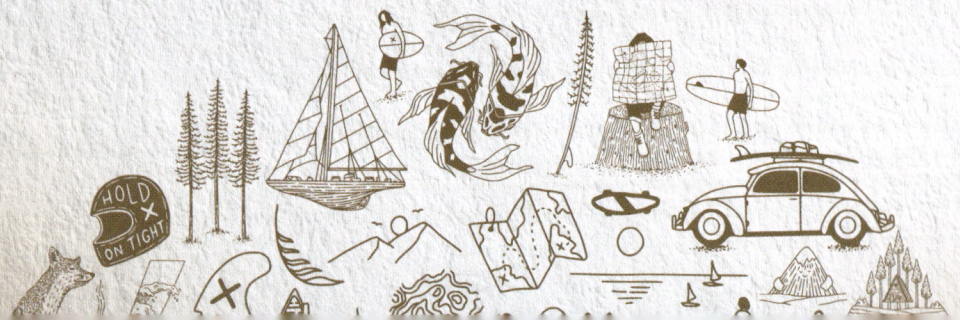

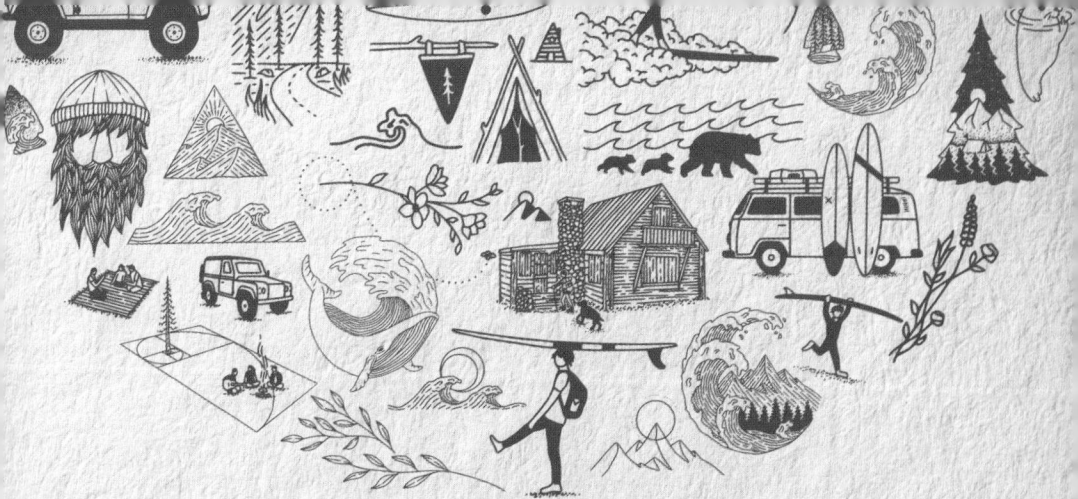

INTRODUCTION

Hey, I'm Ollie Smither. I'm a fine line artist and tattoo designer from Devon, UK. Since 2020, I've been using illustrations to share my ideas, sketches, and feelings, and this book is a collection of those creations.

I spend about half the year traveling in a camper van, complete with my dog, Tucker, a surfboard, and everything else we need for a good adventure. I love the outdoors and am heavily inspired by the adventures and trips I take, discovering majestic waves, hidden trails, and secret parks in quiet places surrounded by nature. The rest of the year, we are at home in a cottage in Devon, spending the days drawing, surfing, hiking, and swimming. This lifestyle gives me the best of both worlds; all these moments shape my work, and this book is filled with designs that have grown out of these experiences.

A lot were sketched quickly in a notebook during an excursion; others came to life back in the studio. In all, I focus on clean, simple, fine-line, hand-drawn designs. I don't aim to be flashy or complex. My art, like my outdoor adventures, is down to earth. I find this style makes my illustrations feel more natural and almost rustic, like the adventures that created them. It's a way of honoring the inspiration behind each piece, whether a pine tree, tent, or mountain range. And I find a lot of value in keeping my gear light, both on the road and in the studio. That's probably why fine line illustration suits me best. It feels still, like a reflection. It's a way of keeping things real.

I've been drawing as long as I can remember. It's helped me make sense of the world. My mother is very artistic, and art was encouraged in our house. At school, I only took artistic subjects, and I excelled in them. I really enjoyed the creative process, whether that was painting, 3-D modelling, or sketching, and those experiences, too, have shaped my work.

I lost touch with drawing for a few years while I went to university, but I reconnected with it about five years ago when I started sketching in my van, little drawings inspired by memories or things I saw on the road. I shared them online without thinking too much about it, with the aim of documenting my work. To my surprise, people really connected with my little drawings. One thing led to another, and people started requesting my drawings for tattoos. I began doing free commissions to get my name out there, from tattoo designs to logos and anything that came through the door. As my portfolio grew, so did my audience. I opened a shop and started selling prints, stickers, and T-shirts, until my business grew into something bigger than I could ever have imagined. But I'm a big believer in the idea that everything happens for a reason. I was always told I would never make a living from art, and I think I proved all those naysayers wrong. They say if you do something you love, you'll never work a day in your life, but I wouldn't say my job is never work. There are long days and challenging projects. But I love what I do, and the experiences this path has given me are ones I'll cherish forever. The fact that I get to earn a living from doing something that started off as a hobby on a tiny makeshift desk in my bedroom is something I'm grateful for every day. I never know where my next project will come from, and I appreciate that freedom and the freedom of illustration—there are no limits, just my pen.

I have now created over one thousand illustrations, three hundred of which are collected here. This body of work includes commissions and logos for outdoor brands, small businesses, and lifestyle labels; I've met some incredible people on this journey. Collaborating with incredible companies and fellow artists on physical products is one of my favorite types of project—it's such a rewarding process.

But more than anything, what I love most is drawing meaningful tattoos for people (though I have no tattoos myself, which just shows how organic and accidental this business has been). Designing something that someone will carry with them every day is just incredible, and I feel lucky that people love my art enough to put it on their bodies—there's something magical about seeing my artwork on people's skin. I feel lucky to be part of their lives.

When I design tattoos and work with clients, the first step is always to hear their story and think about how to balance it with detail and placement. I consider this when I'm designing art for myself too. A great design has a great story behind it.

I've approached this book in the same way. You'll find a lot of my work circles back to themes of nature and through it, connection. I think there's something timeless about these subjects that everyone can relate to, and I hope that my work inspires people to get outside more—nature is so good for us.

As my story continues, I hope to grow as a tattoo artist. I want to keep learning, drawing, traveling, and finding ways to express myself through my art, as well as inspiring others, whether that's through a print or a T-shirt.

This book is a piece of that journey. A collection of designs made along the way. Some are playful, some are thoughtful, but all of them are inspired by the great outdoors and its simplicity. I hope you enjoy perusing it as much as I've enjoyed making it. And maybe, if one of these pieces finds its way onto your skin or into your home, it will become a part of your journey, too.

Thanks for being here.

Ollie

TATTOO TOKENS

Tattooing is a deeply personal art form, and when someone wears a piece I've drawn, I want it to feel true, considered, and fair. If you find a design in this book that speaks to you, something you'd love to carry on your skin, I'm so glad it connected. That's what this book is all about. I've put it together with the hope that it will be shared, loved, and used—but always respectfully.

If you'd like to use one of these illustrations as a tattoo, all I ask is that you please don't copy or lift the artwork without supporting the artist. Instead, support the work by purchasing a tattoo token from my online shop. You'll find a QR code below that'll take you straight there. It's a small gesture, a donation, that helps keep this creative life going. It means I can keep drawing, traveling, creating, and sharing new work. And it means you're honoring the time and care that went into every line.

If you would like a custom design or have seen something in the book that you'd like to change slightly, I'd be happy to help. Just reach out through my website or Instagram and we can chat. I love working with people to shape something unique, something that tells their story as much as it holds my style.

So, if one of these designs speaks to you, scan the code, buy a token, and know that you're doing the right thing. Thank you for supporting independent artists. Thank you for supporting me. It means more than I can say.

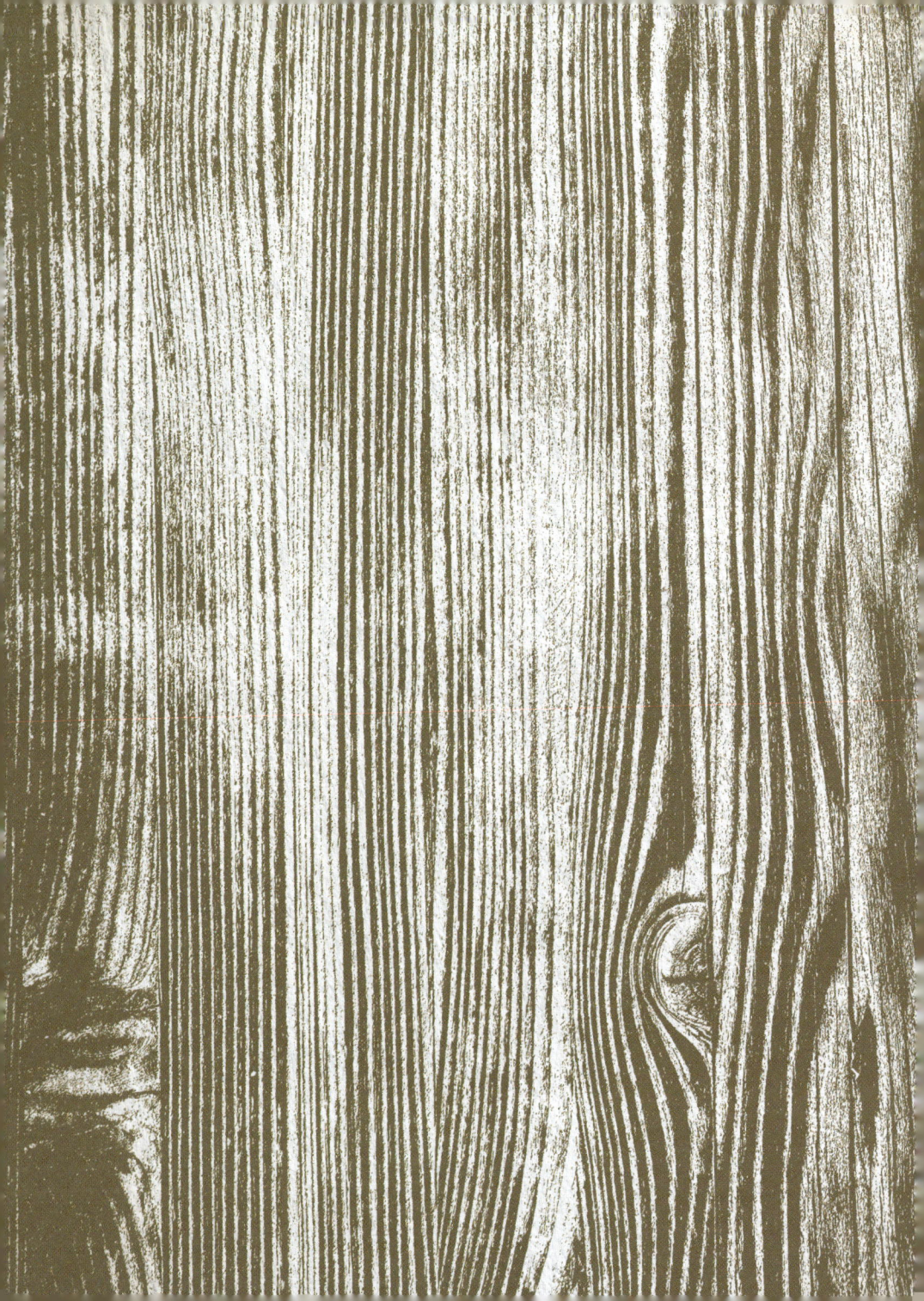

CHAPTER 1

THE GEOMETRY OF NATURE

I find a lot of joy and relaxation in drawing minimal, geometric illustrations. I've always been drawn to simple shapes—triangles, squares, circles—and find they complement the shapes and simplicity I find in nature. The figures always come randomly to me, and sketching out the repetitive forms and patterns feels meditative. They're one of my favorite things to draw.

A lot of these designs started as small experiments in my sketchbook but now make up some of my most popular tattoos. These pieces possess a timeless feel that works well for that purpose. They're a quiet nod to nature and all the details that go unnoticed.

This chapter is for anyone who is also drawn to balance or simplicity. For anyone who finds calm and a sense of grounding in clean, simple designs—and in the natural world. And like art, and nature, often do, these pieces are intended to leave space for the viewer to bring their own meaning. I hope you love them as much as I do.

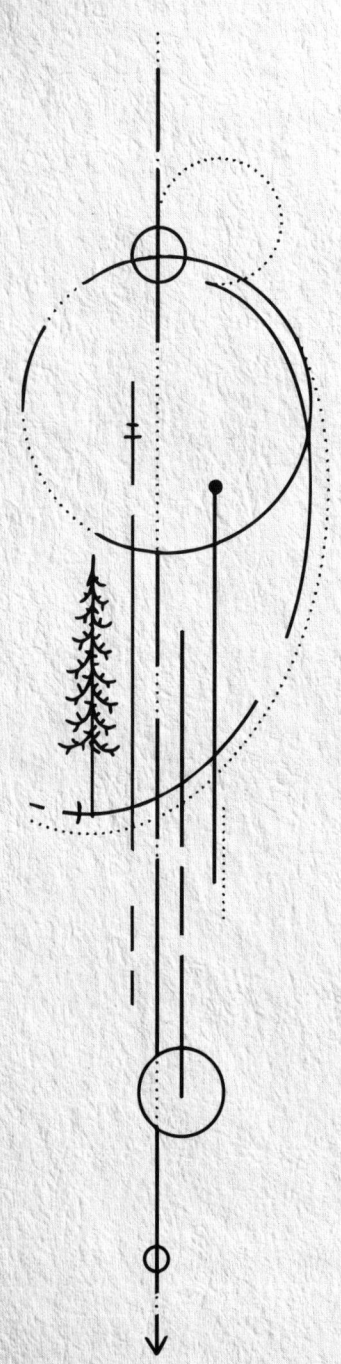

PINE LINE

A single pine stands tall, encircled by rings like ripples of light, moon, and sun. Nature feels infinite in its simplicity. Every line echoes balance: wildness and stillness, growth and quiet strength. In one tree, you see a whole universe of time.

"ADOPT THE PACE OF NATURE: HER SECRET IS PATIENCE."
– RALPH WALDO EMERSON

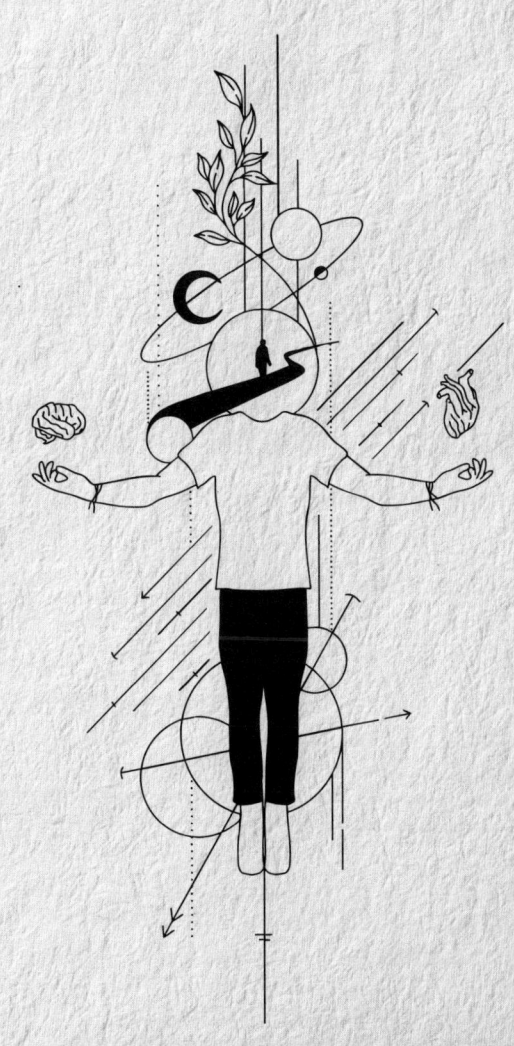

BALANCED

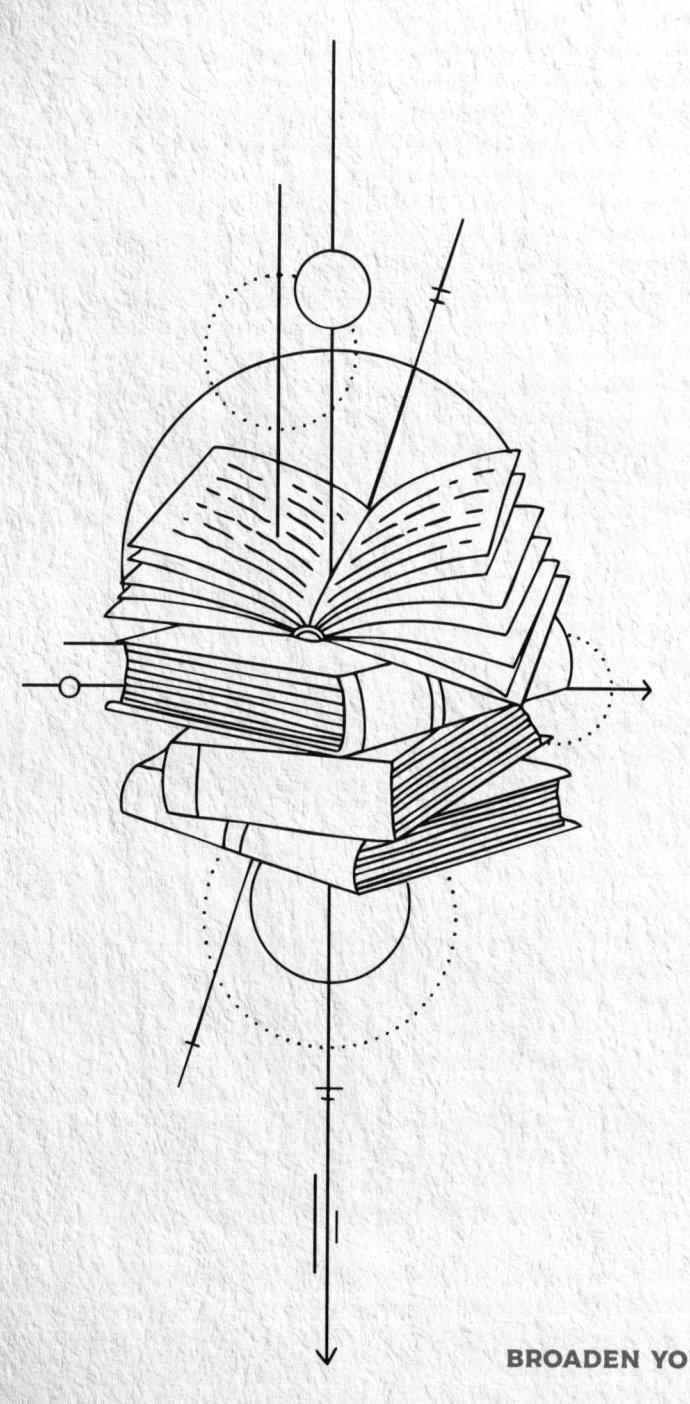

BROADEN YOUR HORIZON

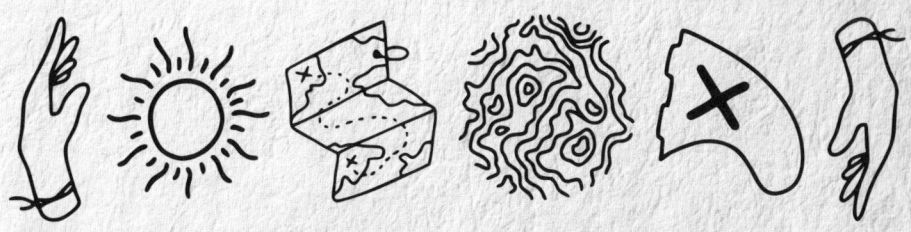

SIMPLE PLEASURE

Symbols travel the sun. A map, an X marking the spot rest between open hands. They remind us that adventure isn't far away. It's always waiting. Journeys can be grand or small, but joy lies in wandering, discovering, and holding space for possibility in your hands.

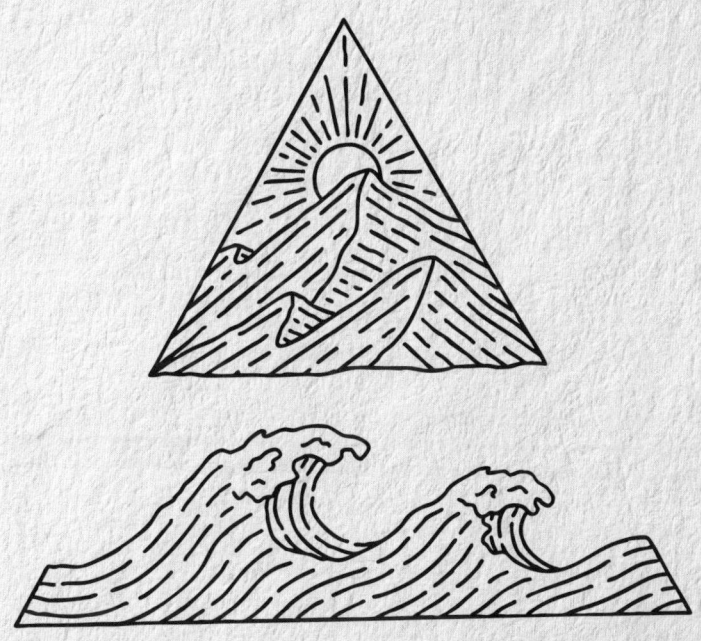

SOLID FOUNDATIONS

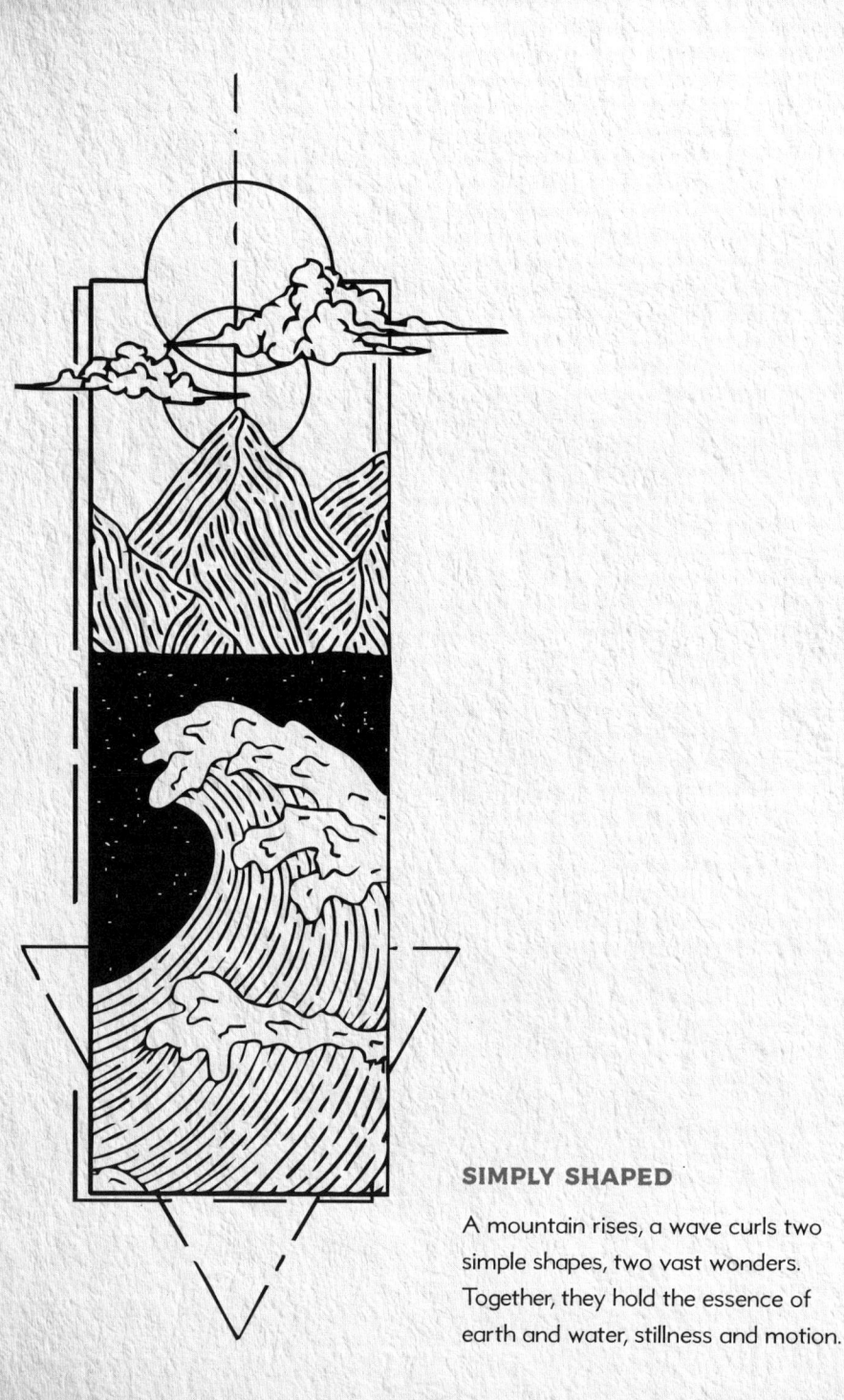

SIMPLY SHAPED

A mountain rises, a wave curls two
simple shapes, two vast wonders.
Together, they hold the essence of
earth and water, stillness and motion.

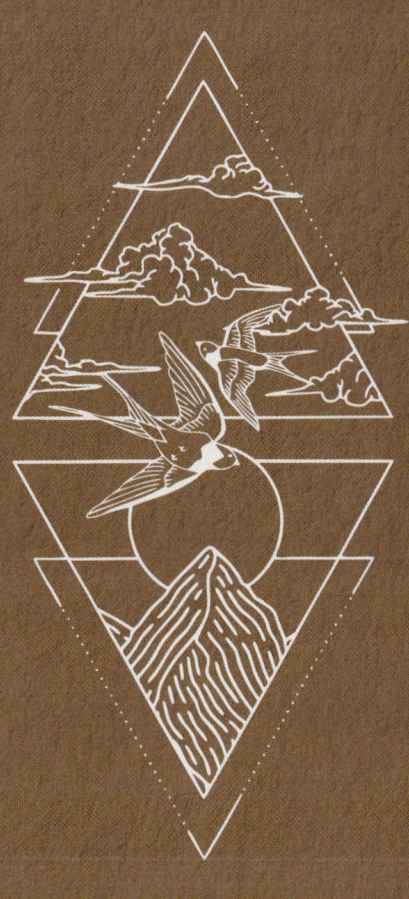

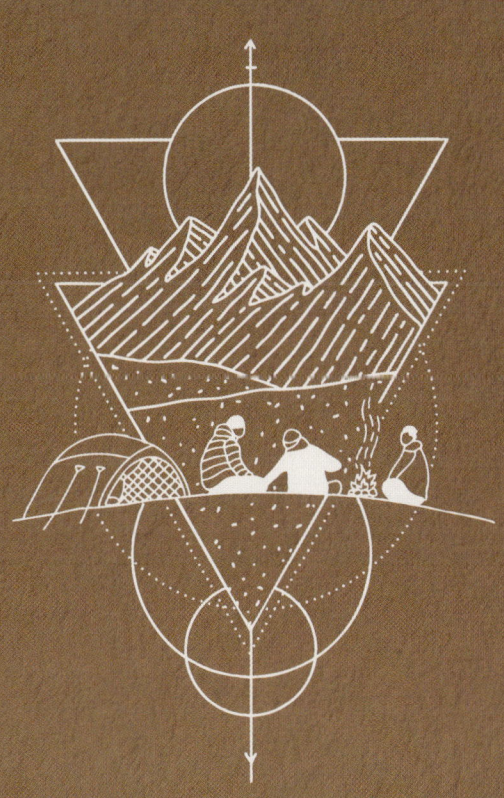

BOUND BY NATURE

Phases of the moon circle a pine tree,
waves crest with white caps, the sun
rests over a mountain. All these voices
speak at once: forest, sea, sky, and
stone. Together they remind us; the
wild hums like music.

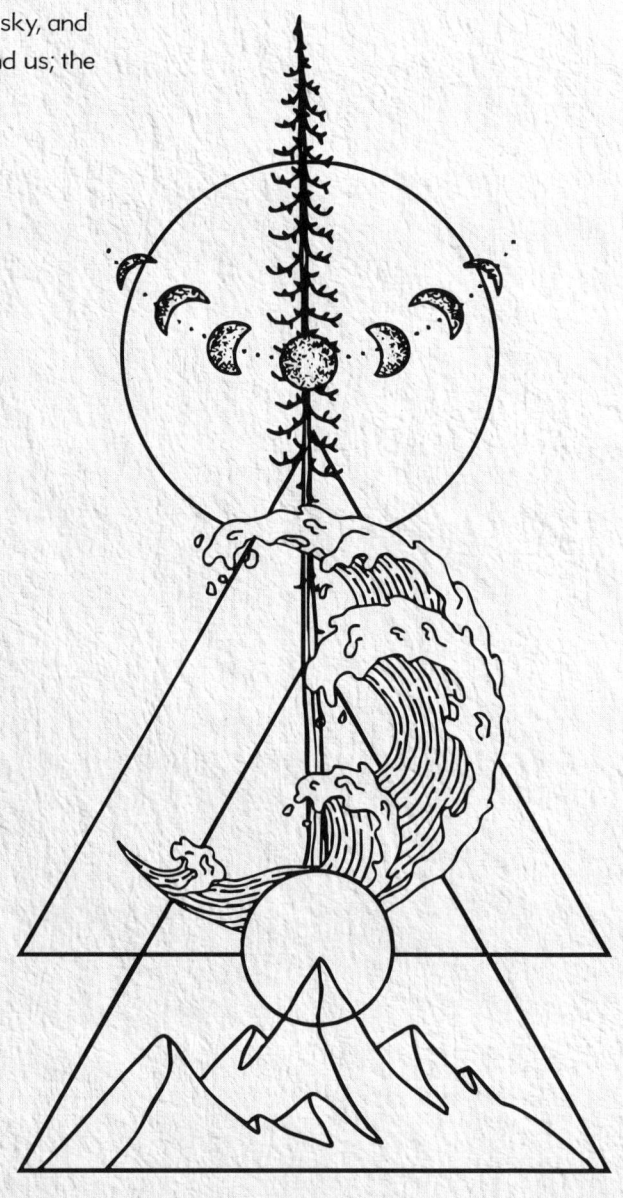

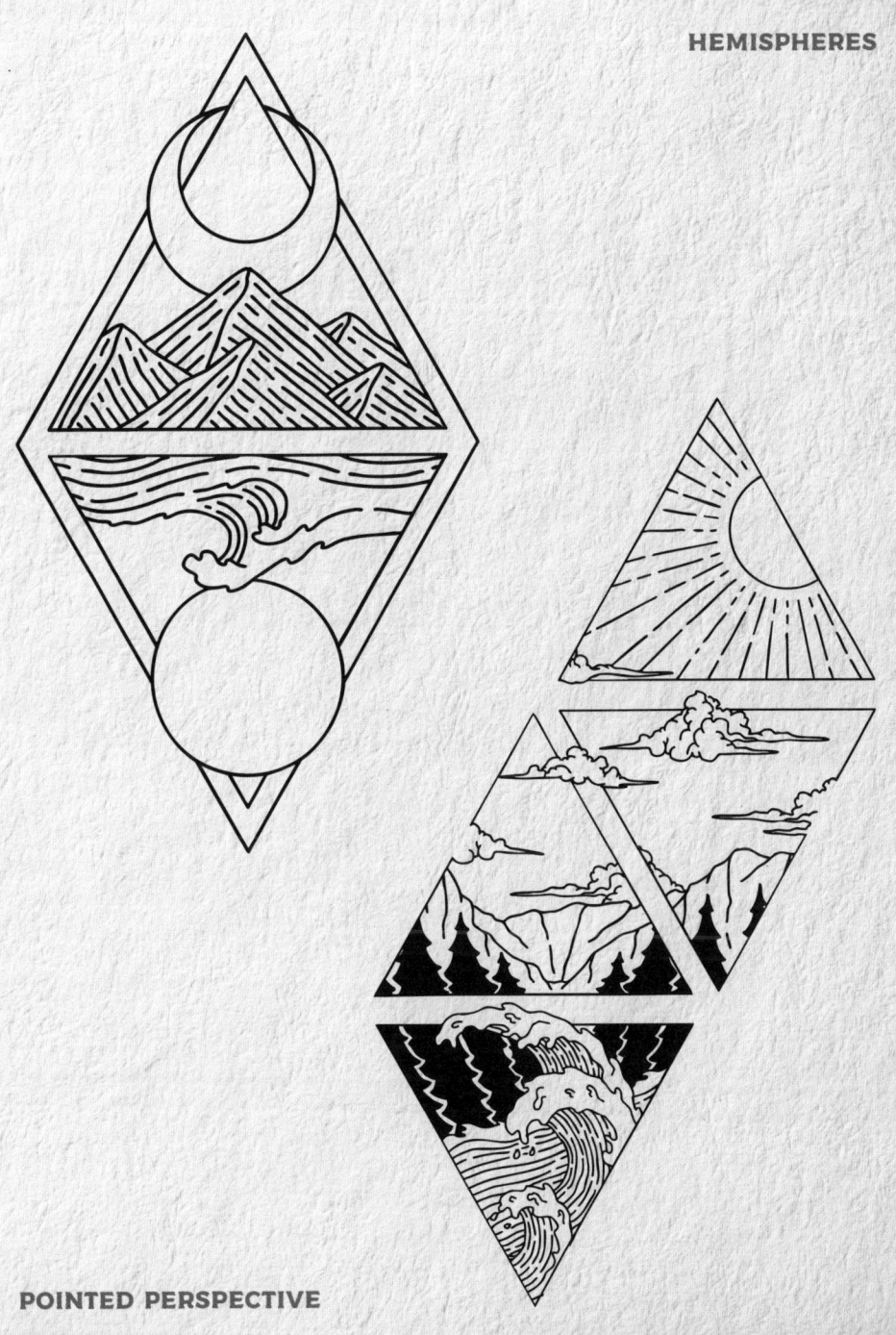

POINTED PERSPECTIVE

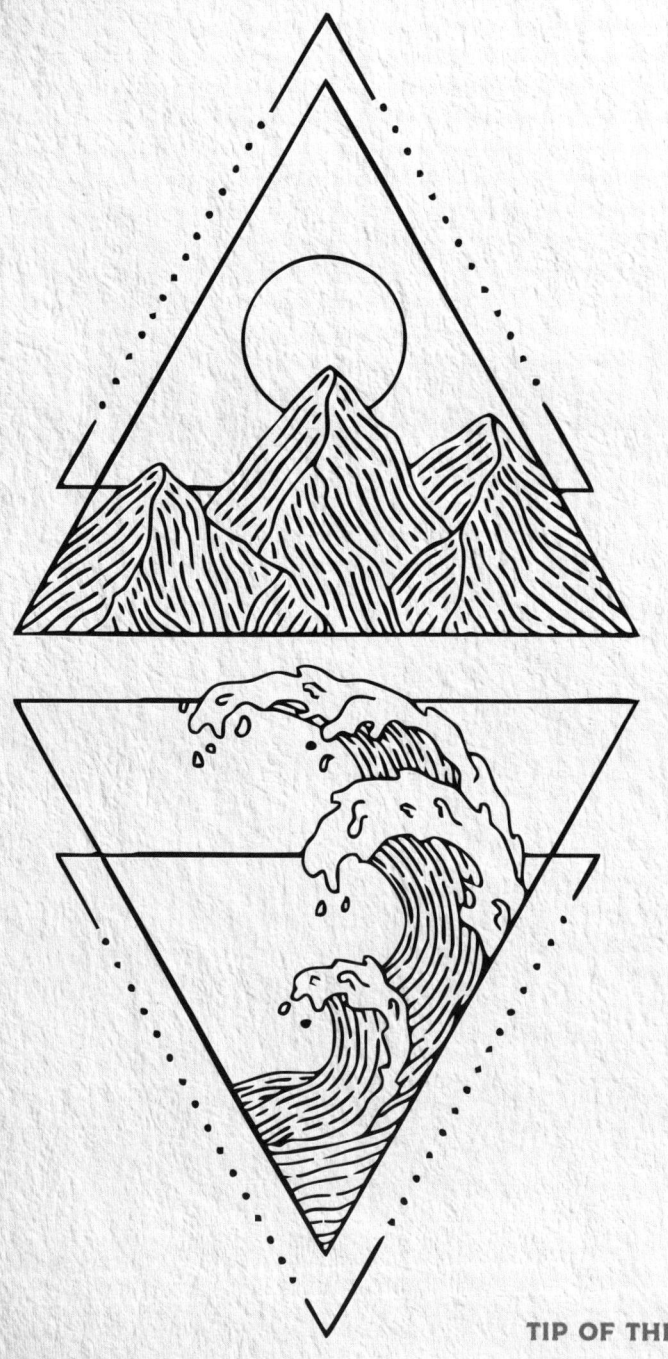

TIP OF THE ADVENTURE

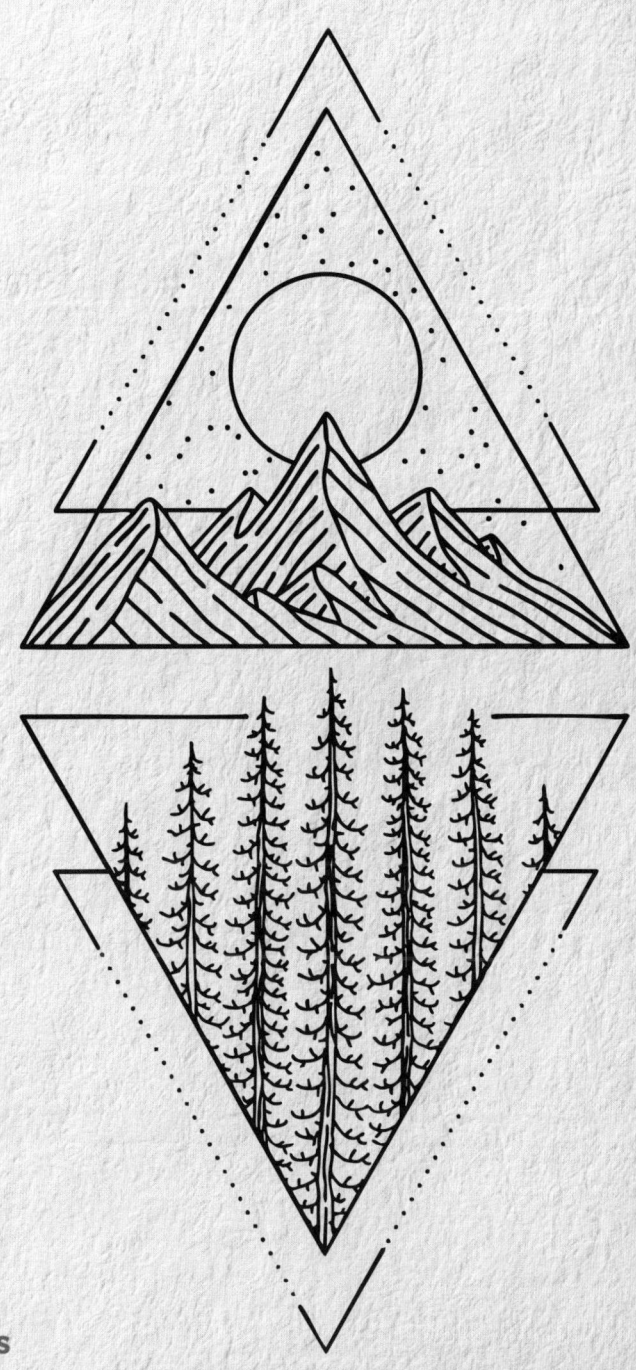

PEAKS TO PINES

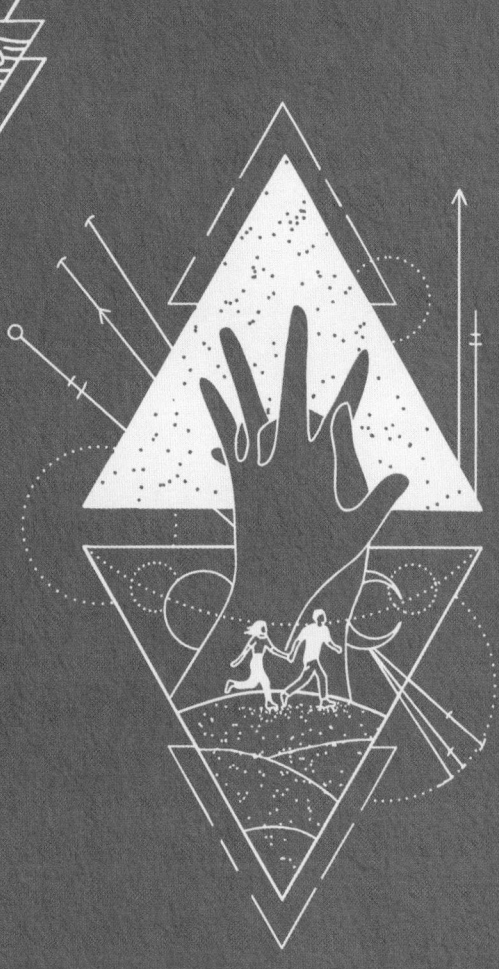

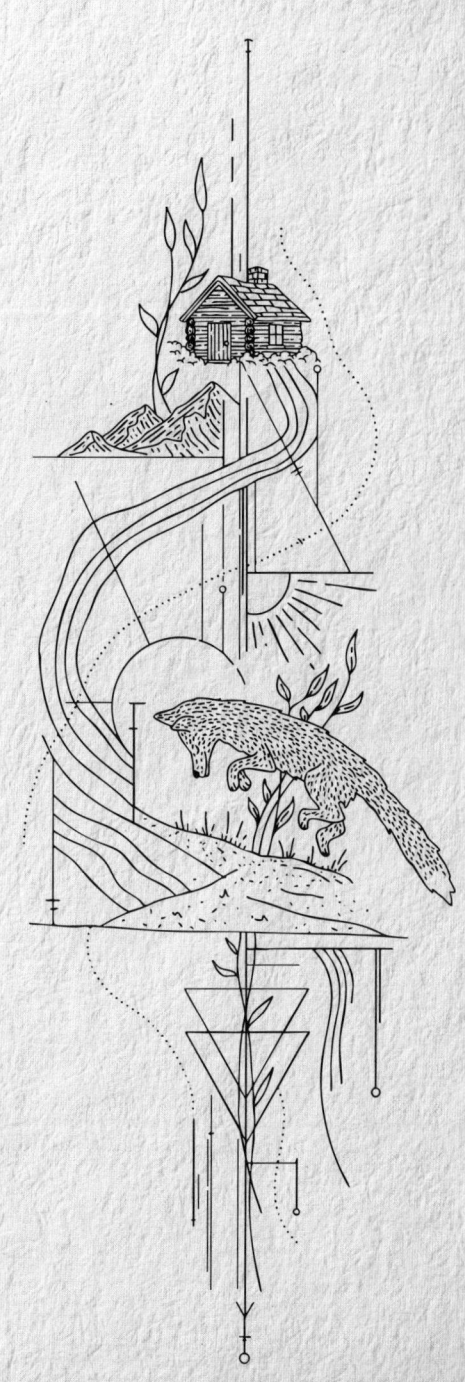

FOX TRAIL

A fox wanders past a cabin, beneath
the moon, toward the sun. The fox
carries curiosity with every step,
reminding us that paths can be quiet,
mysterious, and full of wonder if we
follow them gently.

"NATURE DOES NOT HURRY, YET EVERYTHING IS ACCOMPLISHED."
– LAO TZU

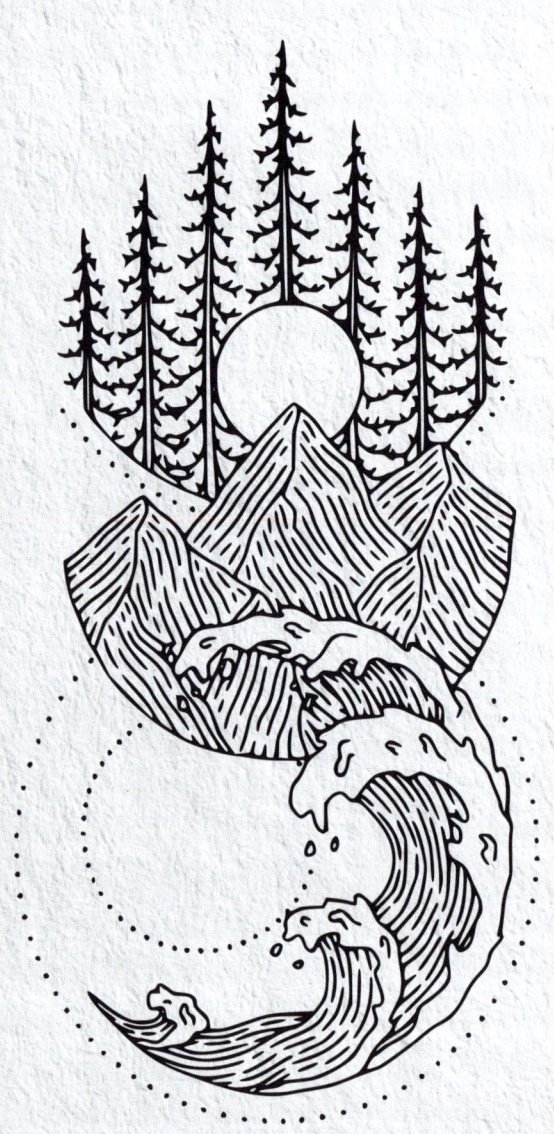

SNOW POINT

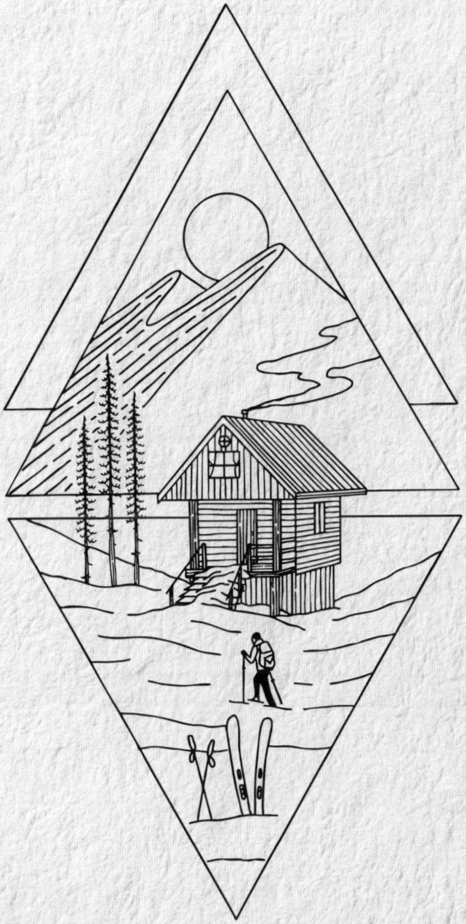

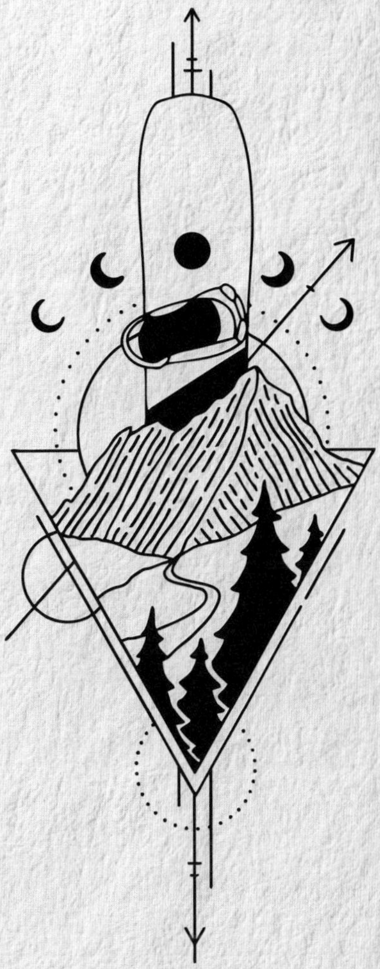

ALPINE ASCENT

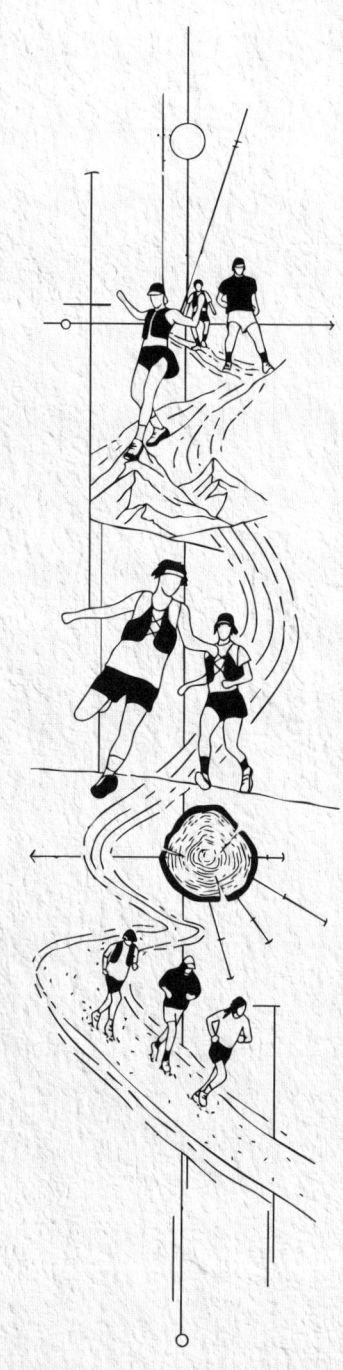

MARATHON

Runners move across an abstract
path, the sun shining, nature unfolding
around them. Each stride a story of
endurance and freedom. The trail
carries them through landscapes both
real and imagined.

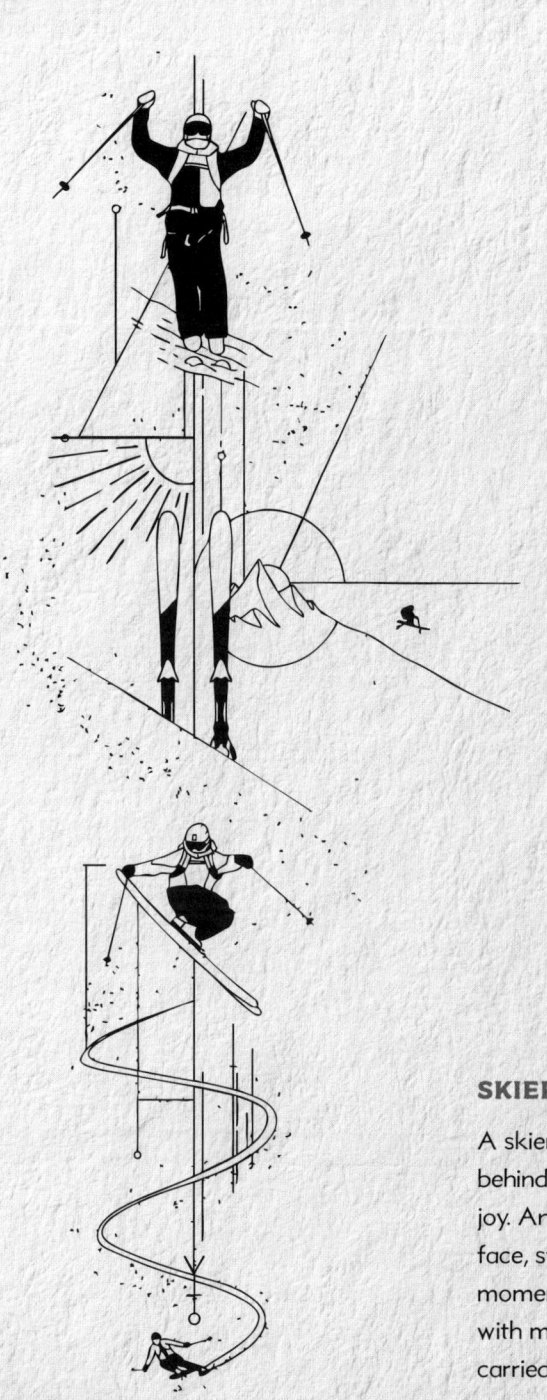

SKIERS' PARADISE

A skier leaps into the air, sun glowing
behind, snow scattering like sparks of
joy. Another carves down a mountain's
face, swift and free. In these fleeting
moments, winter feels endlessly alive
with movement and the rush of being
carried by snow and light at once.

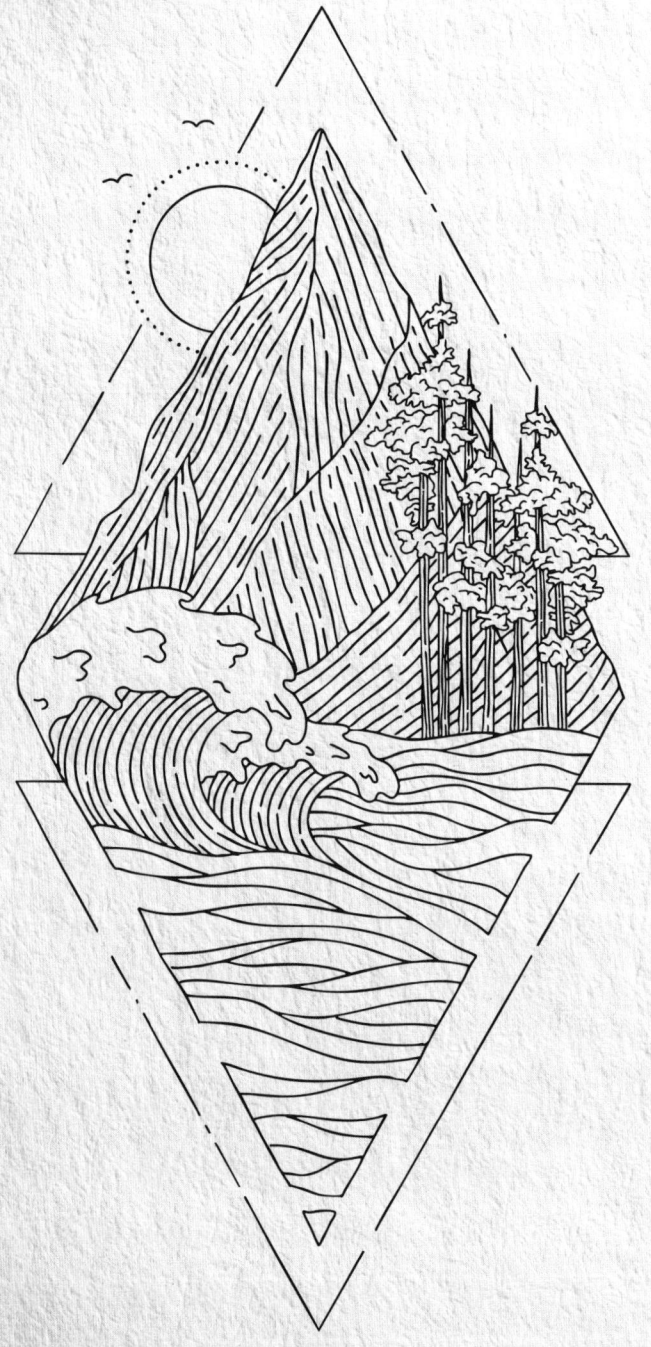

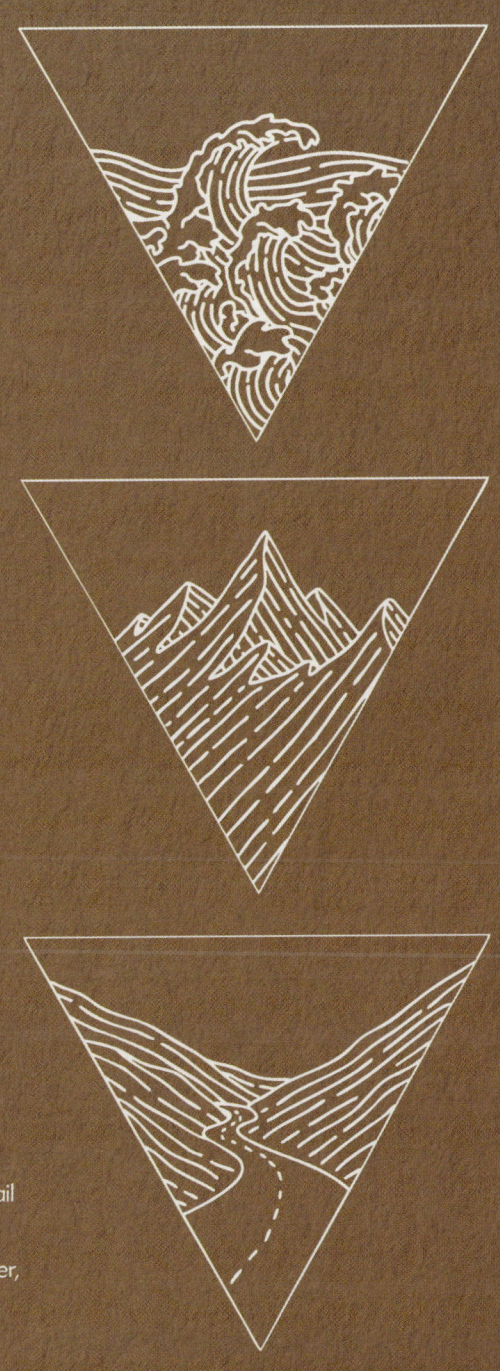

TRIANGLE TRAIL

A wave, a mountain, a road winding
between two hills—three shapes
forming a triangle of journeys. The trail
isn't fixed; it can be water, stone, or
earth. Wherever you choose to wander,
the path becomes your own, carrying
you exactly where you need to go.

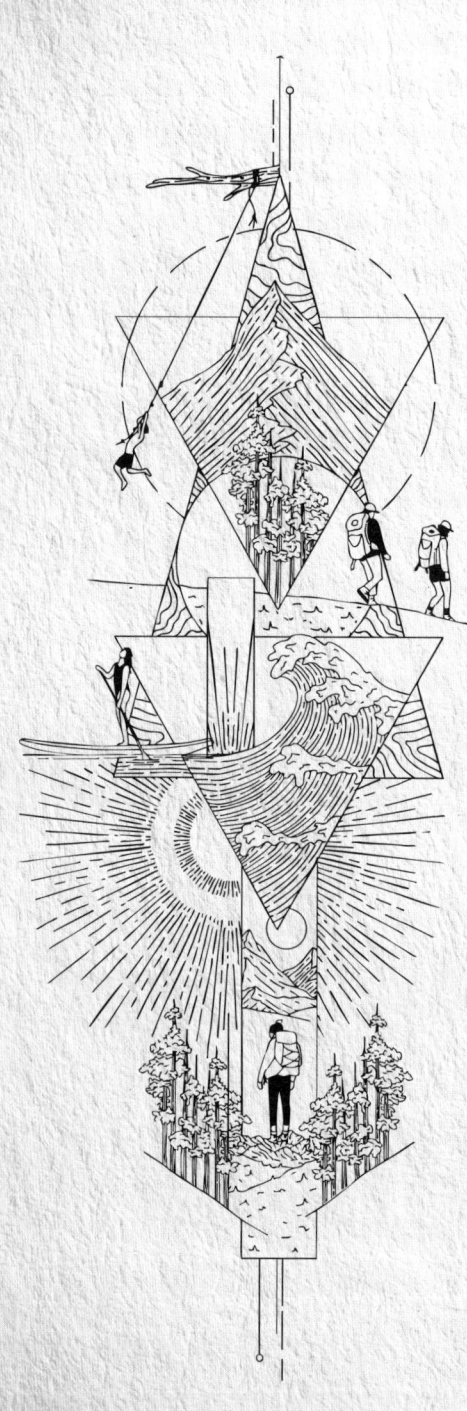

ULTIMATE ADVENTURE

An abstract landscape unfolds hikers on winding trails, climbers scaling rock, wanderers by the sea, travelers under trees. Together, they tell us that the greatest adventures aren't about one place, they're about moving through them all.

WILDER LINES

A mountain, a wave, the sun, a
butterfly, a plant all drawn as one
flowing design. Nature's threads
connect and intertwine earth, air,
water, growth, and light. These lines
remind us that we're never separate
from the wild. It lives in us.

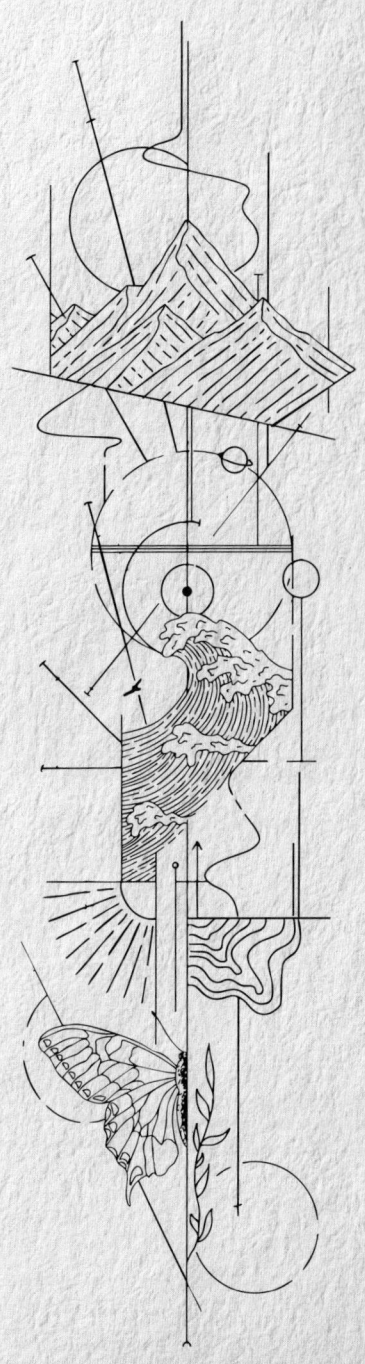

CHAPTER 2

EXPEDITION READY

Strangely, I love packing a backpack for an adventure. There's something really cool about having everything you need right there with you on your shoulders or in your van. About packing your supplies with care, choosing what to bring and what to leave. These aren't just things, they're part of the experience. They hold memories and miles.

The pieces in this collection reflect the tools that help us move forward and embrace the unknown and the adventures that result.

They're for the ones who take joy and find calm in the small rituals of packing and preparing, knowing they're ready for what comes next. I hope they inspire you to chart your own course, whether for a big expedition, long journey, or everyday adventure.

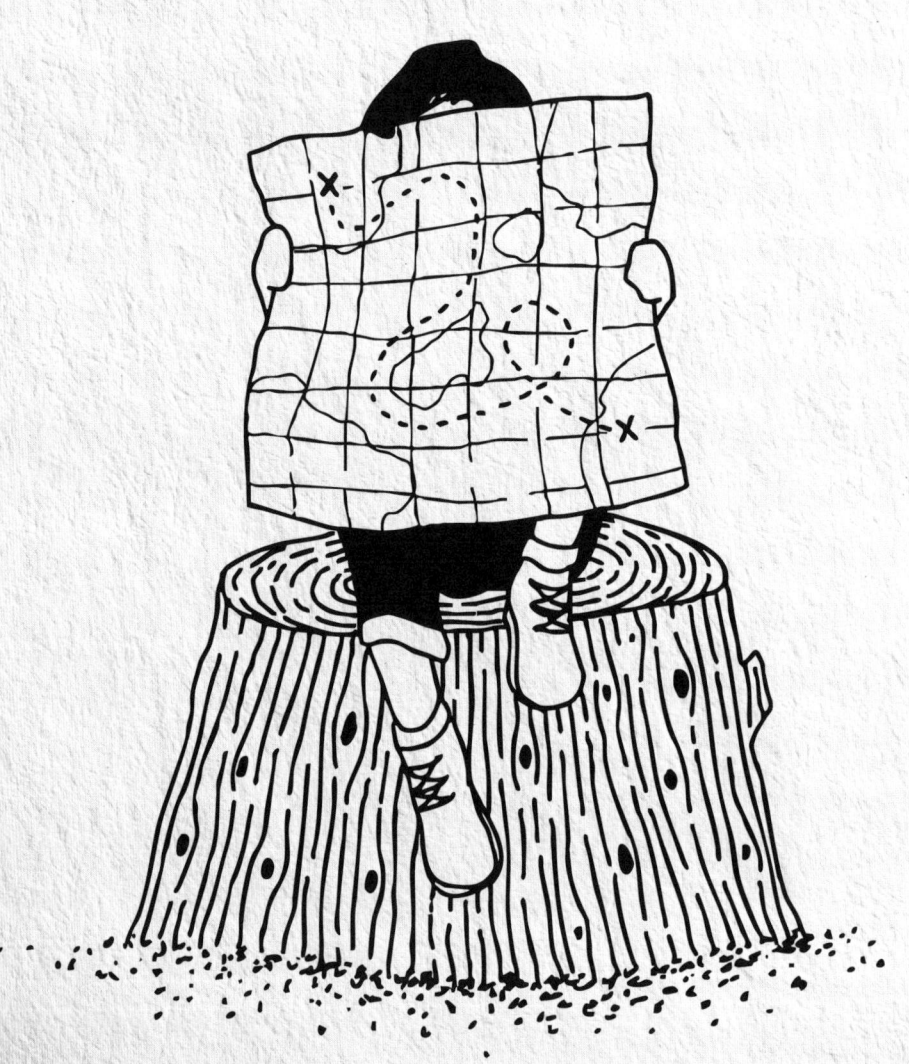

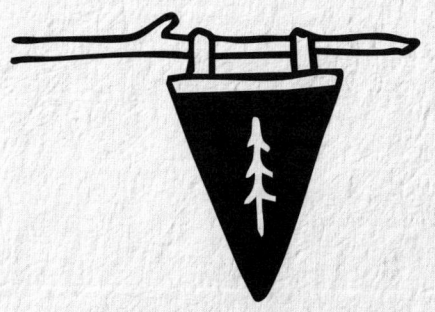

WILD SIGN

A branch holds a small pennant, marked with a single tree. It feels childlike and welcoming, as though pointing the way toward adventure. Simple symbols like these remind us that the forest doesn't need much to speak, it invites you with charm and curiosity.

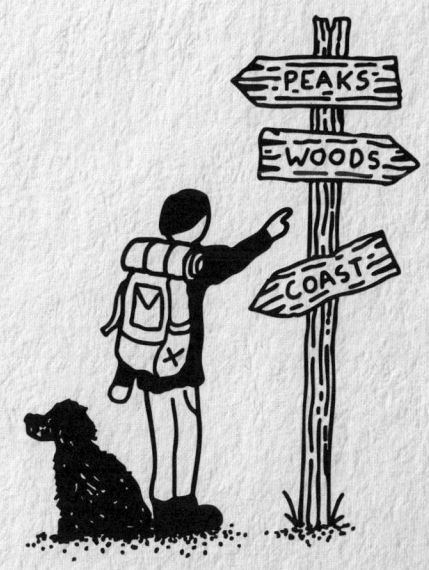

WAYPOINT

A hiker stands with a dog at a crossroads of signs. Peaks in one direction, woods in another, coast in the third. The hiker looks one way, the dog another. Every trail is an invitation, and sometimes the hardest part is choosing where the story begins.

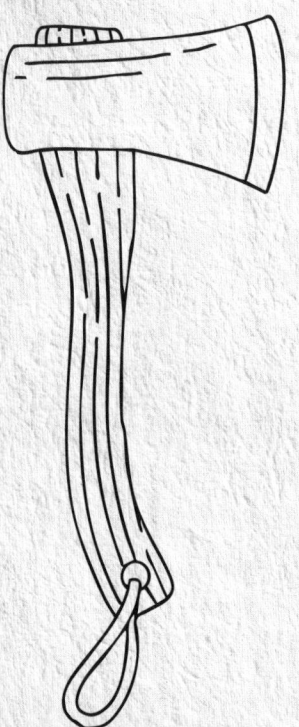

LOG SPLITTER

An axe hangs ready, its leather loop resting easy, drawn with quiet detail. More than a tool, it feels like a companion of cabins and firewood, the scent of pine and smoke.

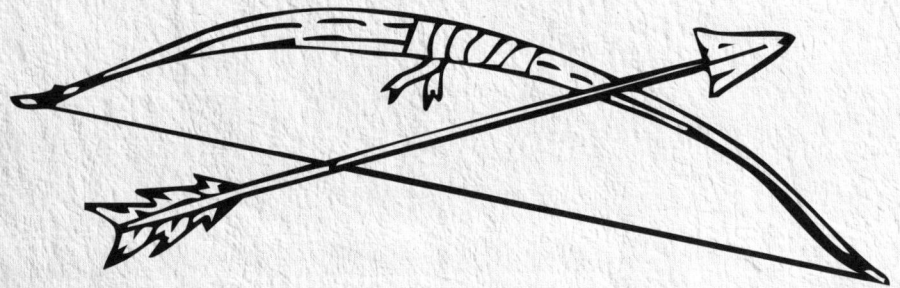

TAKE YOUR SHOT

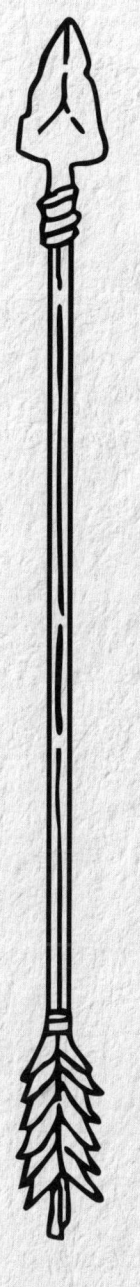

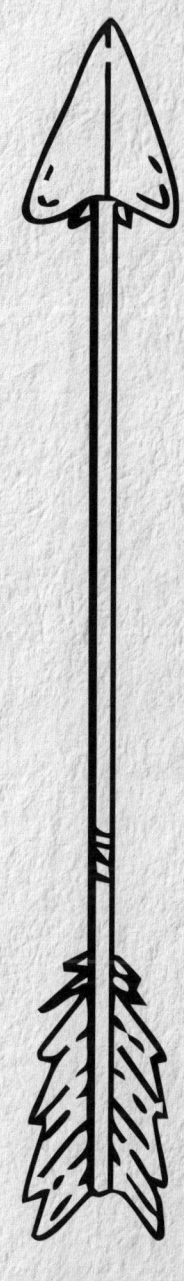

RUSTIC ARROW

WILD ARROW

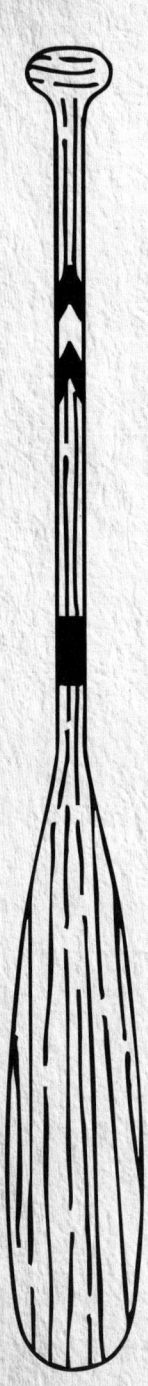

OAR DRIFT

A single oar, carved with care, rests in detail. Its handle holds a design that feels both personal and timeless, like a story etched into wood. It speaks of rivers and lakes waiting quietly.

SET SAIL

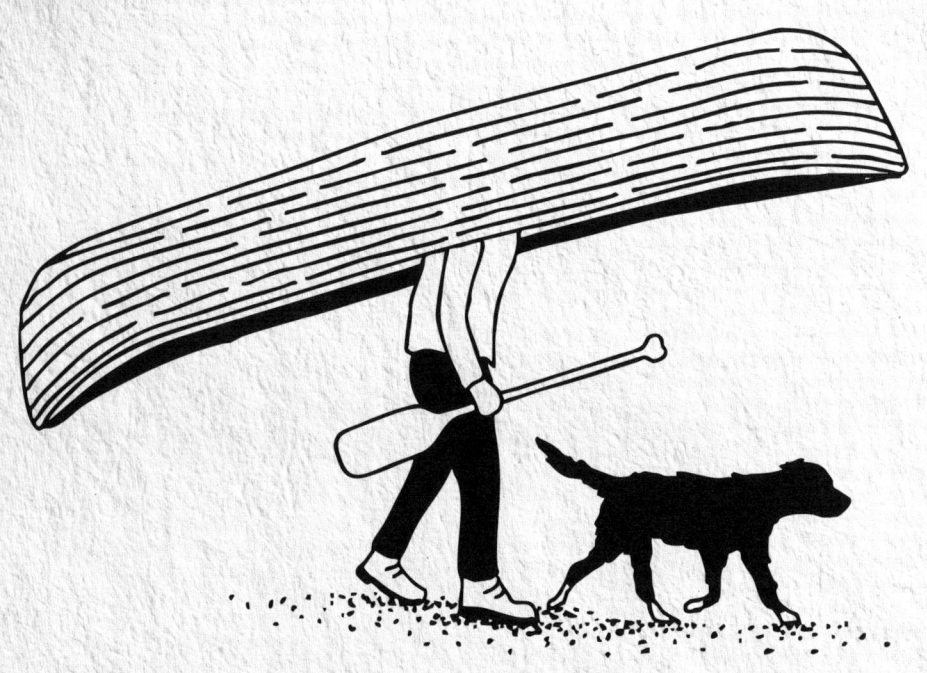

CREEK BOUND

With a canoe balanced above, a traveler walks toward the water, a black dog trotting beside them. The oar rests in hand, steady and sure. The creek hums ahead, promising ripples and quiet. Together, they move toward adventure and the joy of shared company.

"COME FORTH INTO THE LIGHT OF THINGS, LET NATURE BE YOUR TEACHER."

– WILLIAM WORDSWORTH

PADDLE OUT

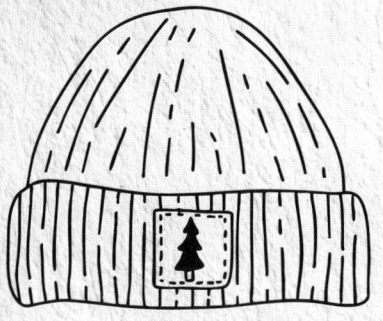

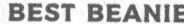

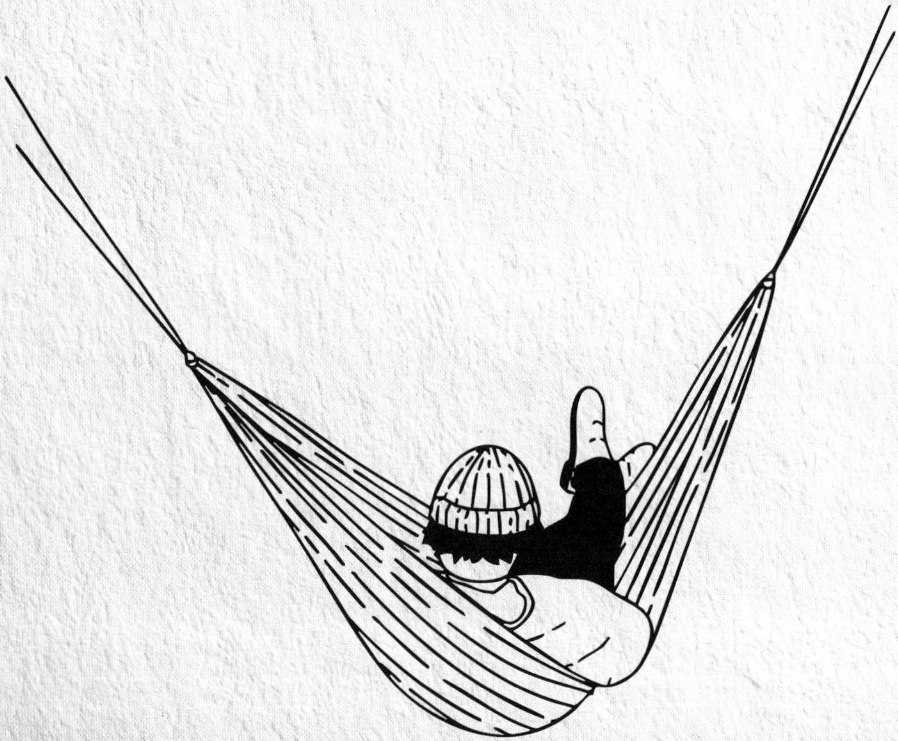

HANG

CHEERS

A cup etched with a pine tree, small and sturdy, feels like a celebration. On a long trail, warmth in your hands is no small gift. Every sip, whether water, tea, or coffee is a reminder that little comforts matter most in the wild.

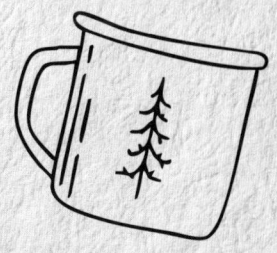

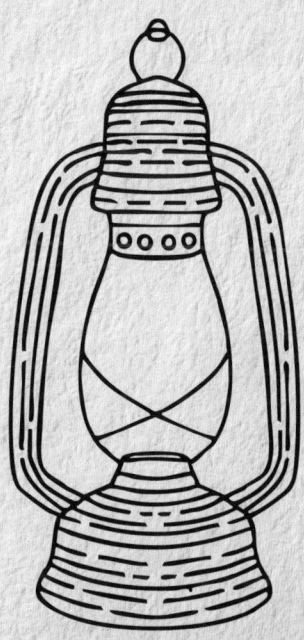

LAST LIGHT

IGNITE

A match flares, small flame alive in the dark. Drawn with care, it feels like both light and promise. In the forest, its warmth, safety, and story reminding us that from a spark comes comfort, and in firelight, we find our gathering place.

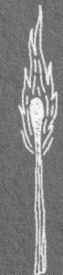

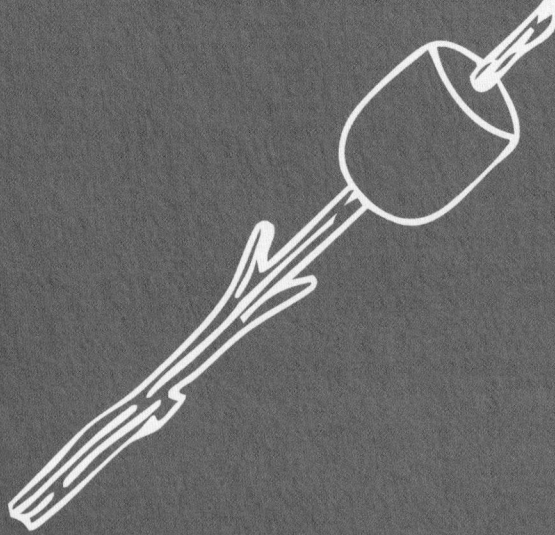

ROAST

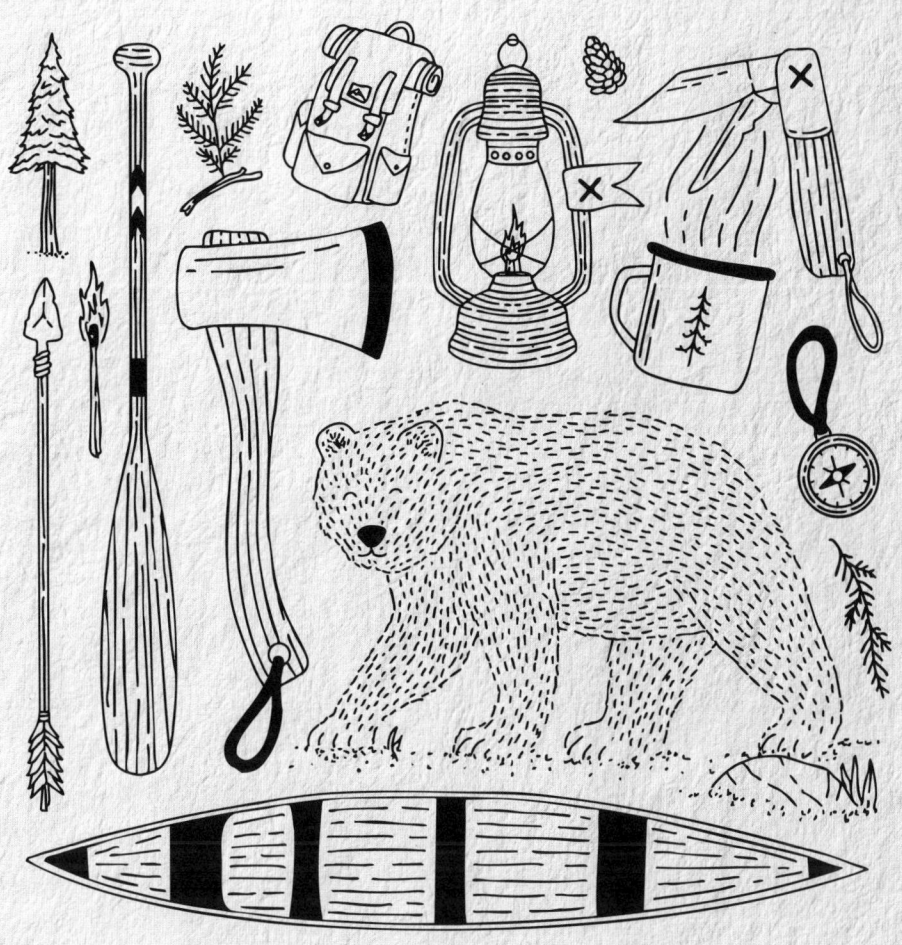

BEAR NECESSITIES

The tools needed in the wild: canoe and paddle, lantern and compass, knife, and matches. These simple tools are enough. The forest is a peaceful place reminding us that life can be simplified to essentials.

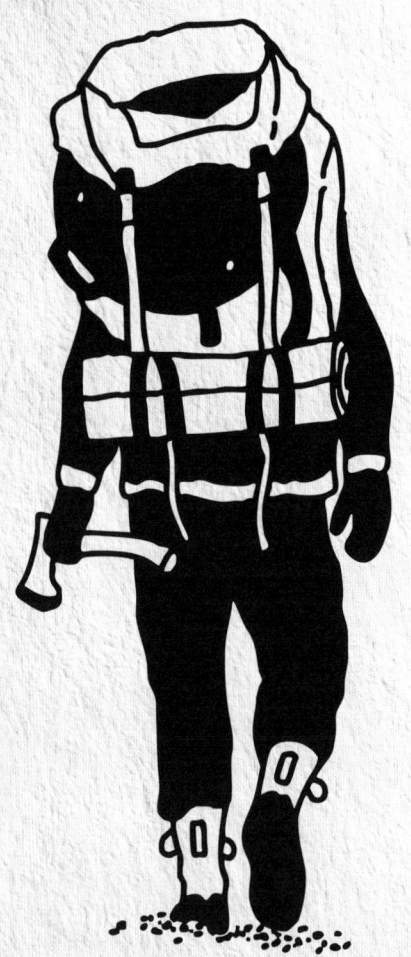

PACKED UP

Backpacks strapped, boots steady, they wander into the wild. Every step carries the weight of gear and the lightness of being free. Together or alone, they walk, grounded by earth and lifted by the promise of adventure.

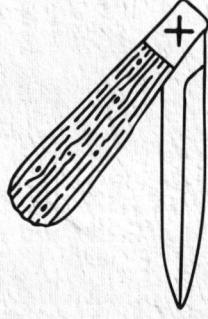

BOARD BUDDIES

A surfer, snowboarder, and skateboarder all sprint together, boards under arms, laughter in stride. Different paths, one spirit, the joy of speed, balance, and adventure. However you ride, whether waves, slopes, or streets, it's the same call: freedom found in motion and outdoors.

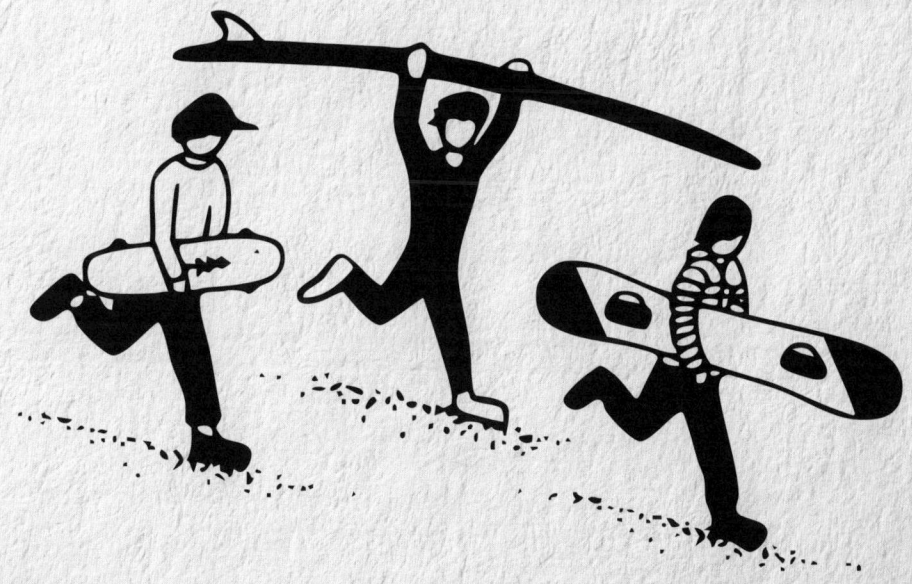

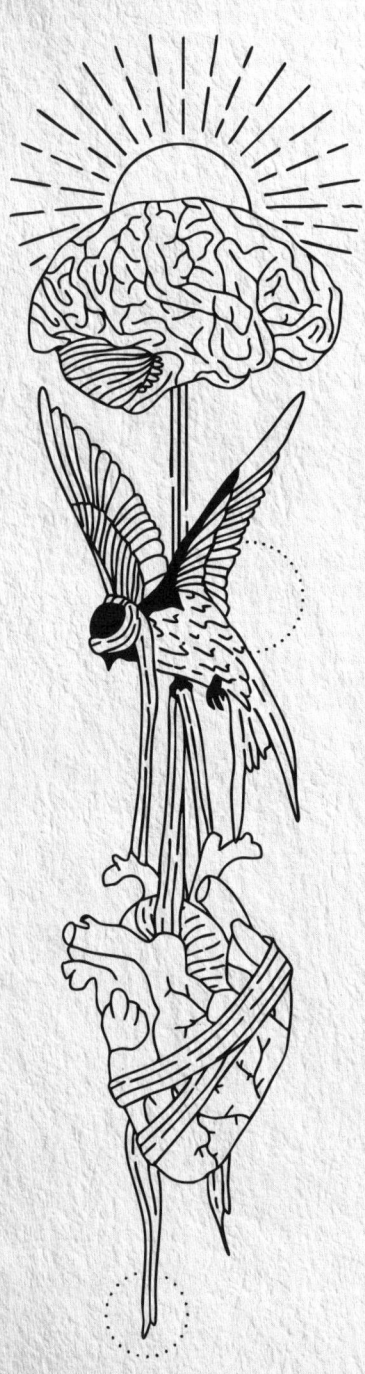

HEAD AND HEART

"HEAVEN IS UNDER OUR FEET AS WELL AS OVER OUR HEADS."

– HENRY DAVID THOREAU

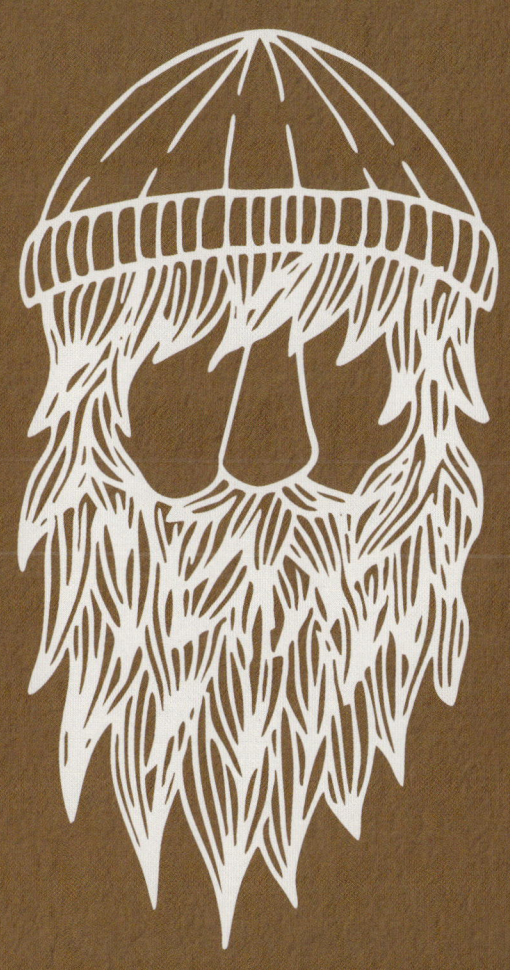

NOMAD

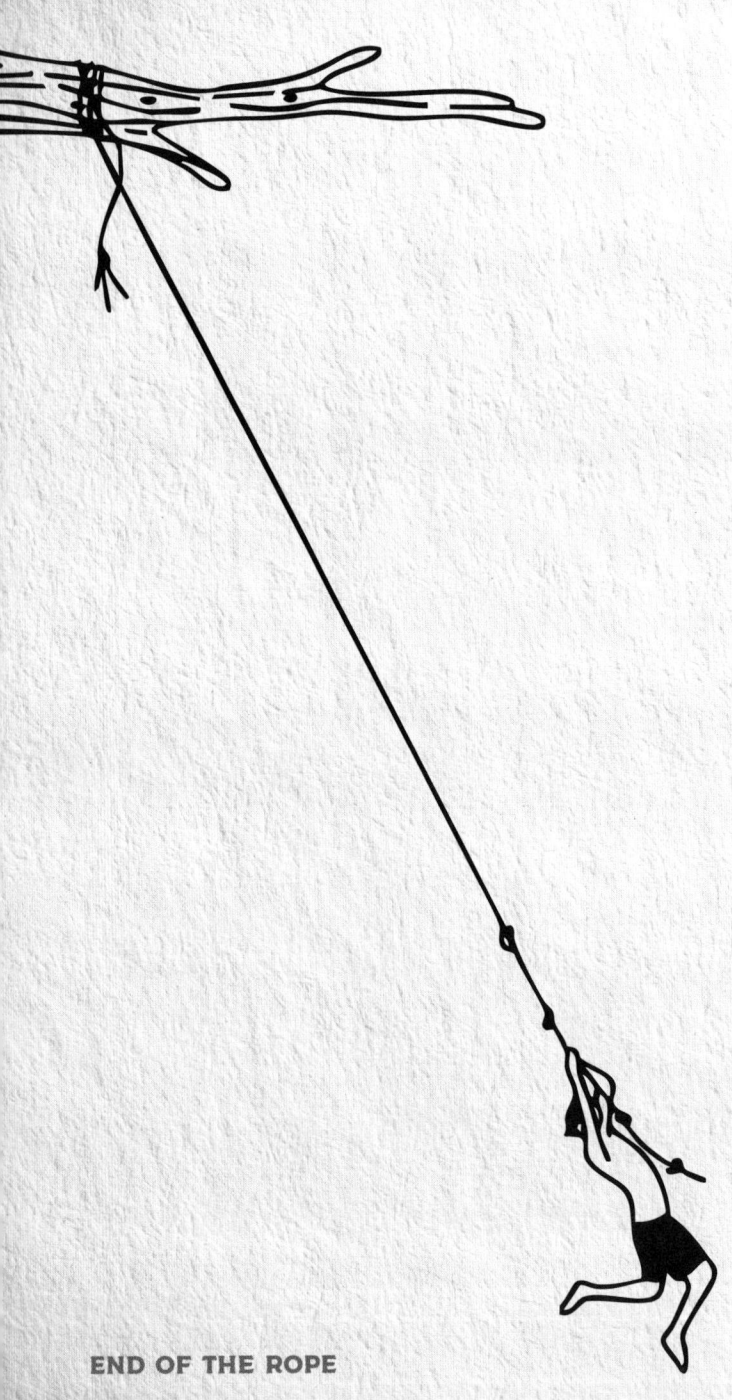

END OF THE ROPE

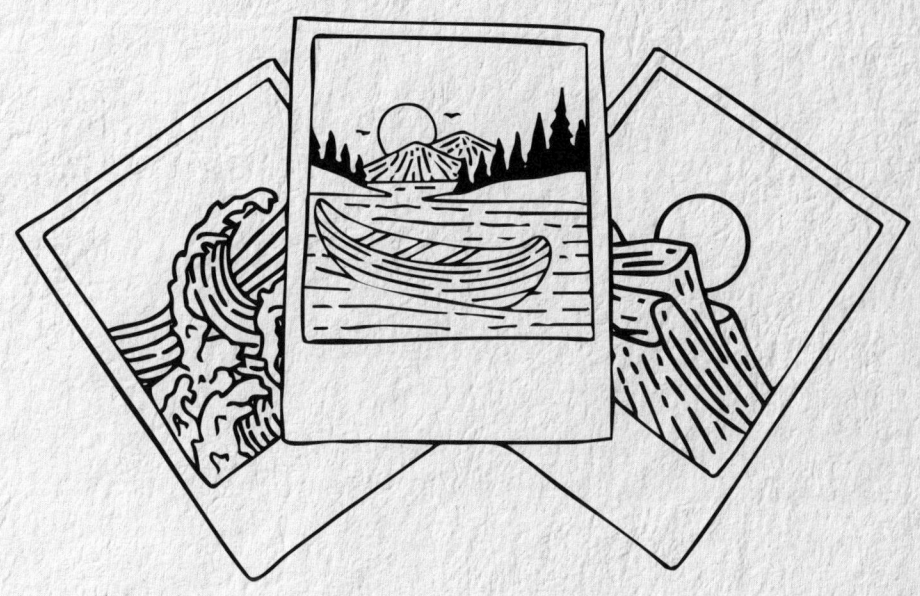

TAKE NOTHING BUT PHOTOS

Three Polaroids capture wild moments: a canoe drifting across sunset waters, a wave frozen mid-crest, a sunrise spilling over mountain peaks. They remind us that the best memories we carry home in images, leaving the wild just as we find it.

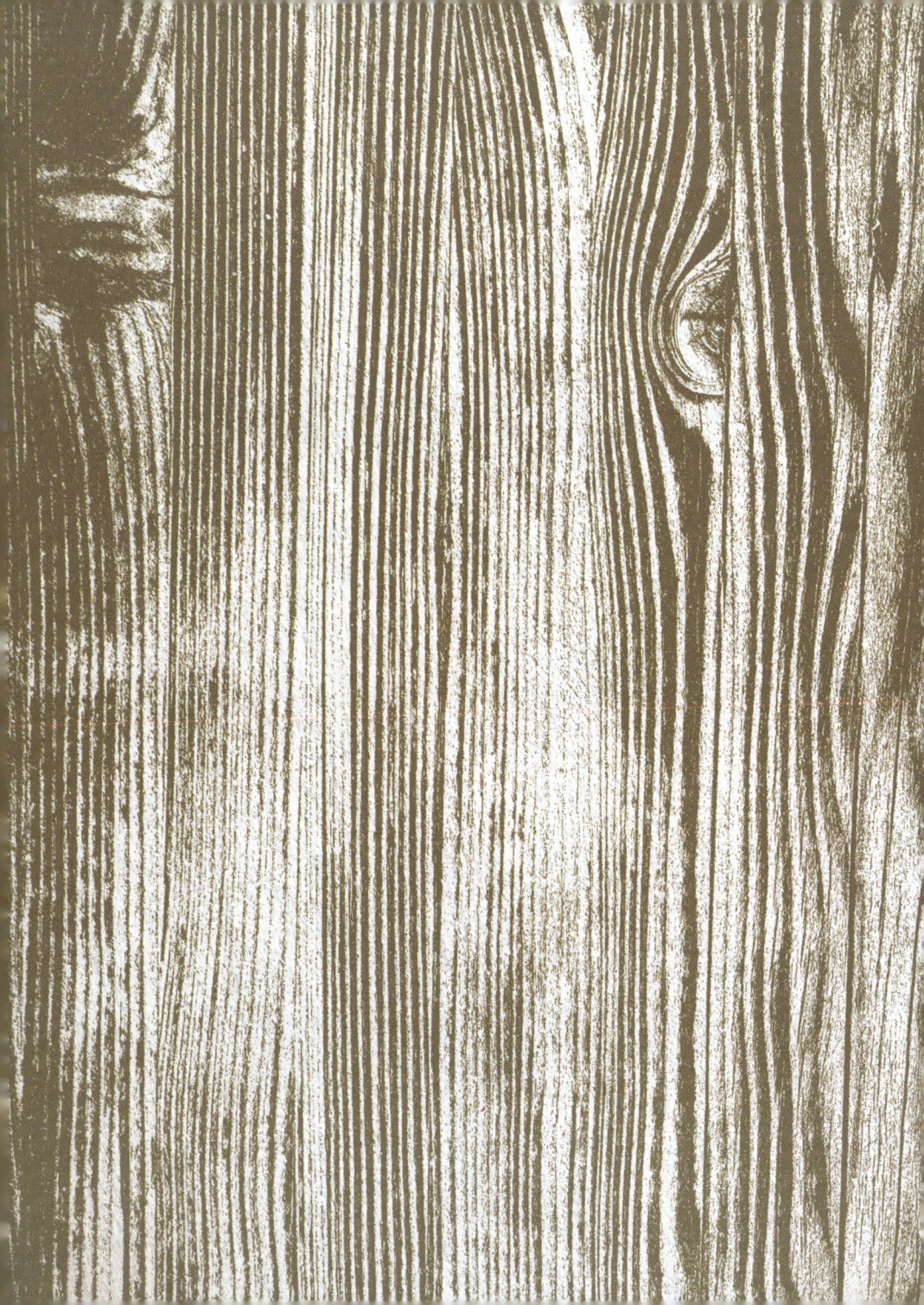

CHAPTER 3

ROOTS
AND
CANOPIES

The woods have always felt like home to me. Whether I'm camping, hiking, or mountain biking through them, whether I'm on a familiar path in a quiet forest or making an unplanned stop somewhere new, there's something quite magical, peaceful, and grounding about their presence. I feel pine trees, my favorite type of tree, particularly capture this spirit, and I draw them often.

My goal with this group of drawings is not to copy nature exactly, but to reflect on the feeling it gives you. Some trees stand alone, and others overlap into full groves. They reflect different avenues of shelter, stillness, growth, and connection.

This chapter is for those who appreciate the power of trees. The people who can't help but stop and look up any time they pass a big one. For those who collect leaves, feel the bark, and walk barefoot along the trails. For the wanderers who love taking the long way and making a route through the pines. Whether you're deep in the forest or just dreaming of one, these illustrations will help you on your way.

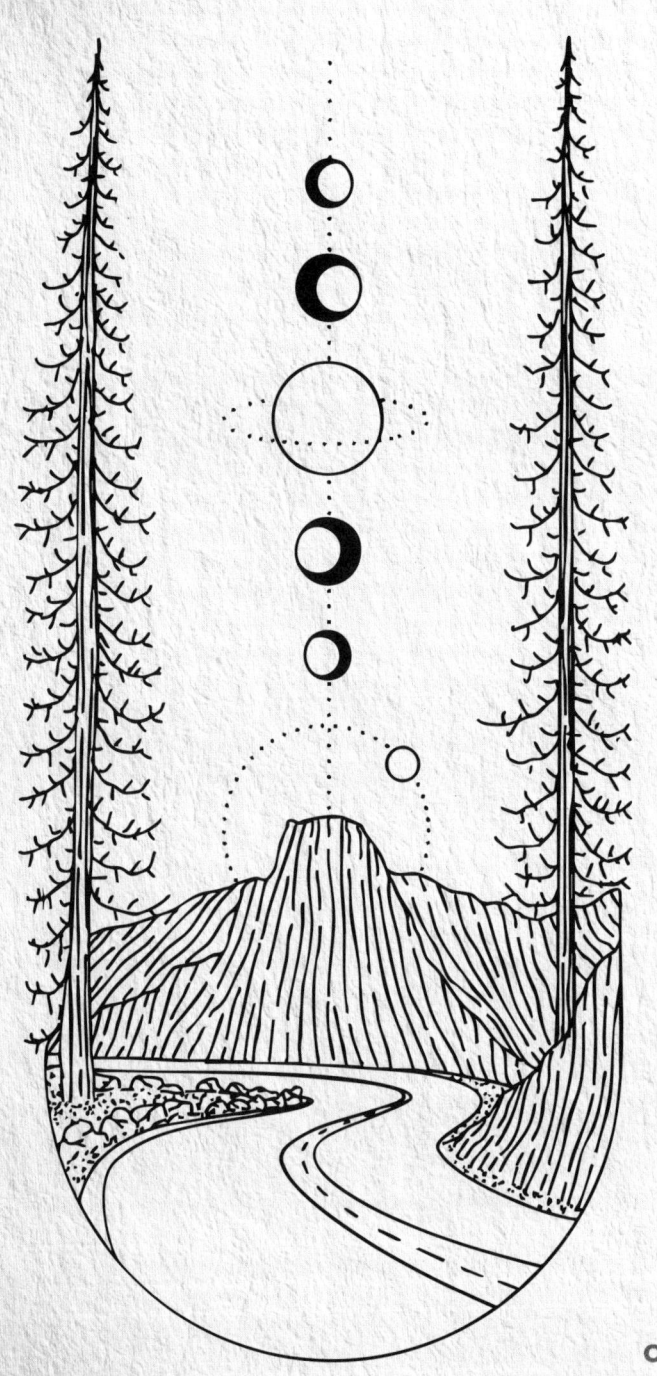

COSMIC DIRECTION

THE LESS-BEATEN PATH

A trail disappears into a forest thick with trees. It feels like an invitation. Quiet, steady, alive with unseen creatures. The path is old yet waiting, reminding us that every step deeper into the woods carries you closer to wonder and discovery.

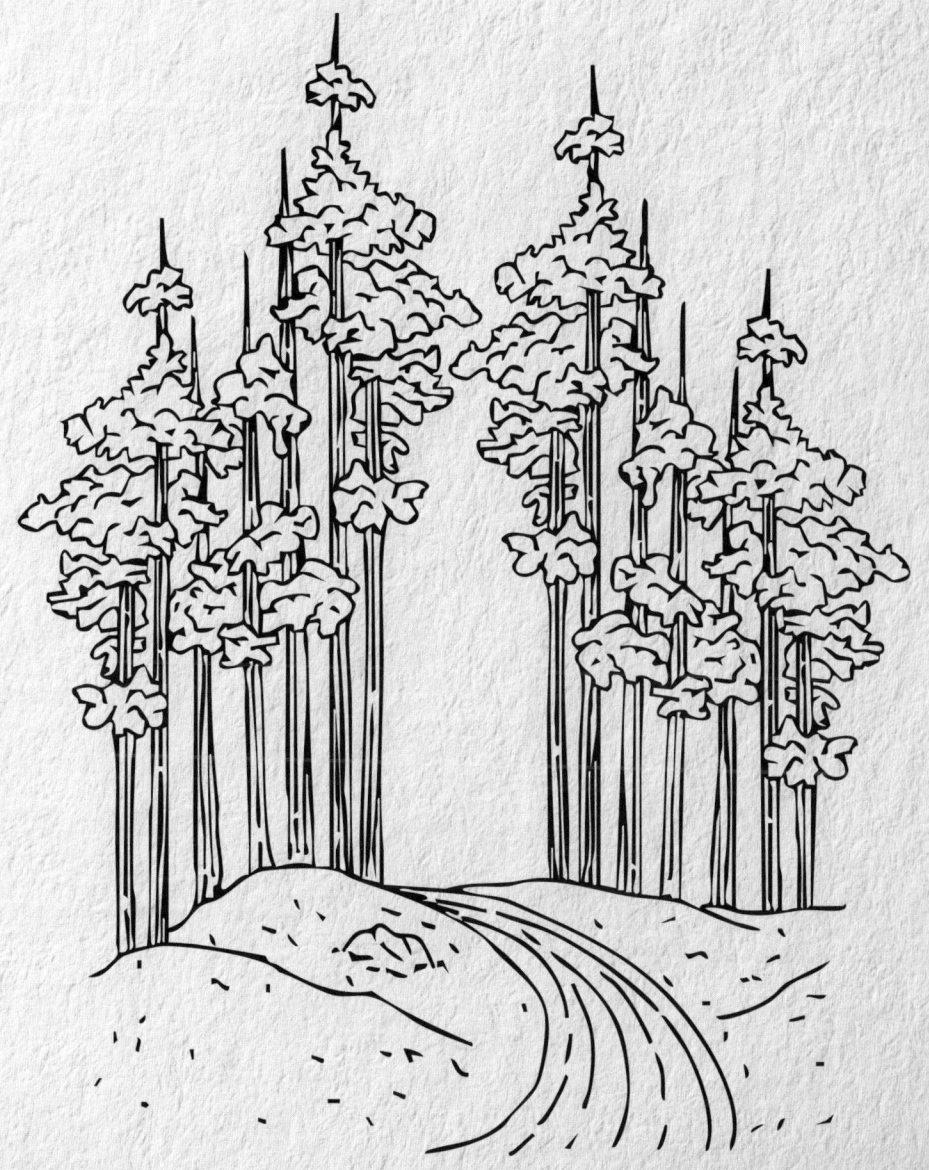

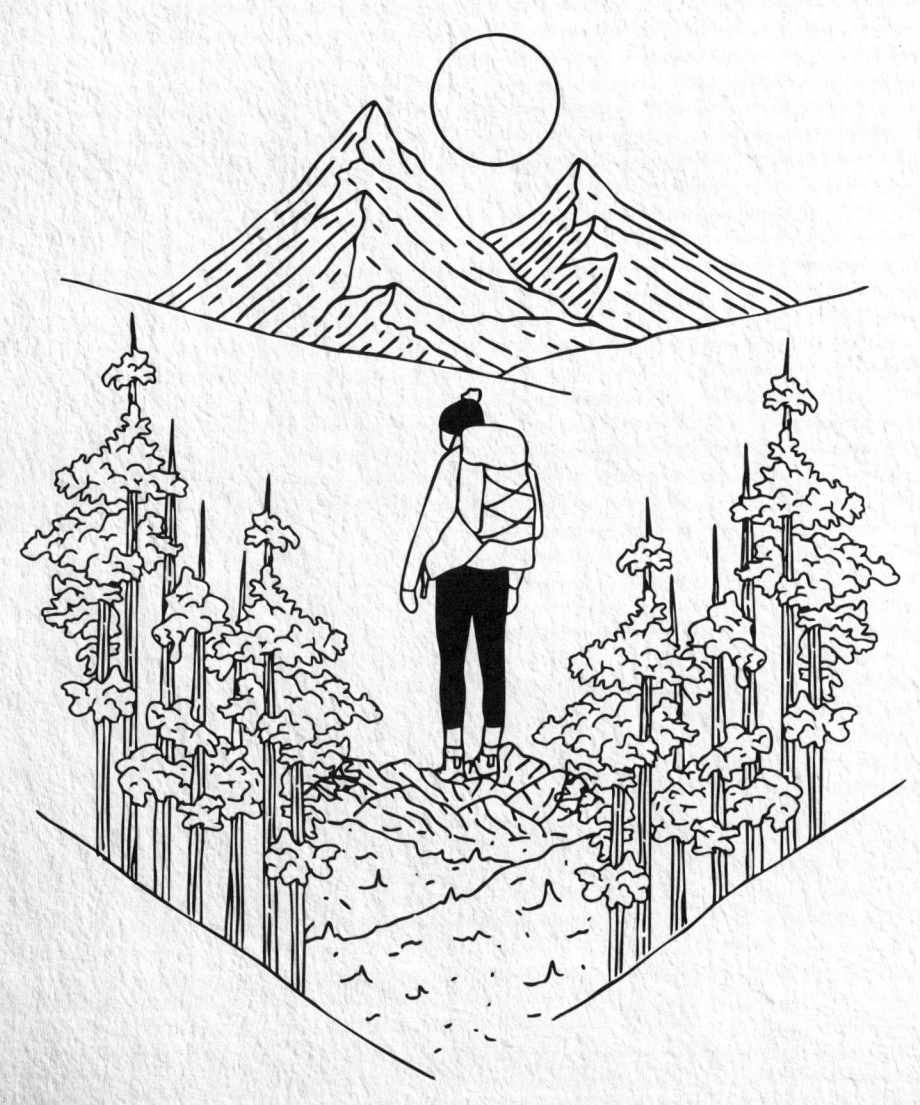

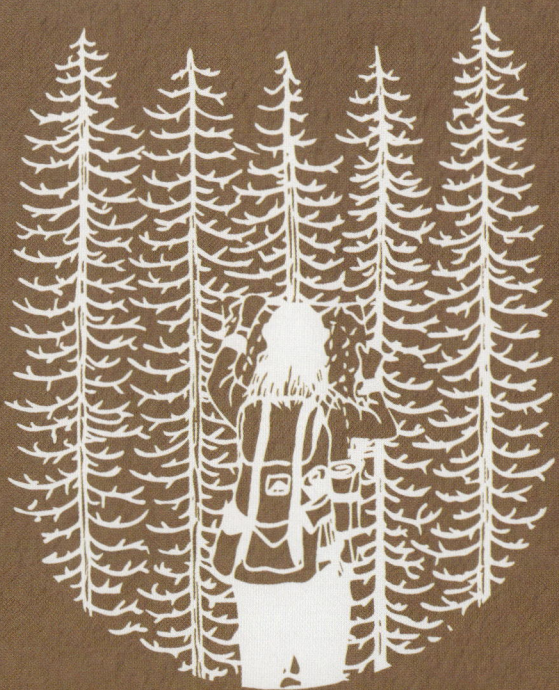

EVER GREEN

Two tiny fir trees stand side by side,
each its own world yet together in
charm. Small, resilient, they whisper
of growth and companionship. They
remind us that every towering forest
begins with little trees rooted close,
reaching quietly toward the sky.

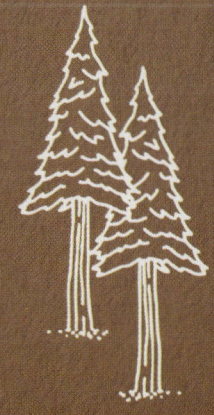

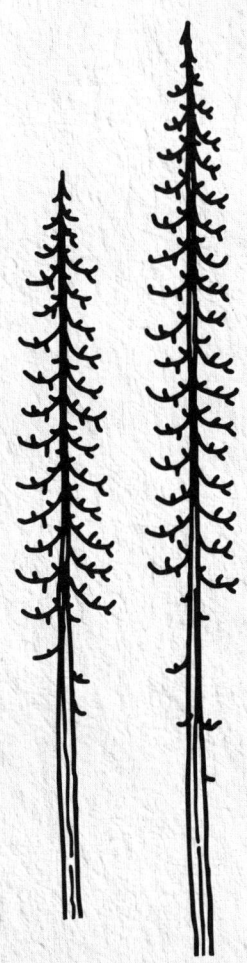

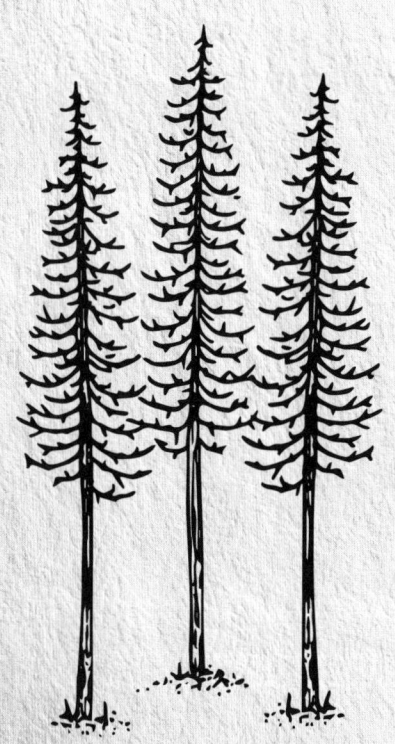

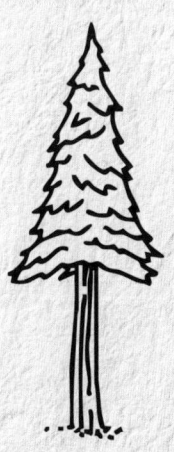

TIMBERLINE

Five fir trees rise in different heights: siblings, parents, children. Each carries a story of age and weather, standing together against wind and storm. United and quiet, they remind us that strength isn't always solitary. Sometimes it's found in being rooted side by side, season after season.

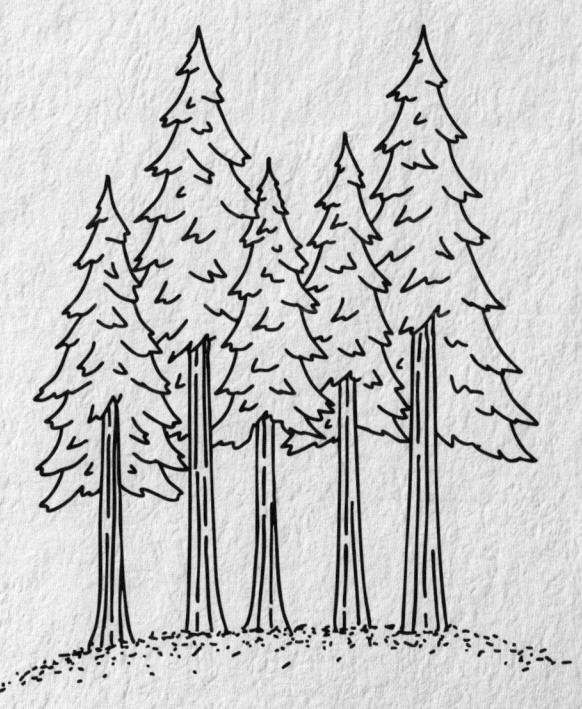

REDWOODS

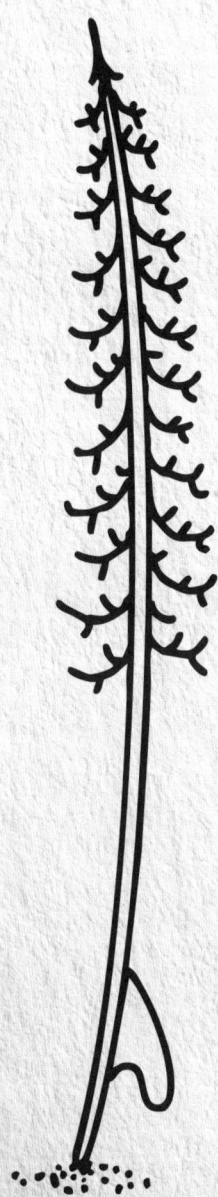

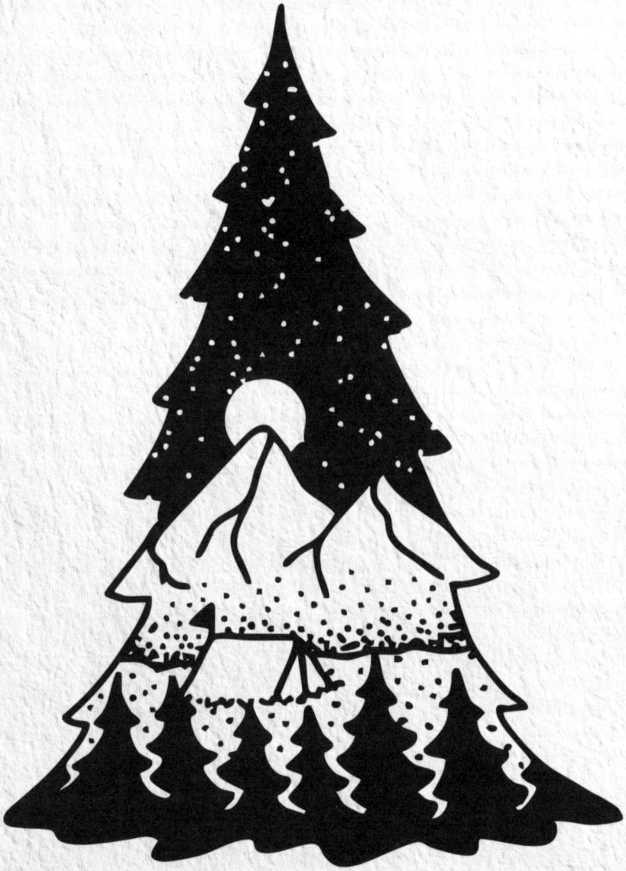

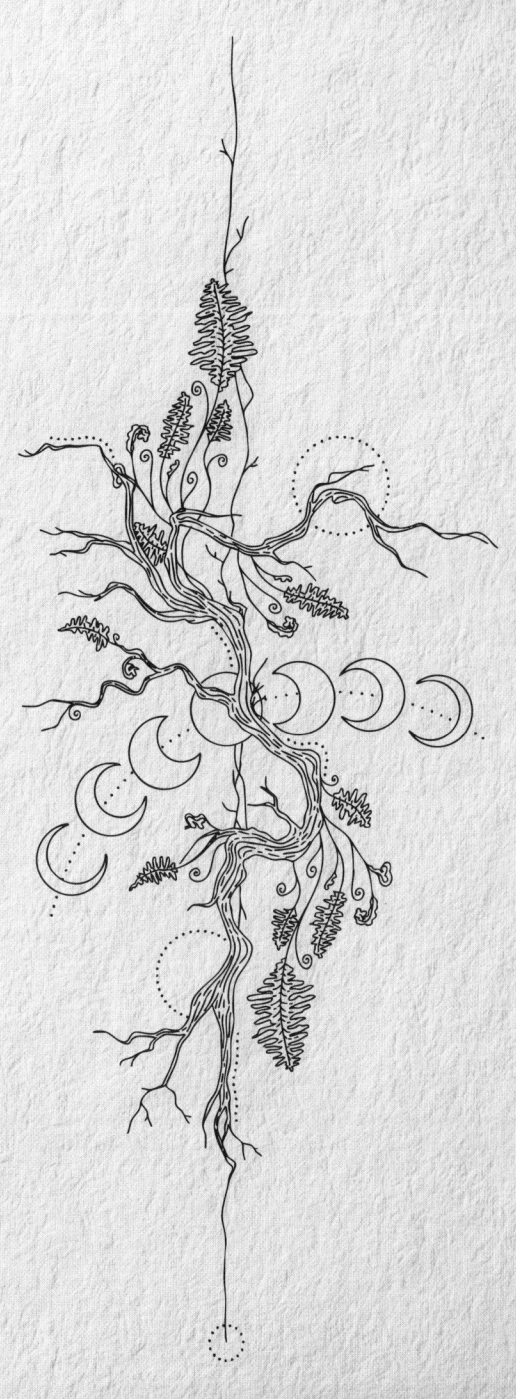

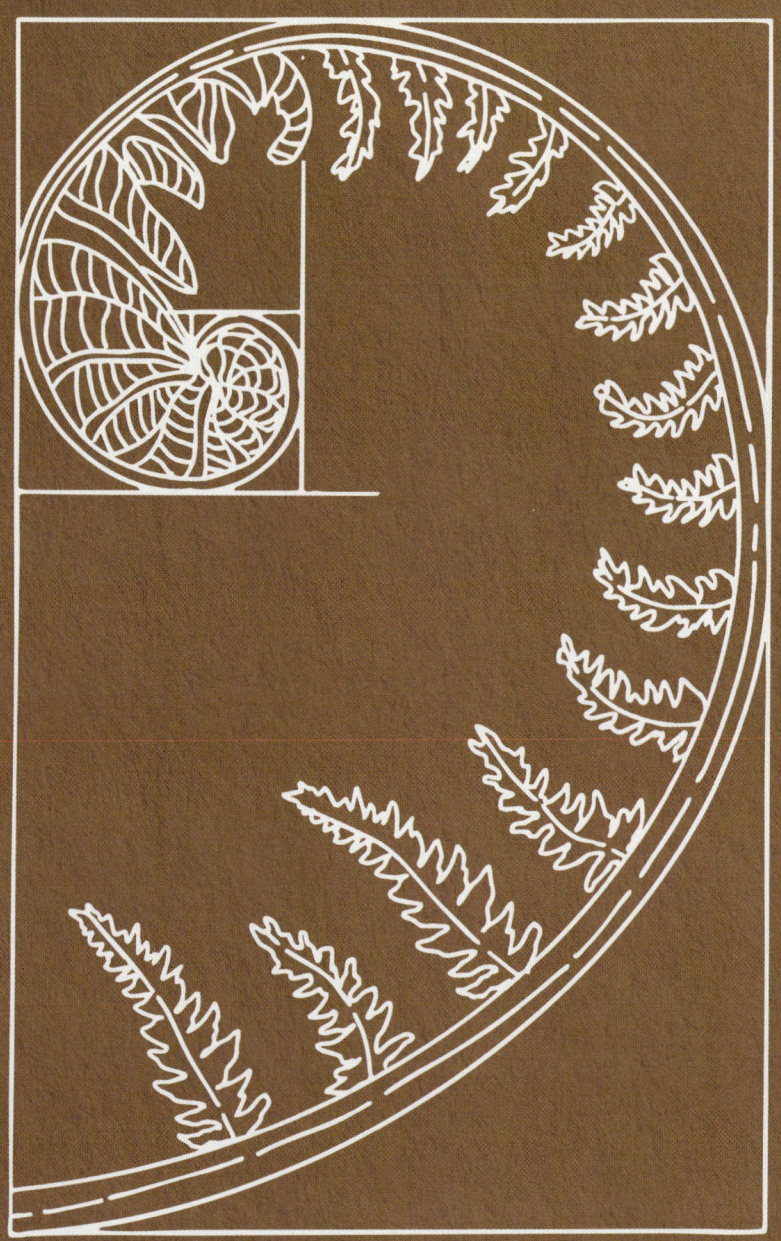

GOLDEN FERN RATION

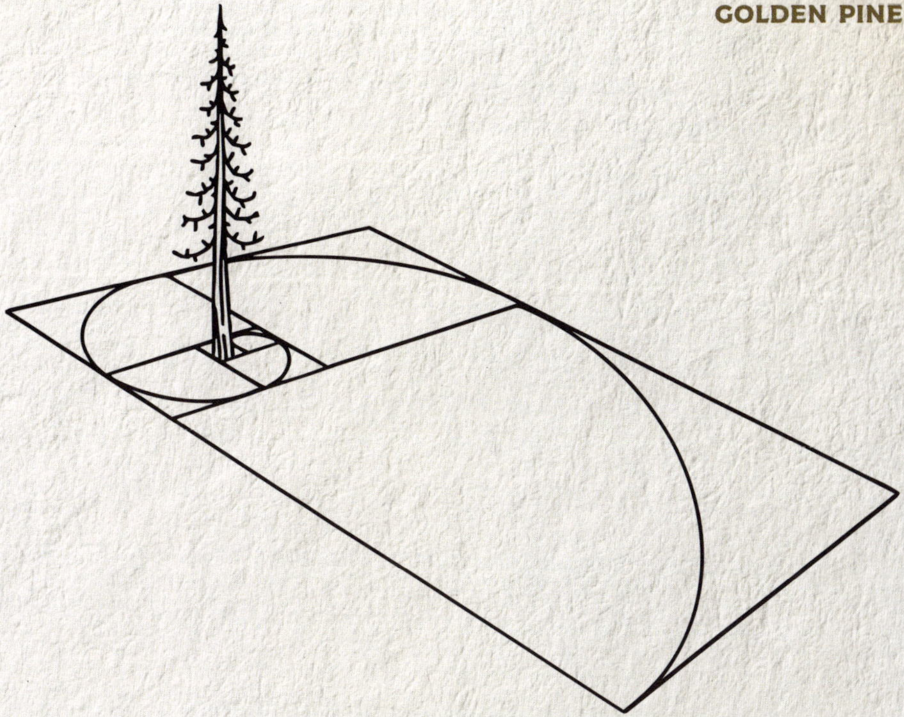

CLASSIC TOADSTOOL

Beneath shaded trees, a mushroom
rises bright, charming, mysterious.
Both invitation and warning, it feels like
something out of folklore. The forest
floor is full of such secrets, where
beauty is tinged with danger, and magic
hides in the most unexpected places.

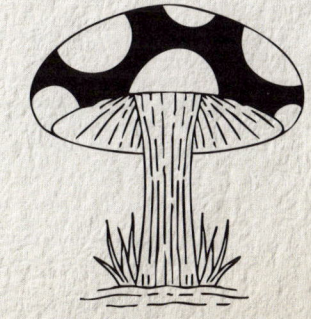

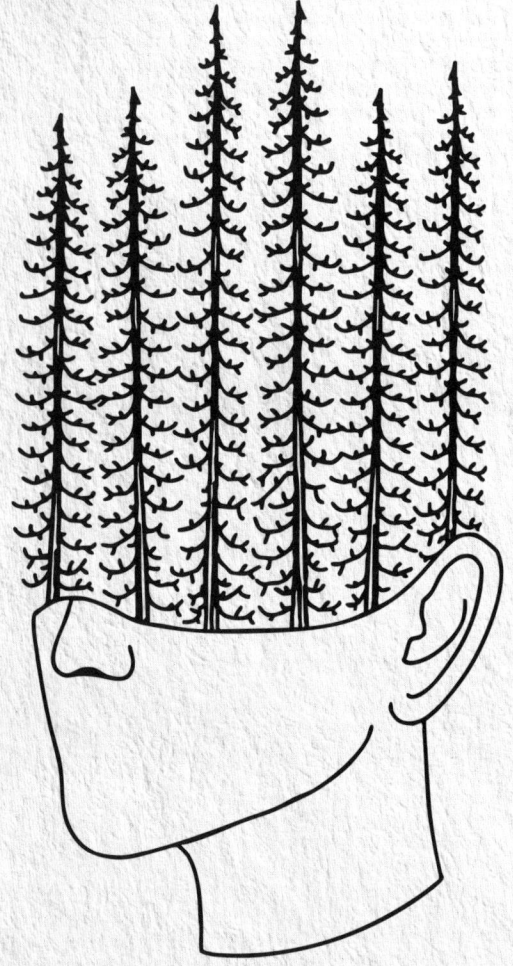

TREE HUGGER

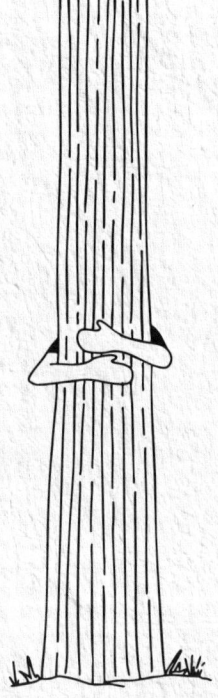

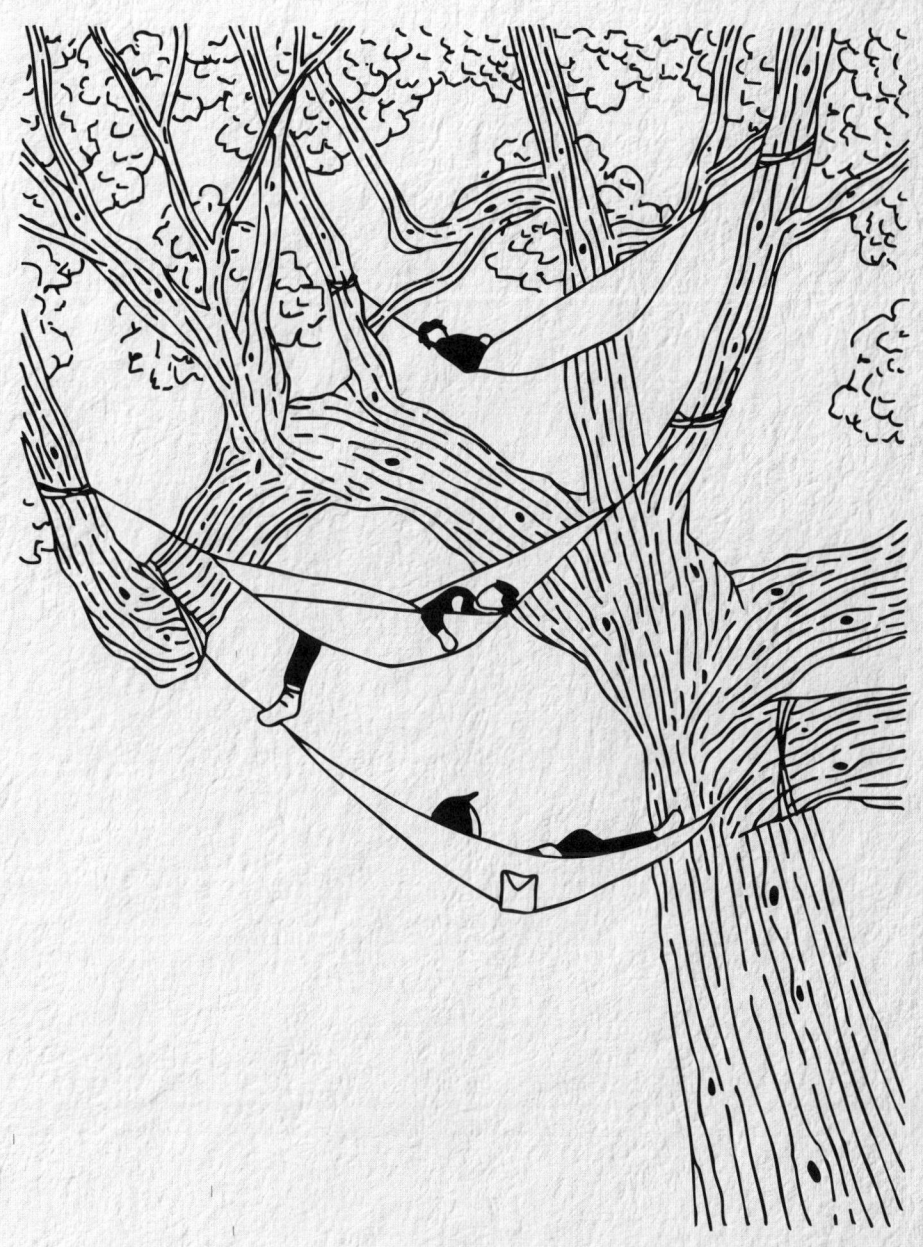

BED IN THE BRANCHES

TREE HOUSE

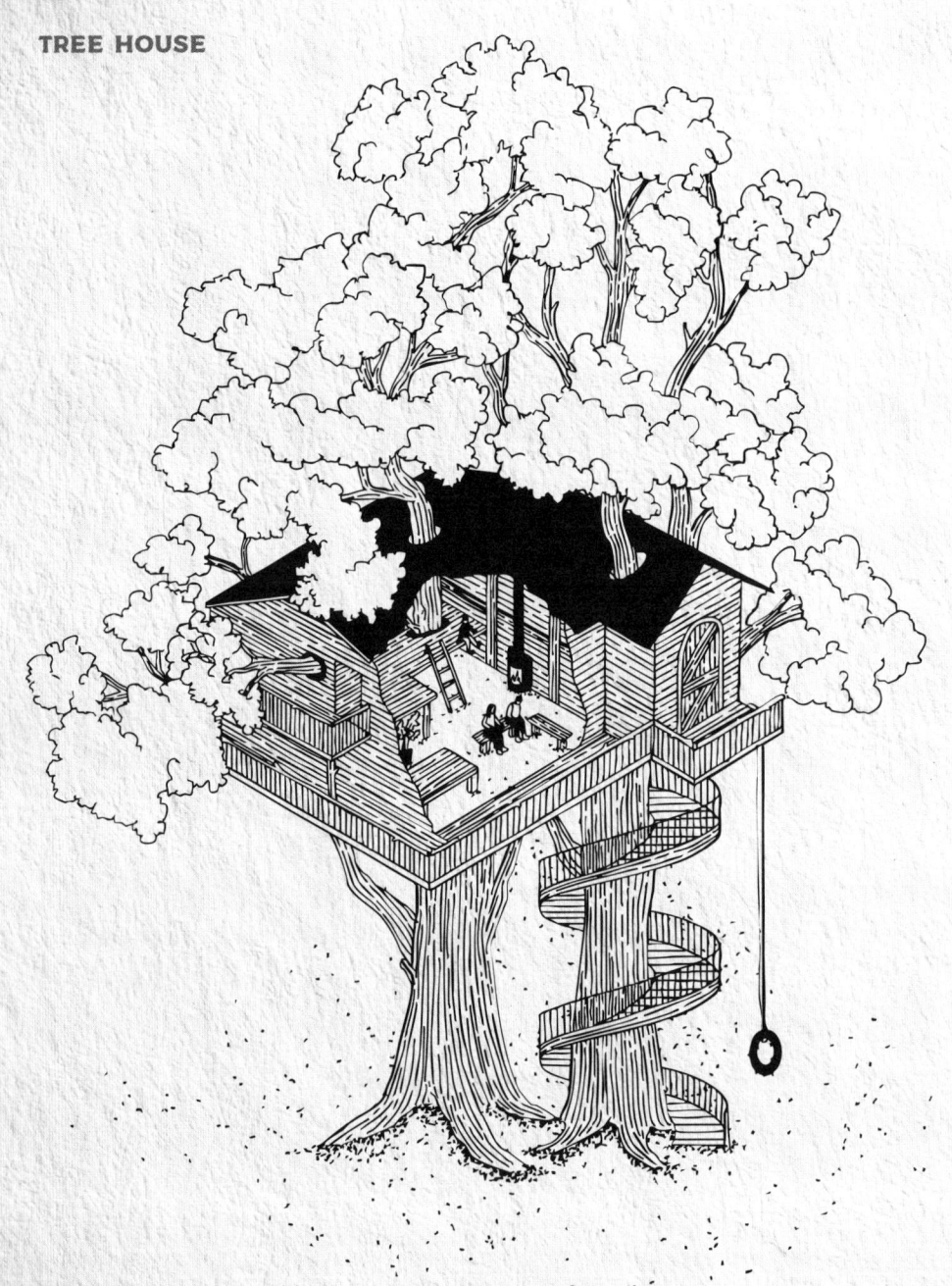

"AN EARLY MORNING WALK IS A BLESSING FOR THE WHOLE DAY."

– HENRY DAVID THOREAU

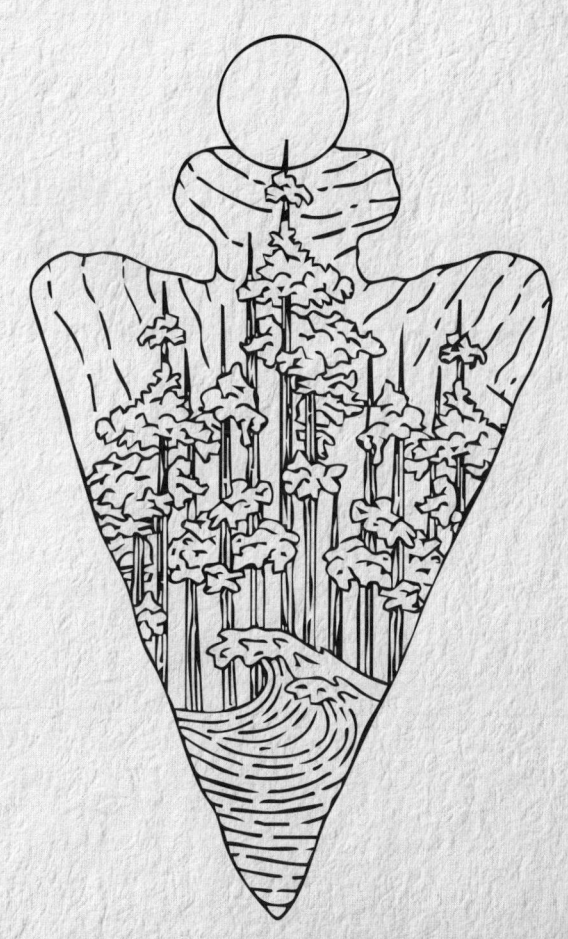

WOODLAND FLINT

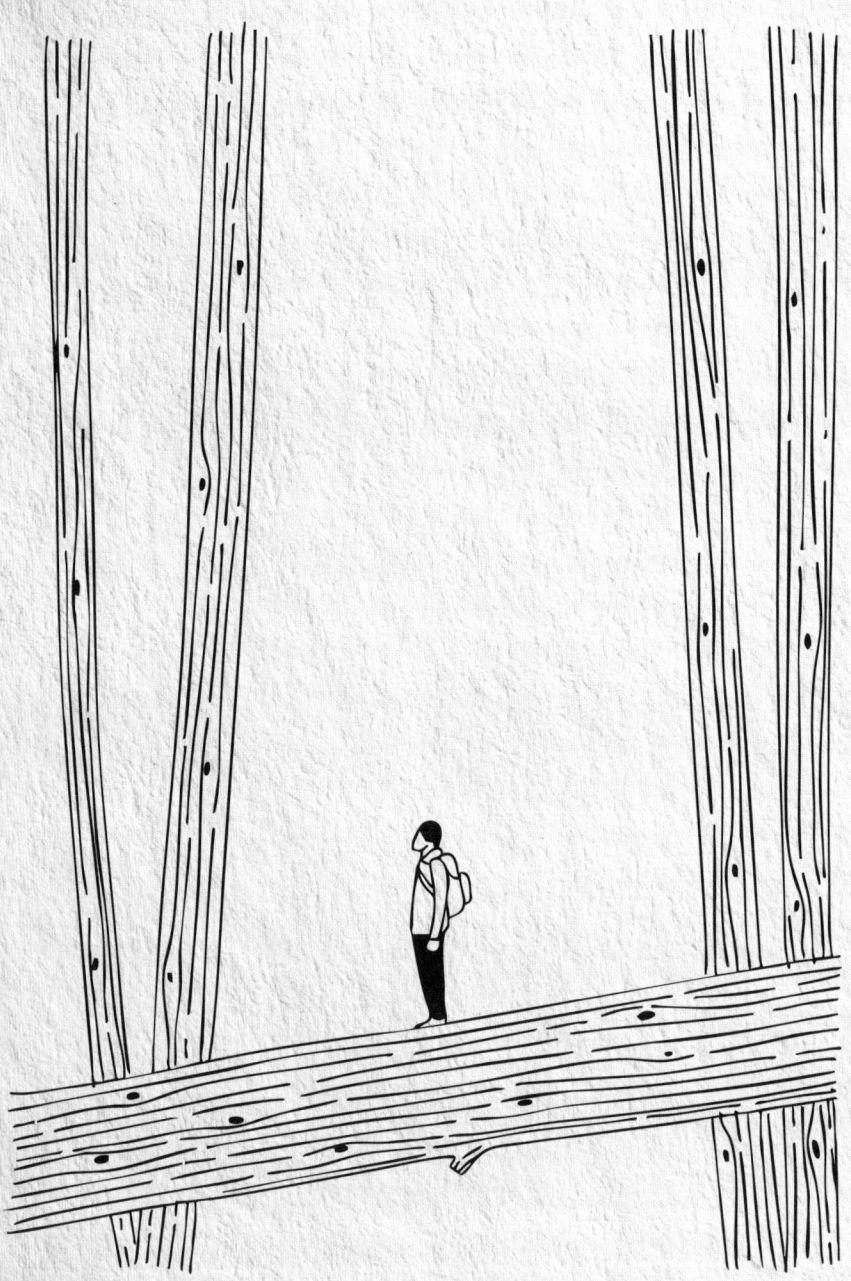

BRIDGE ACROSS

LIFE LINES

Tree rings fill a frame, circles upon
circles, each one a season endured.
These lines hold storms, droughts,
sun, and years. An entire life etched in
wood. They remind us that the forest
is history itself, written slowly, layer by
layer, in patience and time.

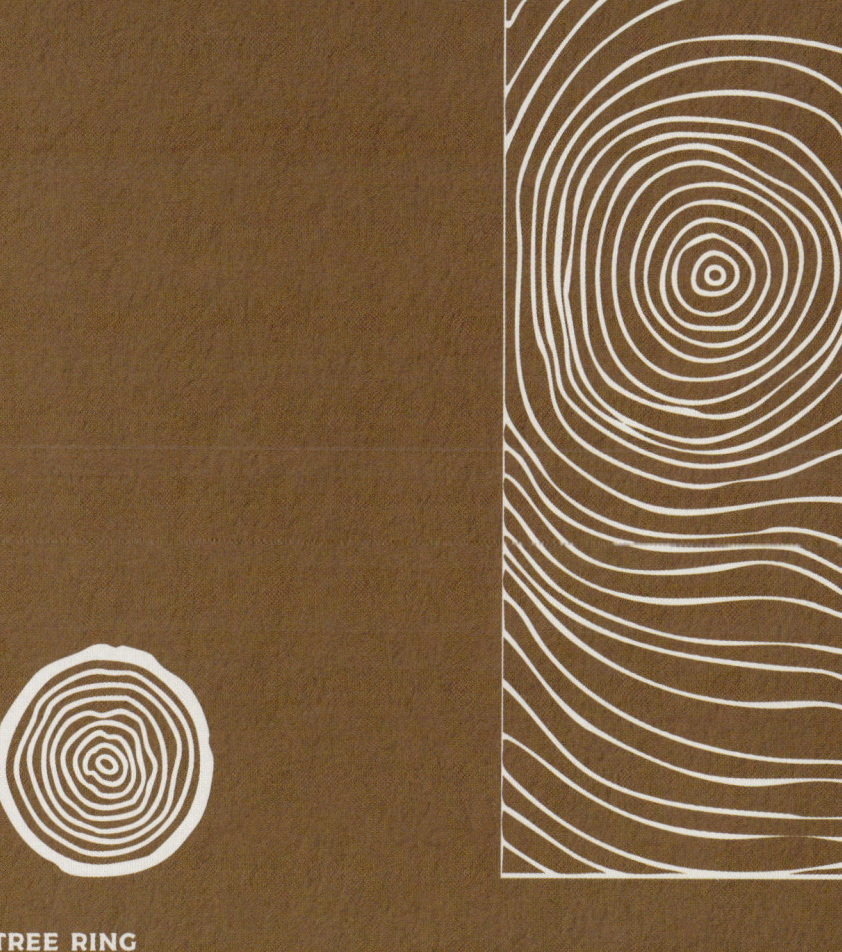

TREE RING

"I WENT TO THE WOODS BECAUSE I WISHED TO LIVE DELIBERATELY, TO FRONT ONLY THE ESSENTIAL FACTS OF LIFE."

– HENRY DAVID THOREAU

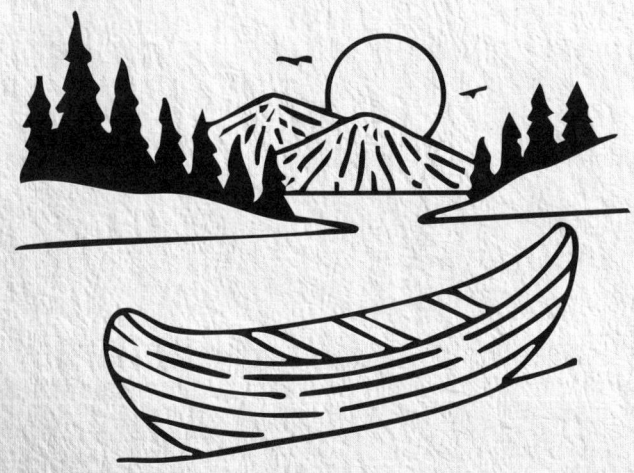

WOOD FRAMES

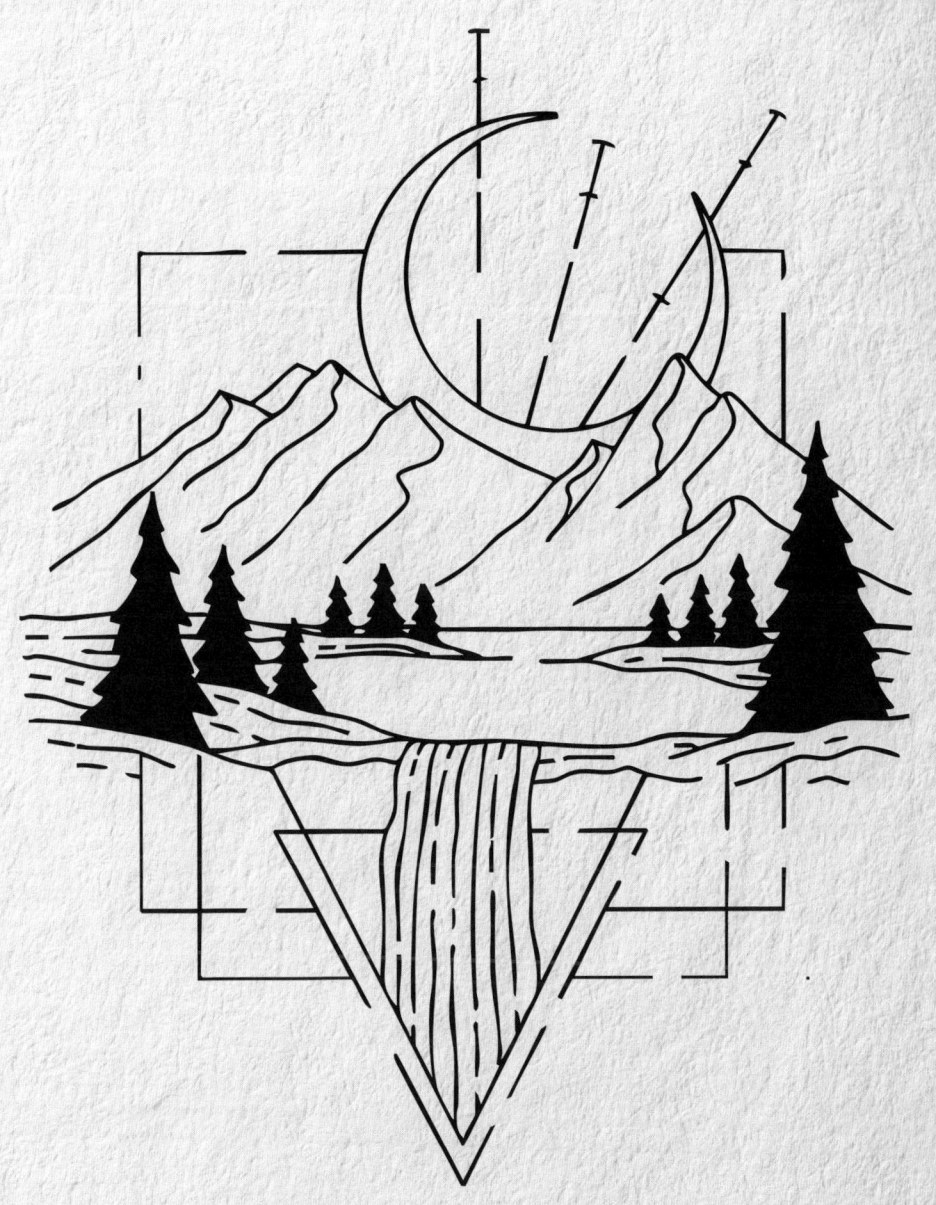

PINE ECHOES

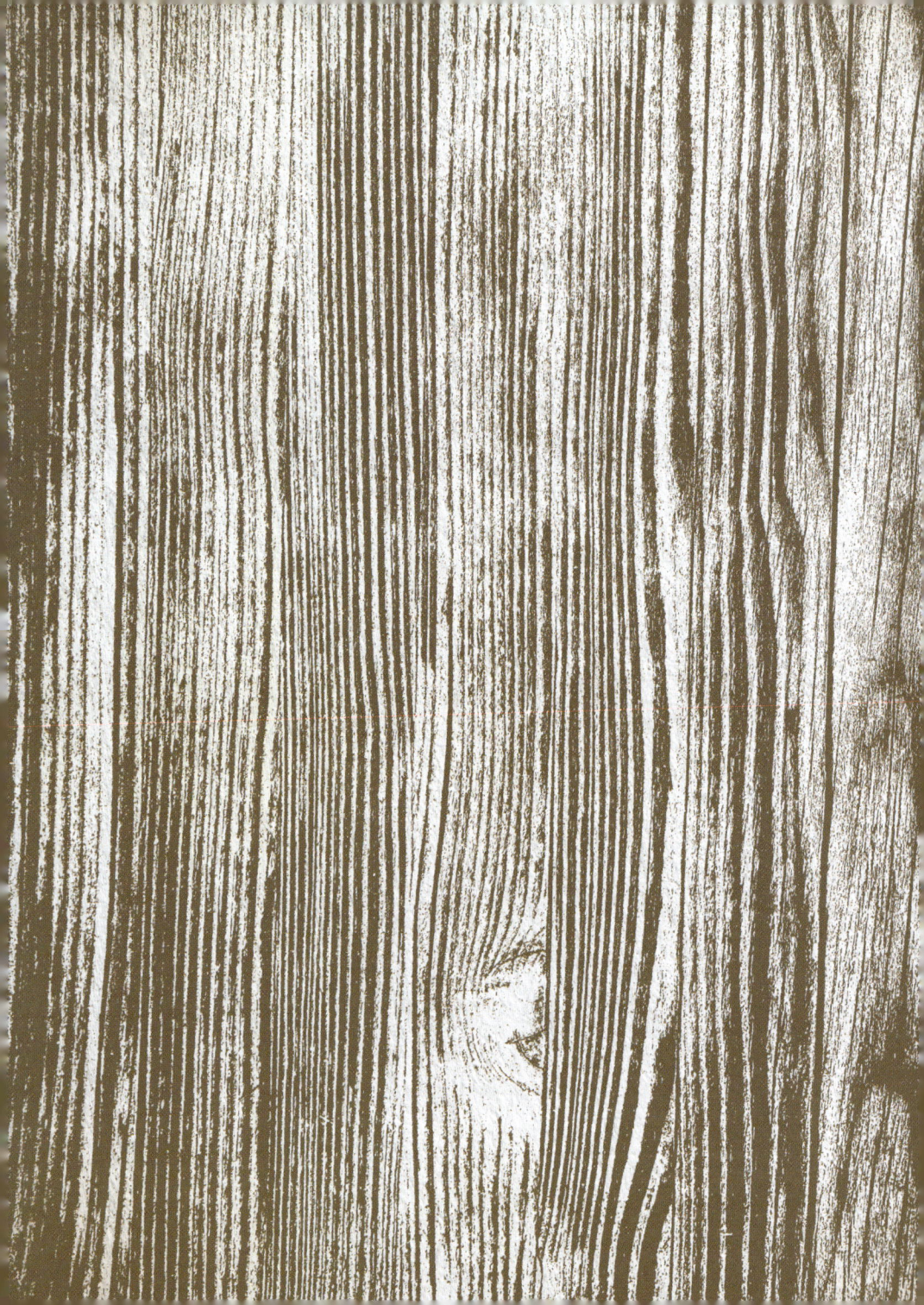

CHAPTER 4

FLORAL FLOURISHES

There are so many types of flowers, and each holds its own special beauty. They grow where they want to, they bloom only when they're ready, and in the wild, they'll thrive without needing any attention. They can carry deep meaning, acting as symbols of birth months, as thoughtful gestures, and as atmospheric shorthand for the wonders of nature.

This chapter is dedicated to the simple joy found in that spirit of individuality.

Many of these designs began as studies. I wonder how many types of flowers and plants you can identify in these illustrations—from ferns to wild blooms and tiny sprigs, stems, leaves, buds, and even scattered petals. I've drawn each one with its simplicity and lightness in mind. Just like the real thing, there are no heavy lines here, no overworked details, just an appreciation for the beautiful and diverse world they represent.

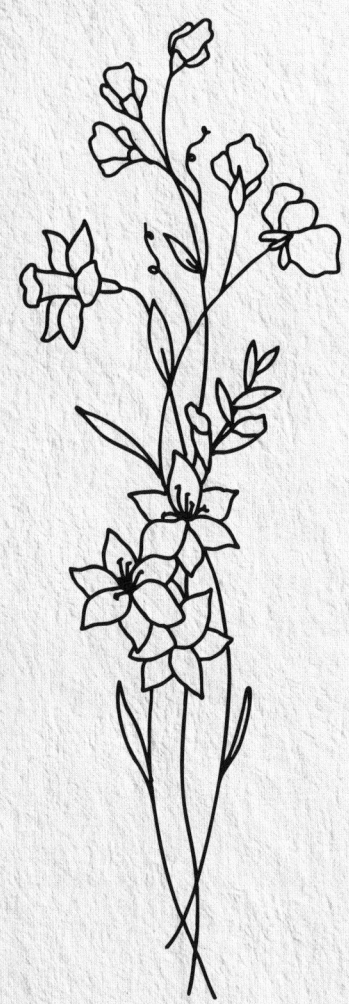

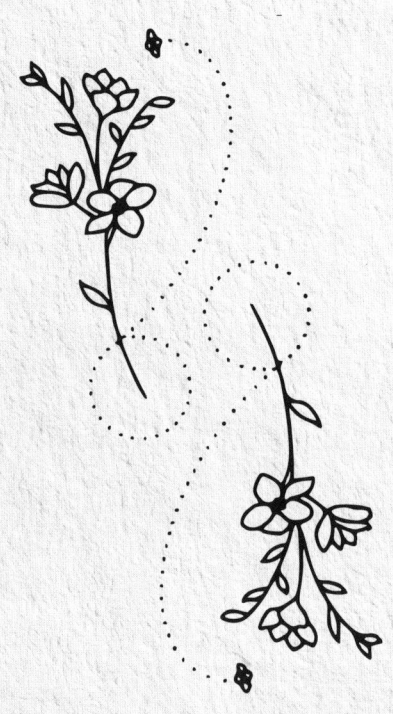

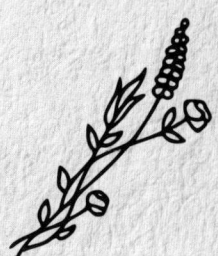

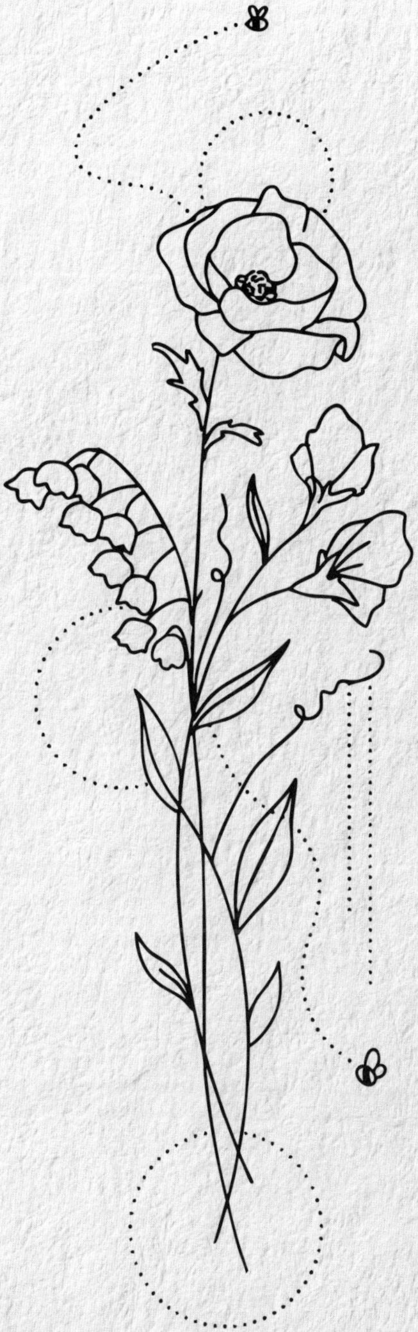

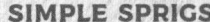

FLIGHT OF THE BUMBLEBEES

WILD BOUQUET

WILD ACORN

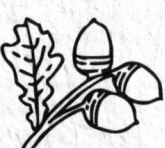

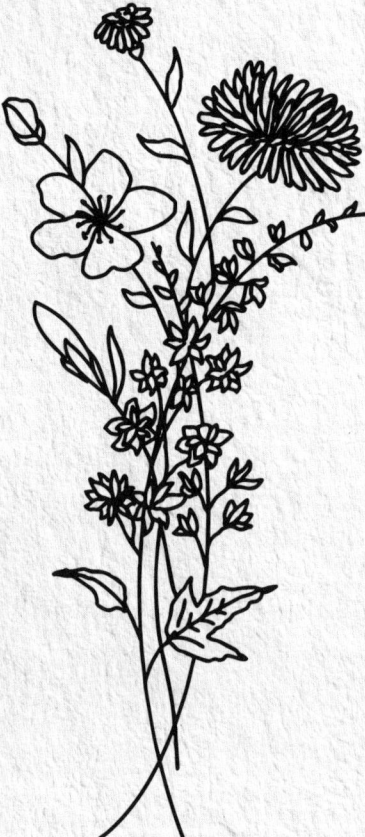

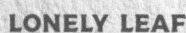

LONELY LEAF

AUTUMN BOUQUET

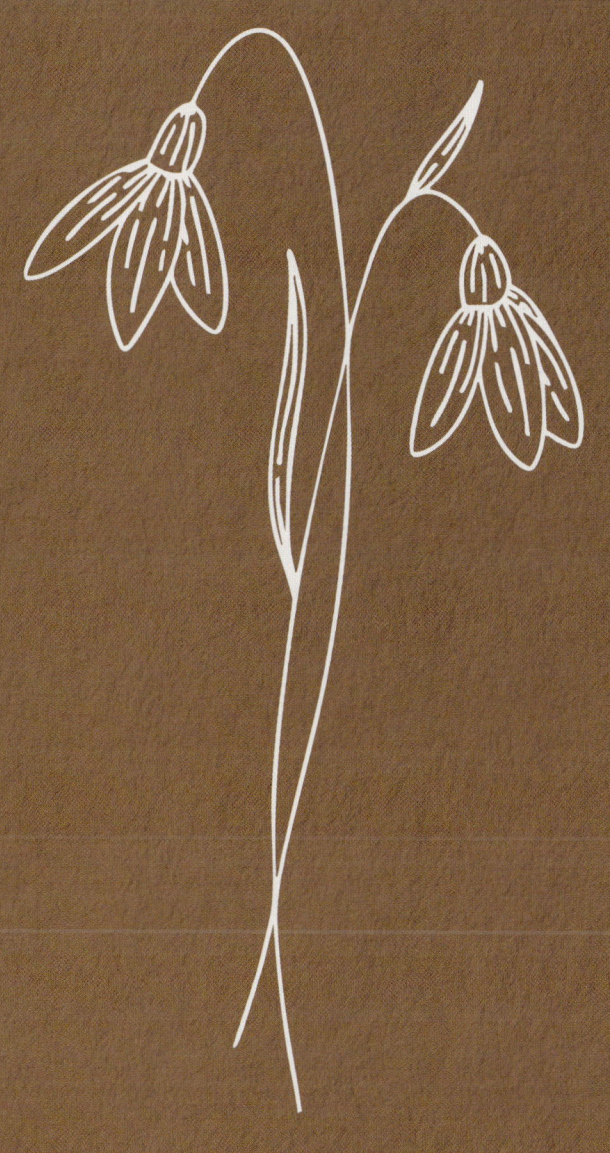

JANUARY — SNOWDROP

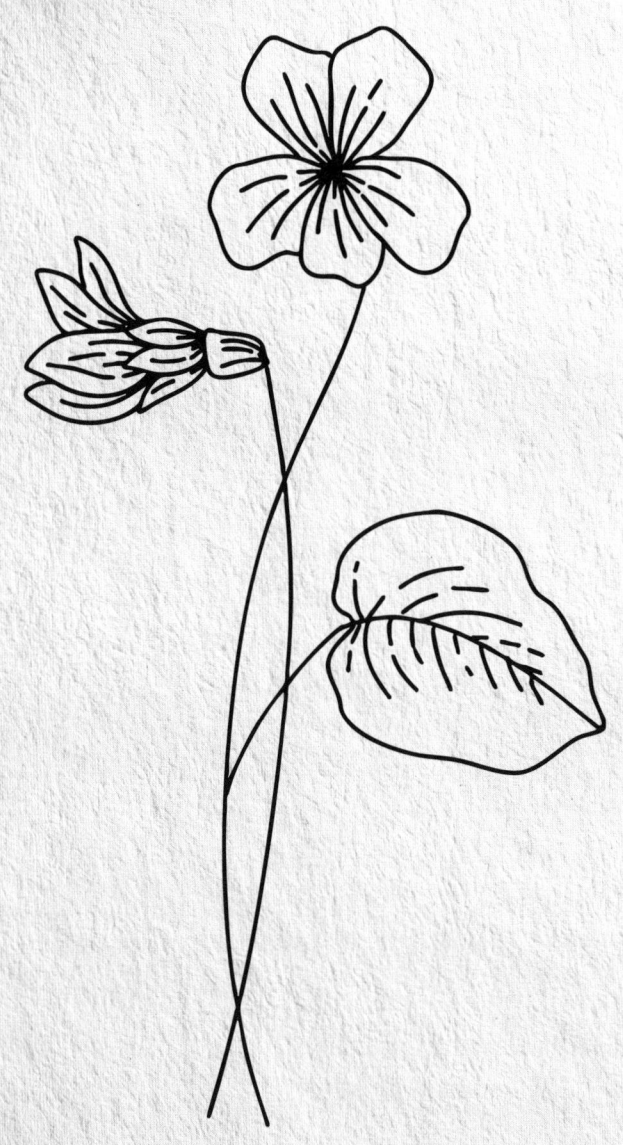

FEBRUARY — VIOLET

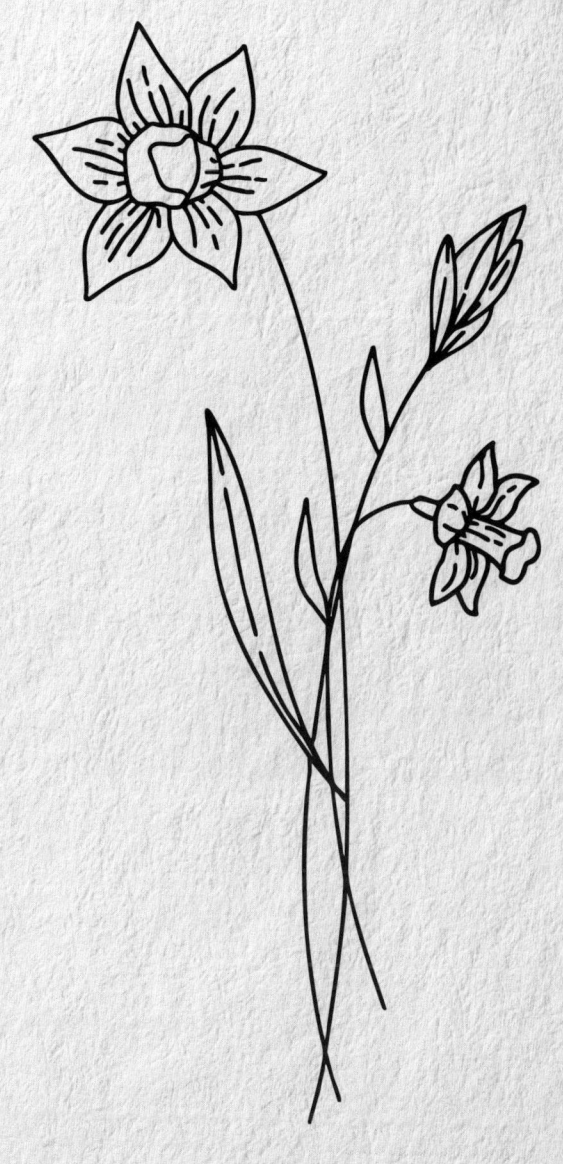

MARCH — DAFFODIL

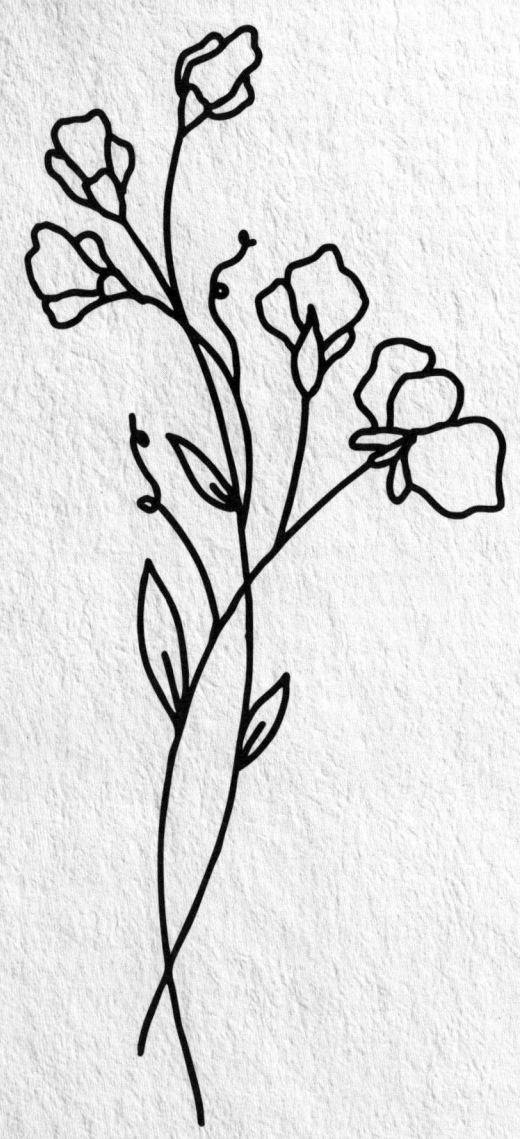

APRIL — SWEET PEA

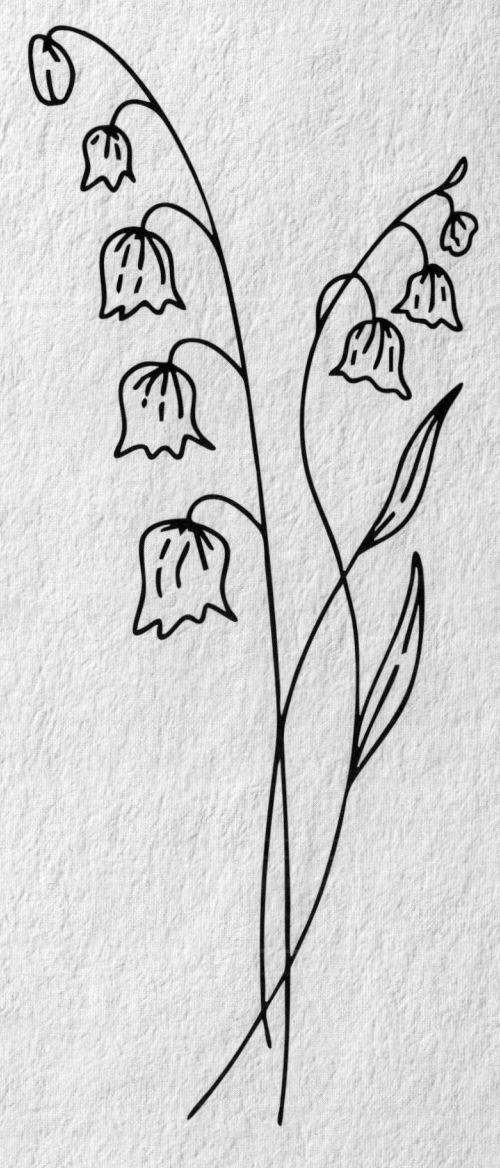

MAY — LILY OF THE VALLEY

JUNE — HONEYSUCKLE

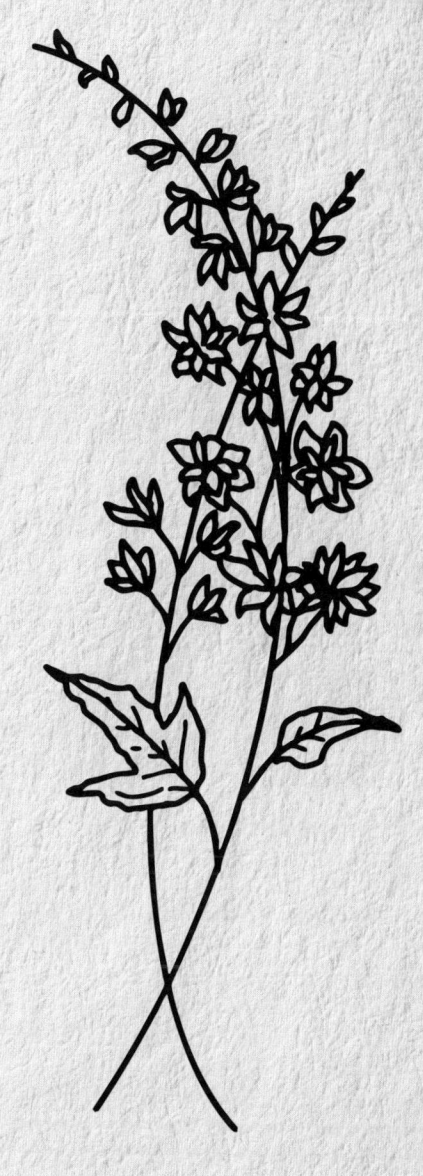

JULY — LARKSPUR

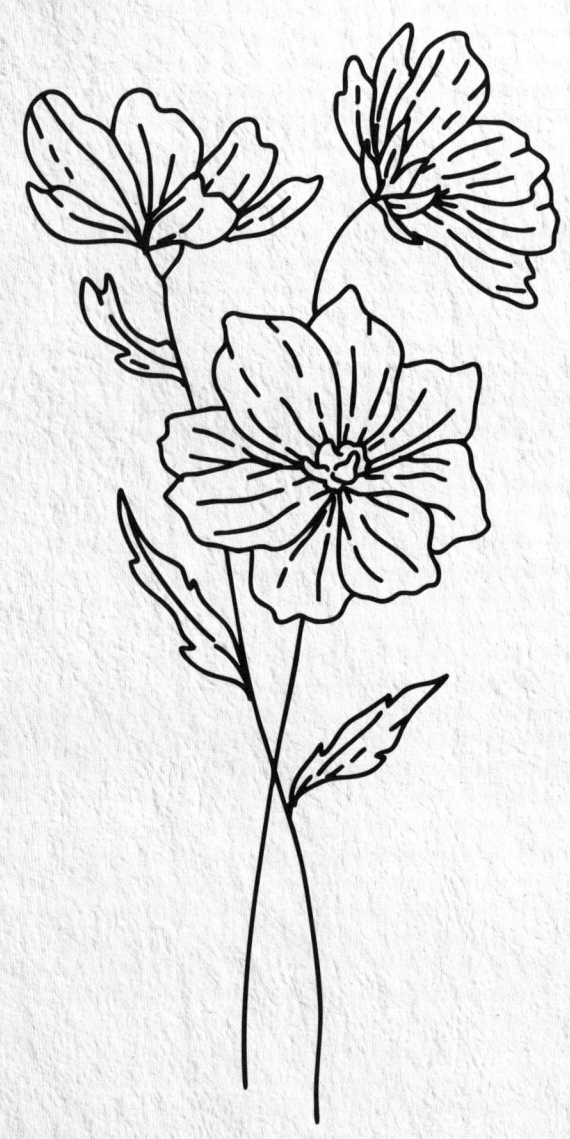

AUGUST — POPPY

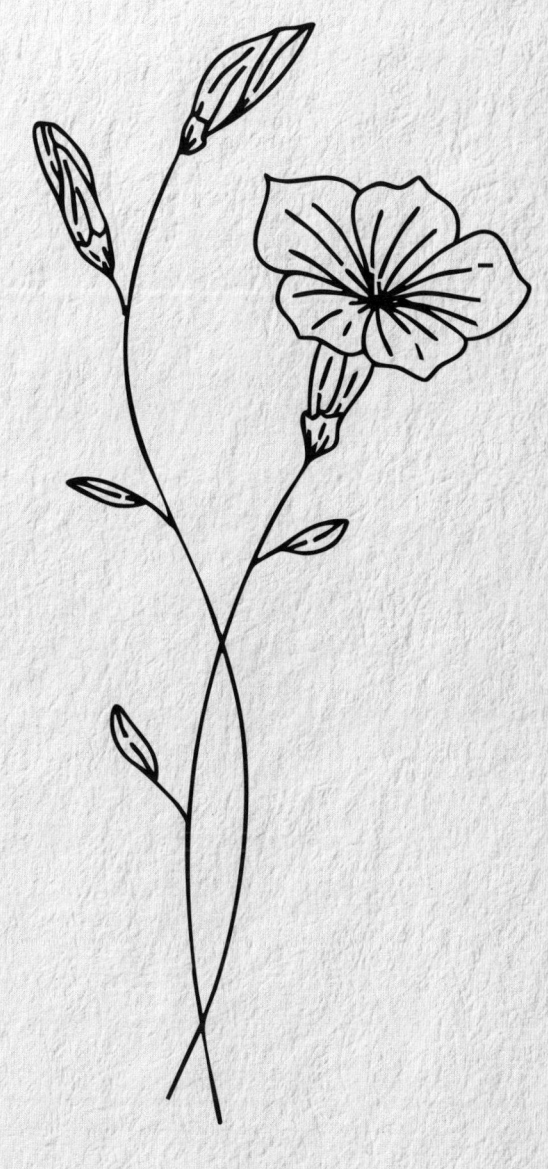

SEPTEMBER — MORNING GLORY

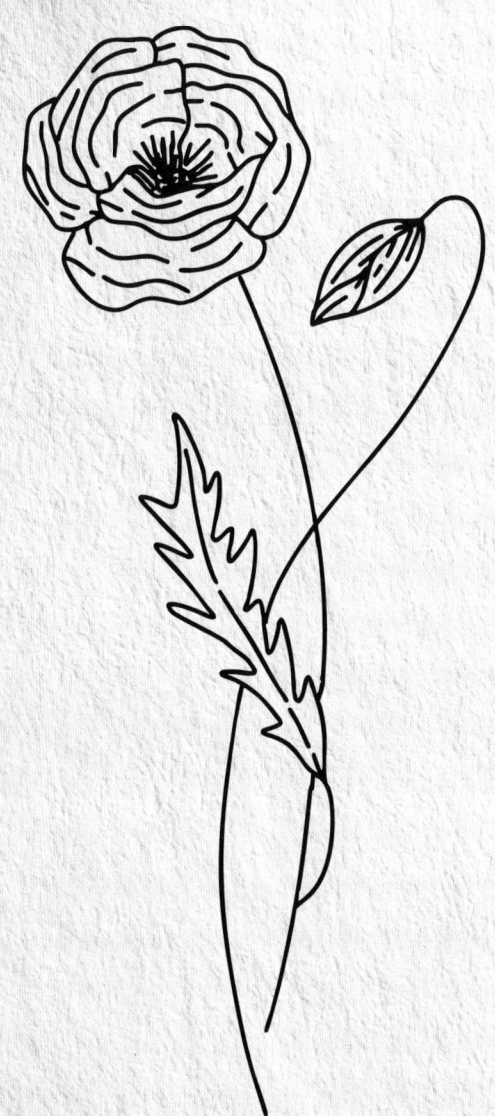

OCTOBER — COSMOS

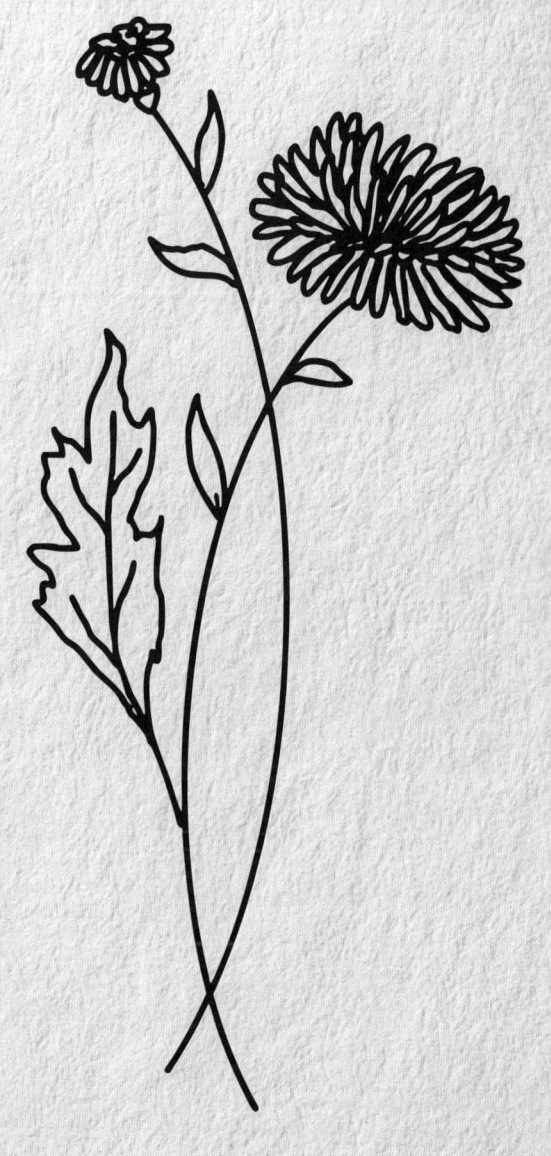

NOVEMBER — CHRYSANTHEMUM

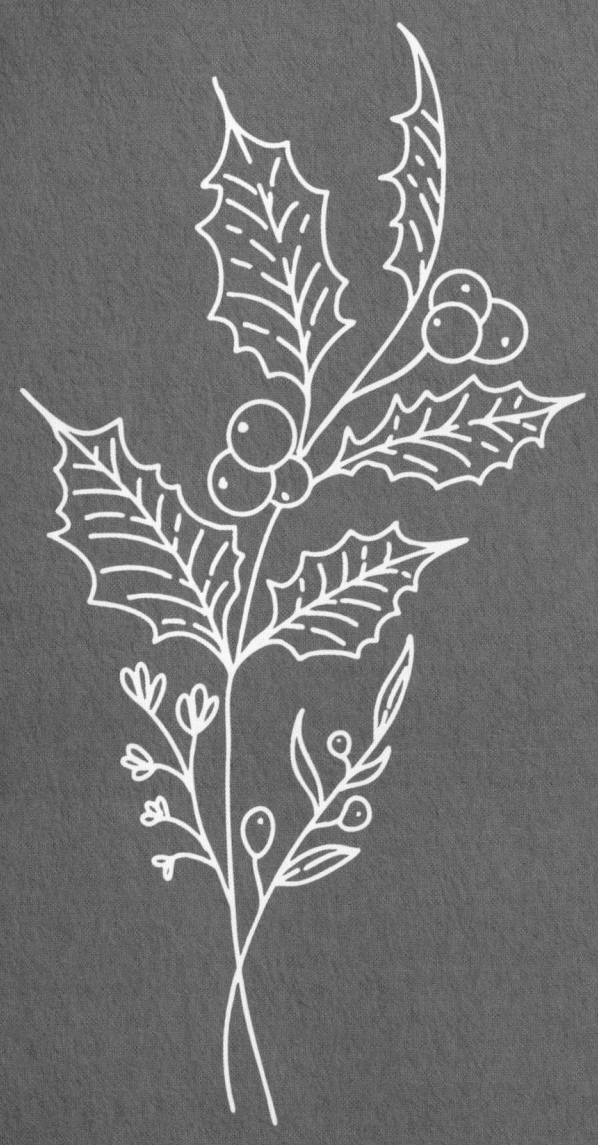

DECEMBER — HOLLY

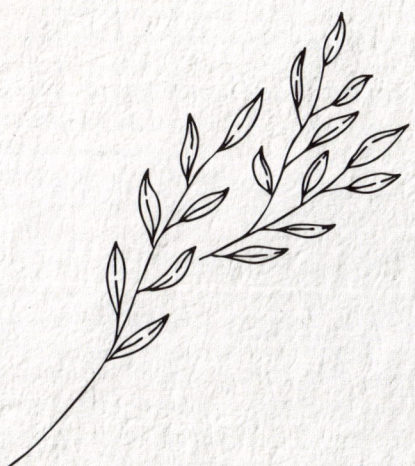

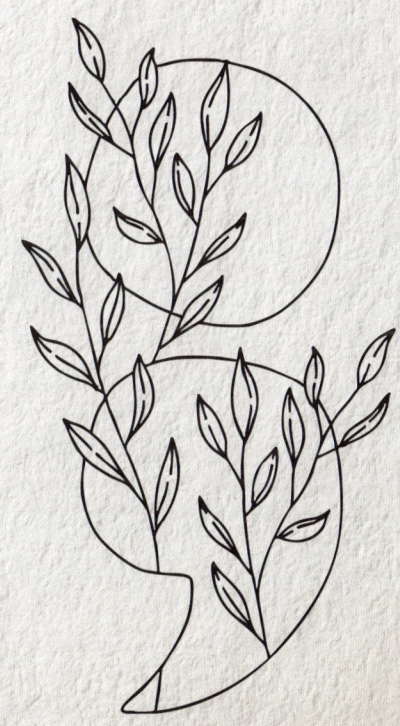

GROWTH

Three sprigs of green push upward, delicate yet determined. They grow above a semicolon pause, continuation, beginning again. It's a symbol of resilience: life starting fresh. In every small leaf, there's a promise that growth is always possible.

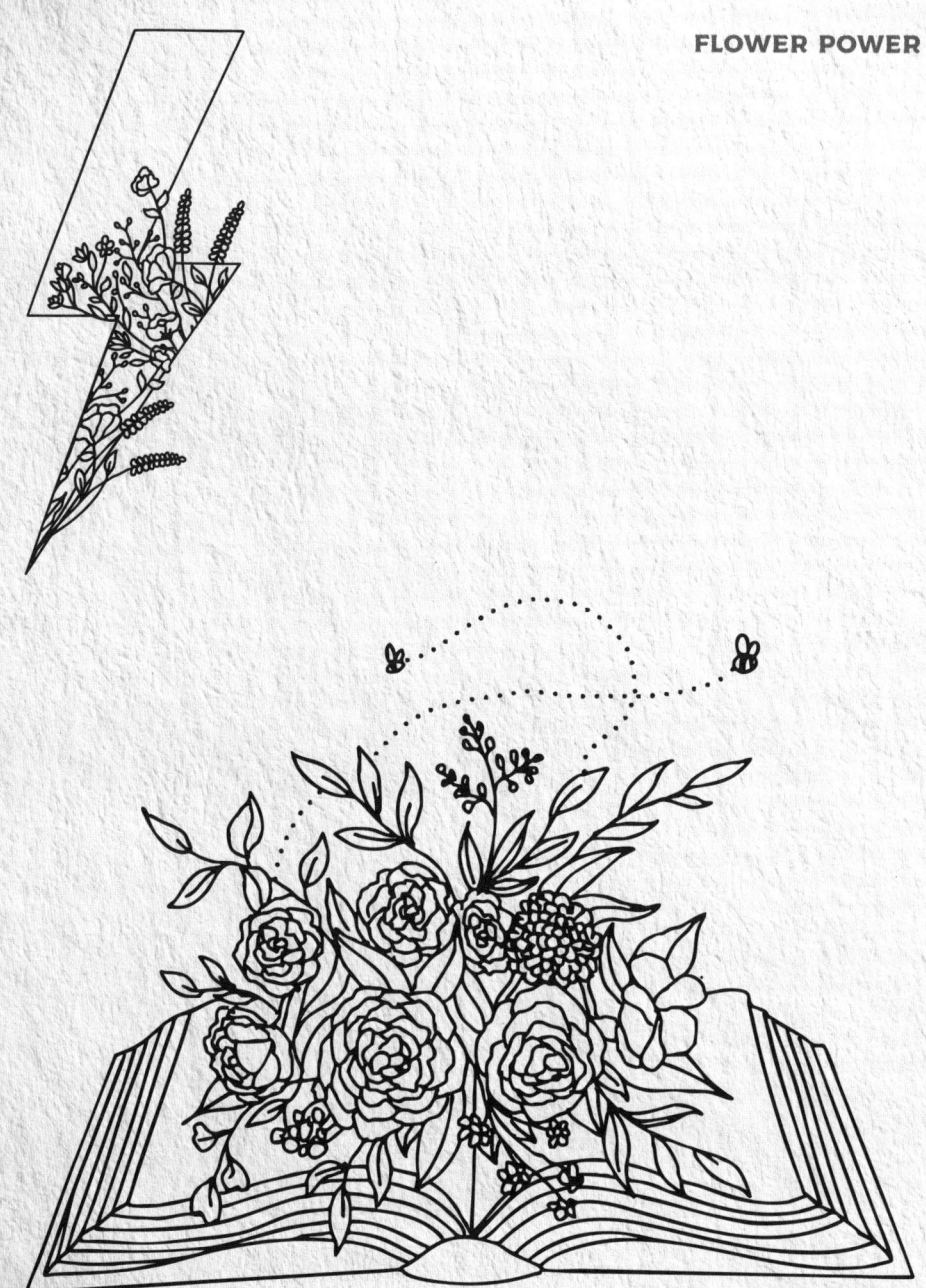

BOOK IN BLOOM

LOVE BLOSSOMS

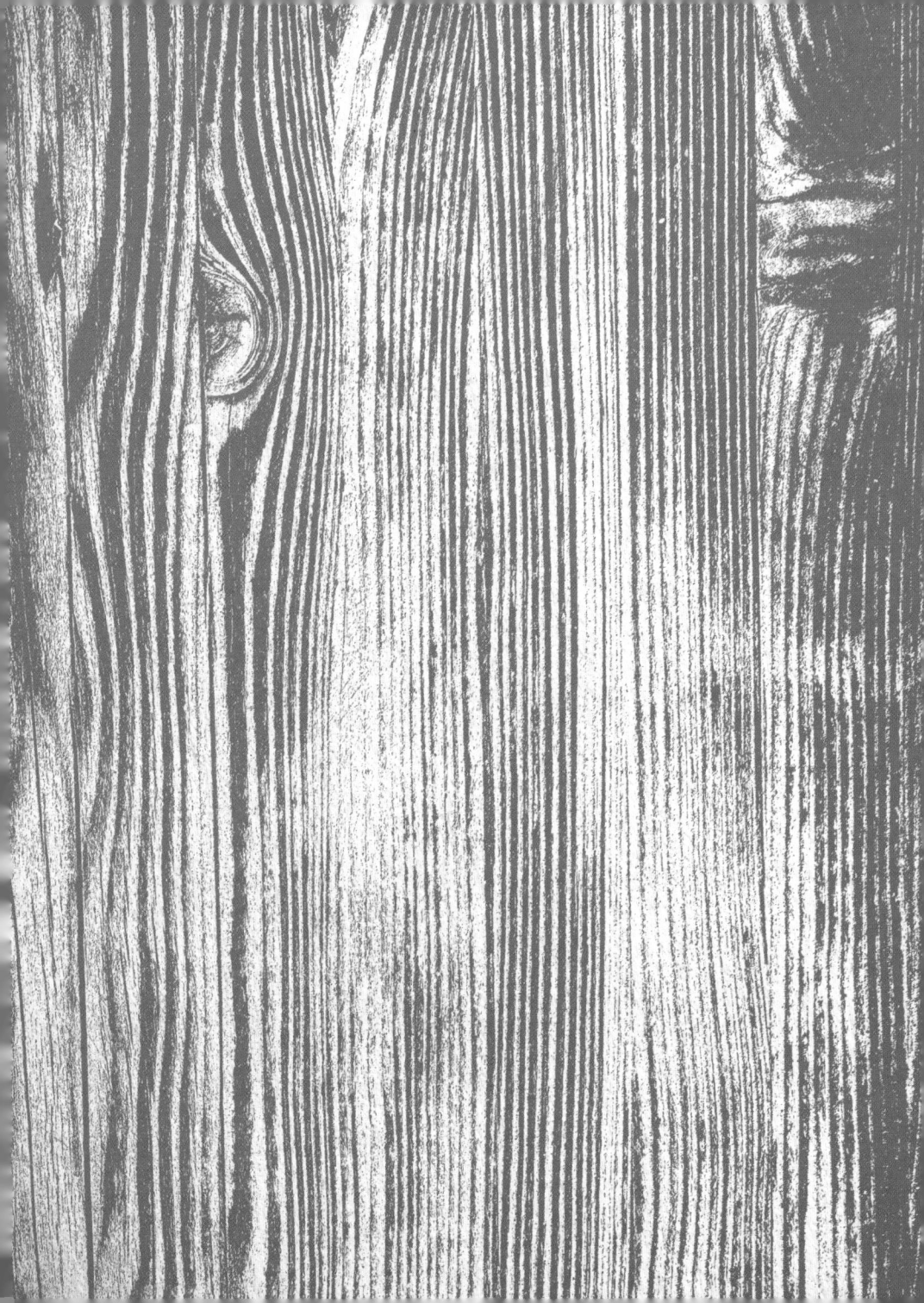

CHAPTER 5

ELEMENTAL FORCES

It's no secret that I love the great outdoors. I love everything from wide open spaces to mountain ranges. I love it when the view stretches out ahead of me, the sky seems to open up, and it's impossible not to think about how much life is in that landscape.

This chapter is a reminder of that feeling, and an evocation of the simplest building blocks that shape the ridge lines, rolling hills, crashing waves, and everything in between.

When I'm out on an adventure, I'll often find myself pausing in front of a scene to take out my sketchbook or camera and quickly capture what I see. It's never the kind of snapshot that's meant to be perfect but a way to mark the moment and record essential elements.

These designs are like that—they're little reminders of the places that have made me pause and will make you pause too.

They're meant for anyone who has ever stood on the edge of a viewpoint and been in awe. For people who seek reminders of the elemental connection that we all share. These designs will transport you to a place of quiet appreciation for this beautiful world we call home.

"LOOK DEEP INTO NATURE, AND THEN YOU WILL UNDERSTAND EVERYTHING BETTER."

– ALBERT EINSTEIN

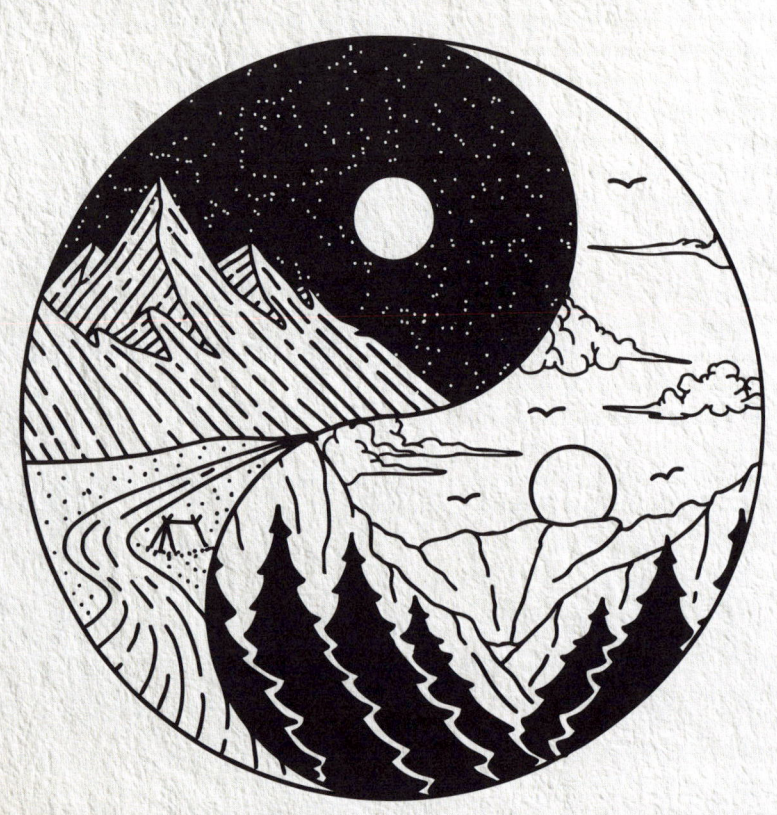

WORLD IN BALANCE

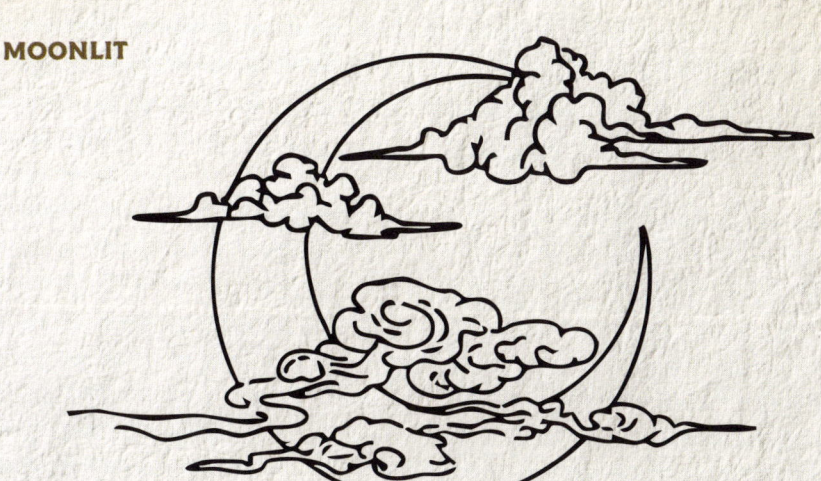

MOONLIT

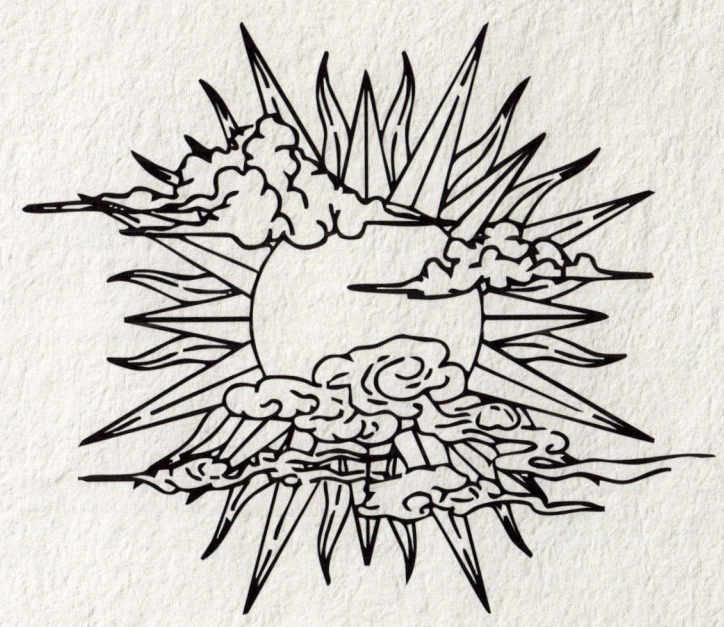

SHINING THROUGH

CELESTIAL TIDE

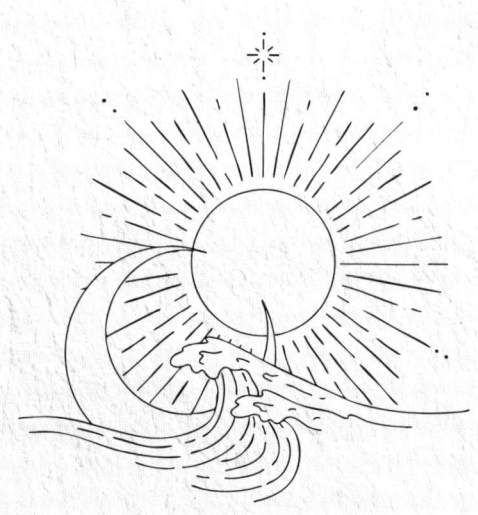

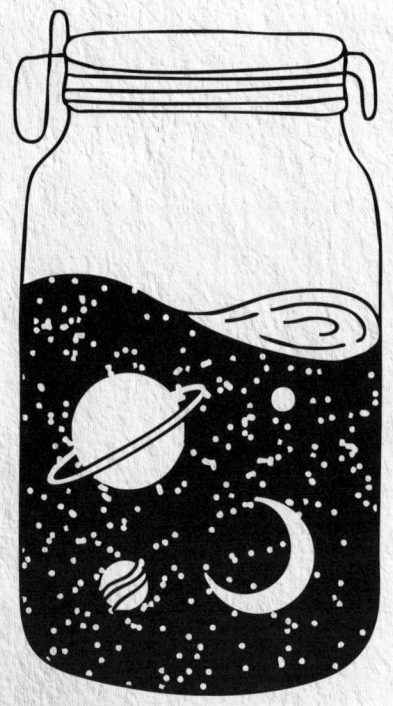

SPACE SAVER

TAKEAWAYS

Three jars sit side by side—one holding a mountain, one a wave, another five small pines. Little keepsakes of the wild, gathered and saved. They feel like memories bottled up. Reminders that adventure always lingers somewhere inside you.

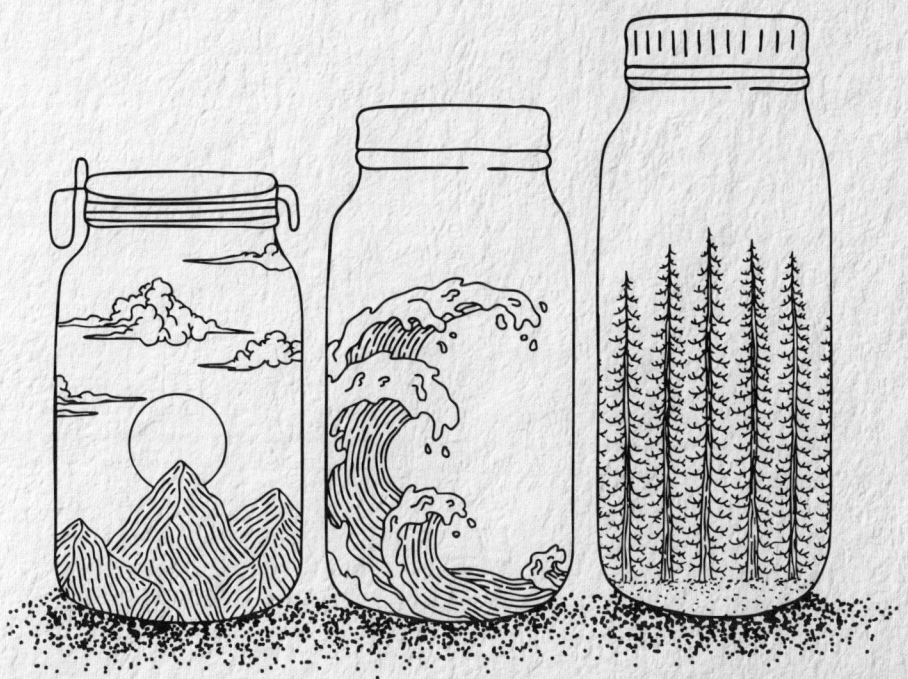

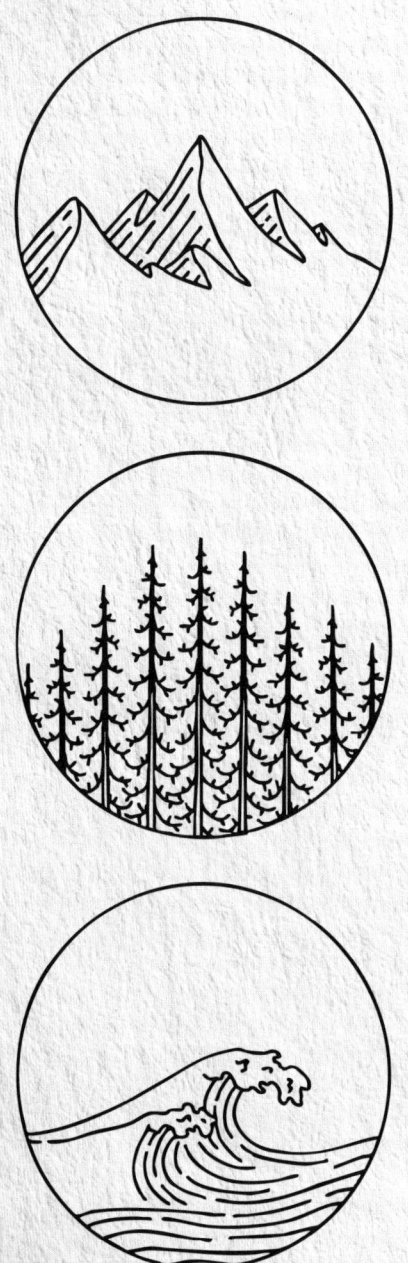

OUTSIDE THE BOX

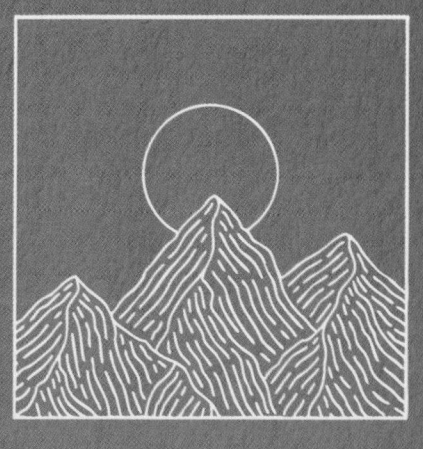

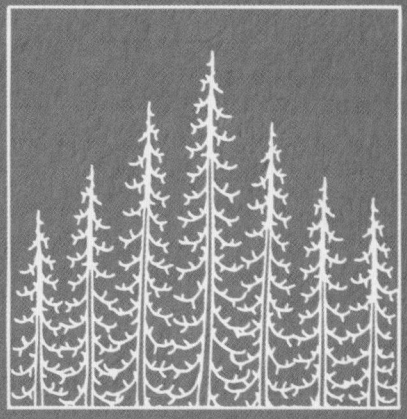

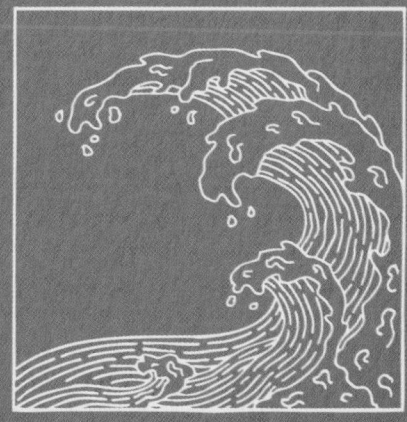

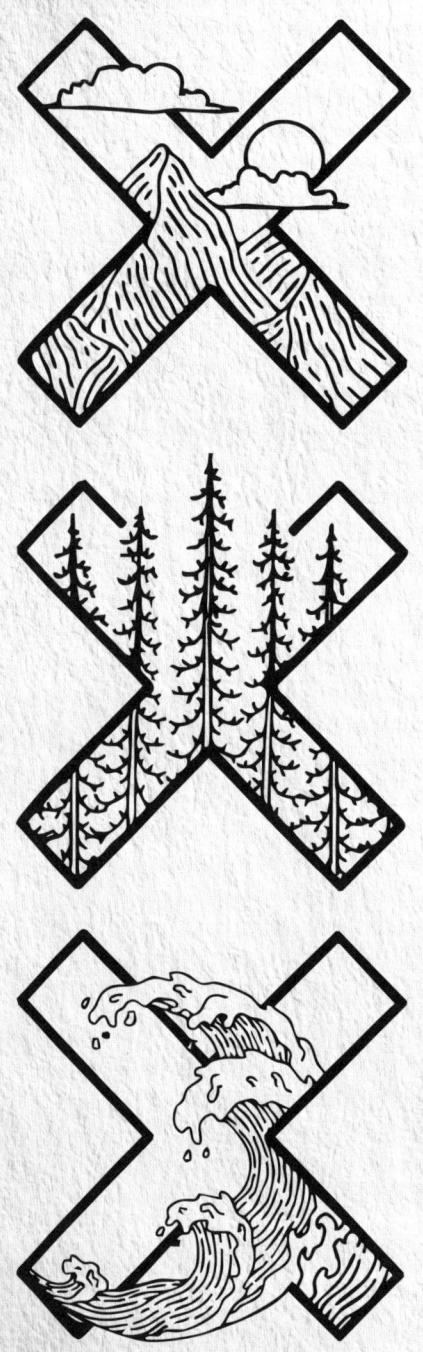

EXTRA SPACE

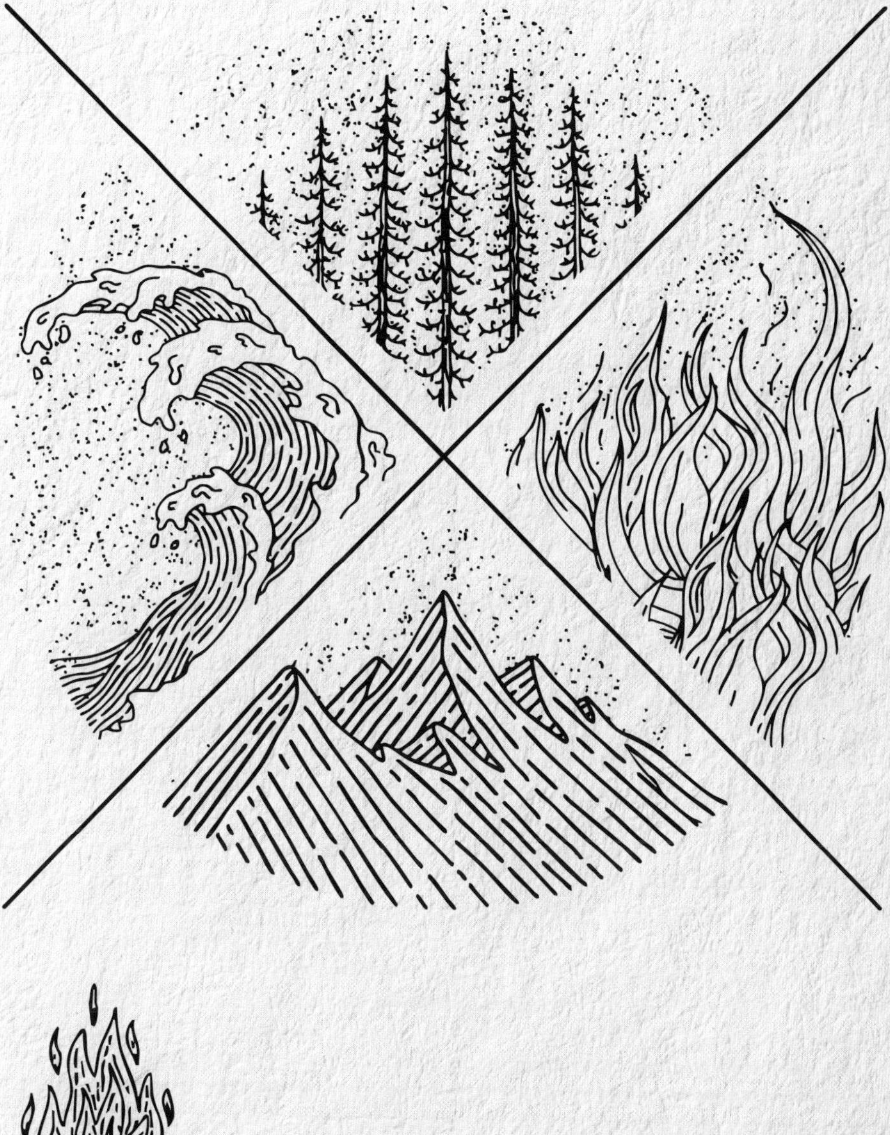

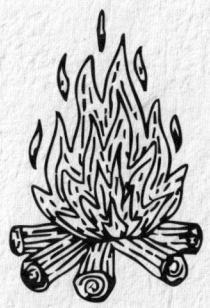

EMBERS

ELEMENTS OF THE WHOLE

WATER

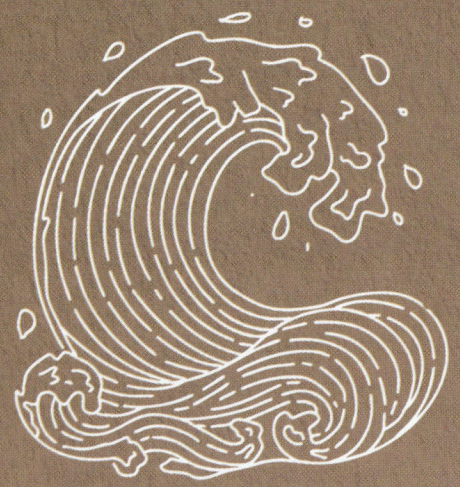

EARTH

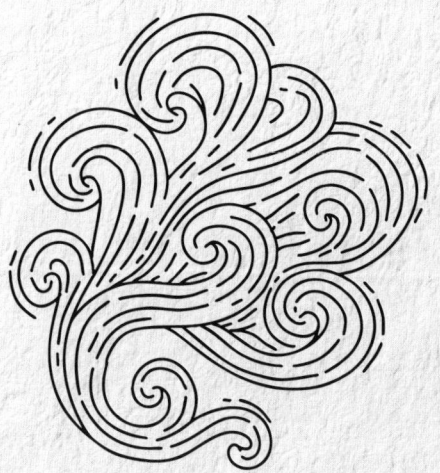

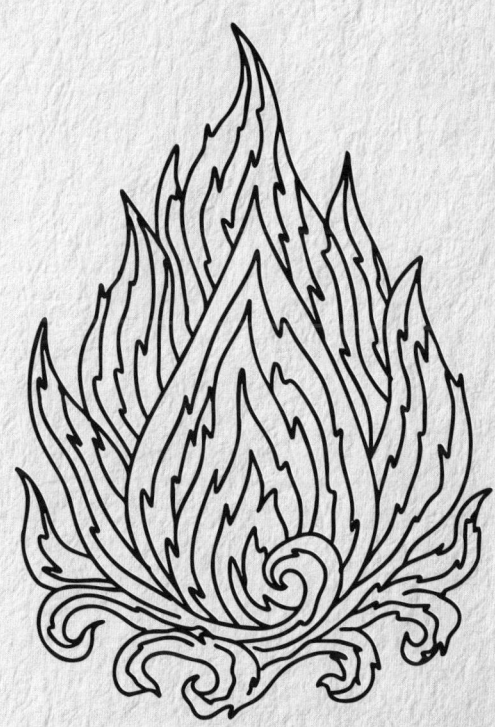

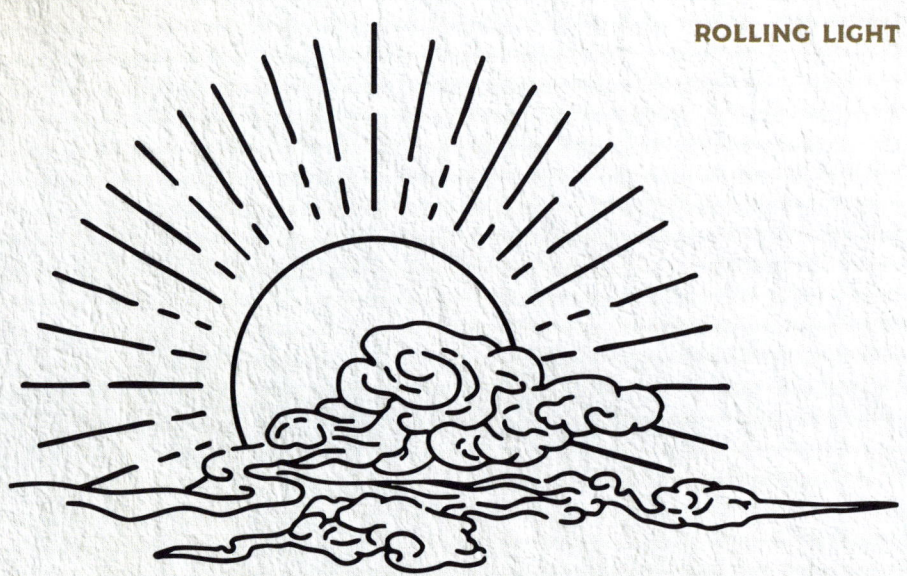

SUNKISSED

A single hand opens to the sun, warmth resting in its palm. The light feels soft yet steady, a reminder that the world can be gentle. In that glow, there is the kind of comfort only nature can give.

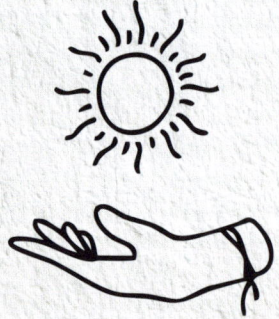

"THE EARTH HAS MUSIC FOR THOSE WHO LISTEN."

– GEORGE SANTAYANA

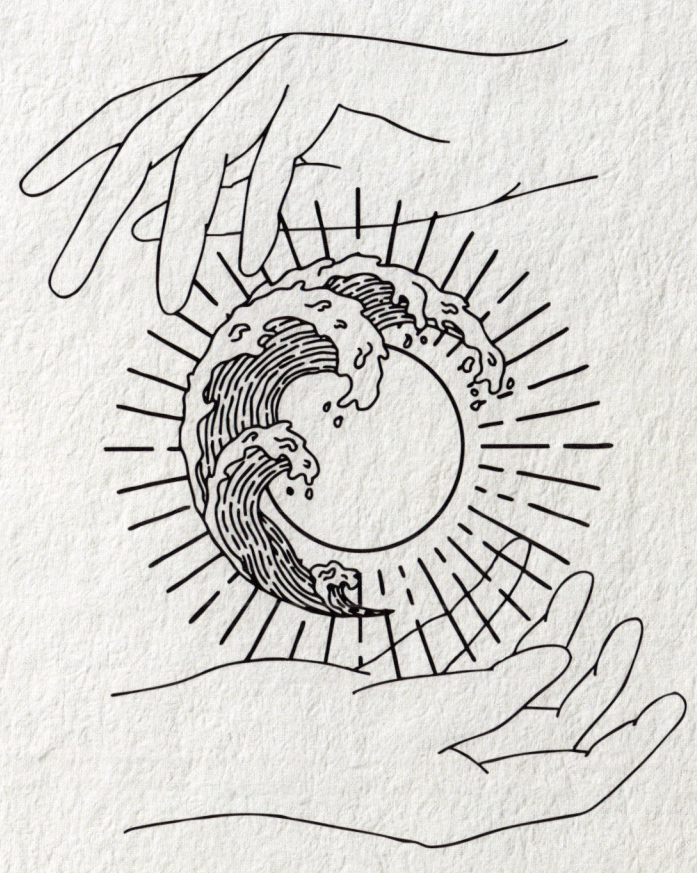

TIDAL HARNESS

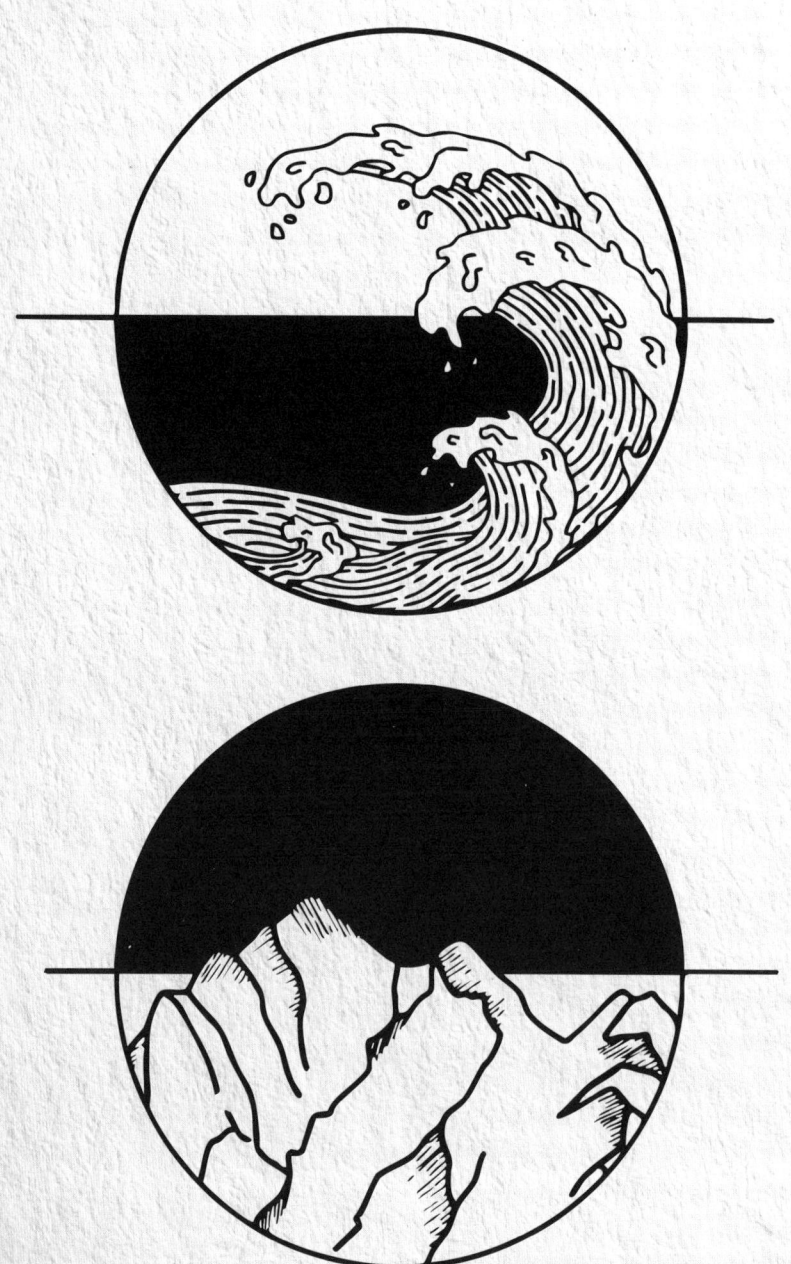

SEA PEAKS

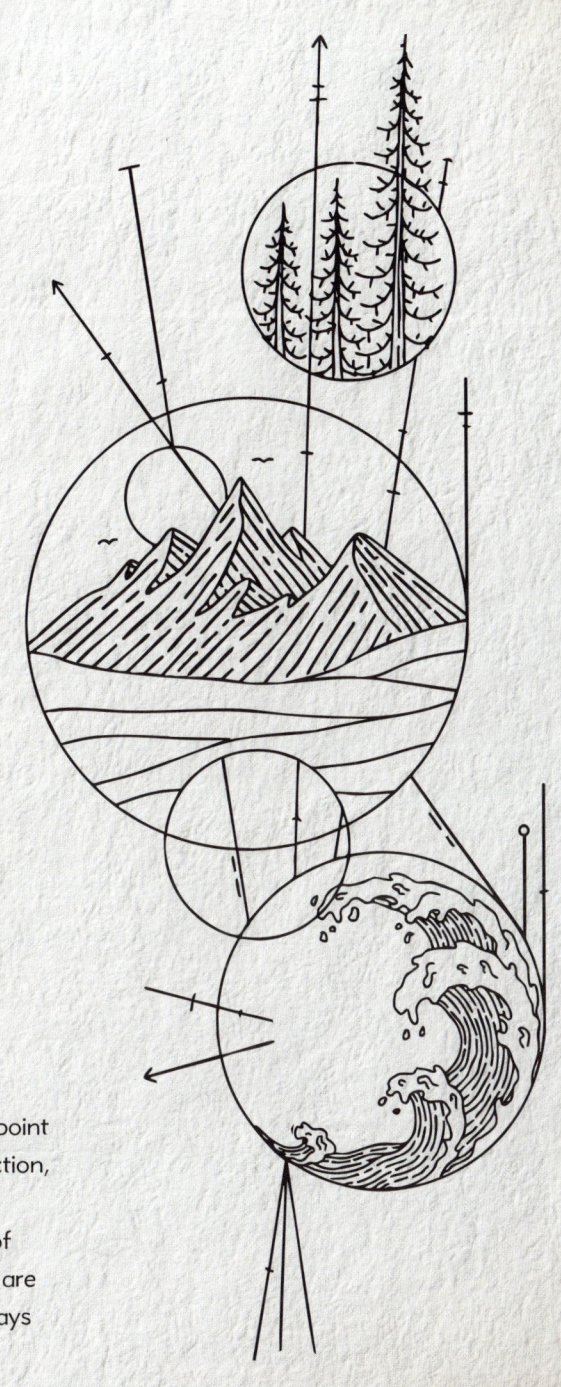

SOLSTICE

Four circles hold the seasons;
mountains and sunrise, moonlit
skies, waves in motion. Arrows point
outward, breaking in every direction,
marking change. The solstice is
more than a day; it's a turning of
time, reminding us that endings are
beginnings, and the earth is always
moving forward.

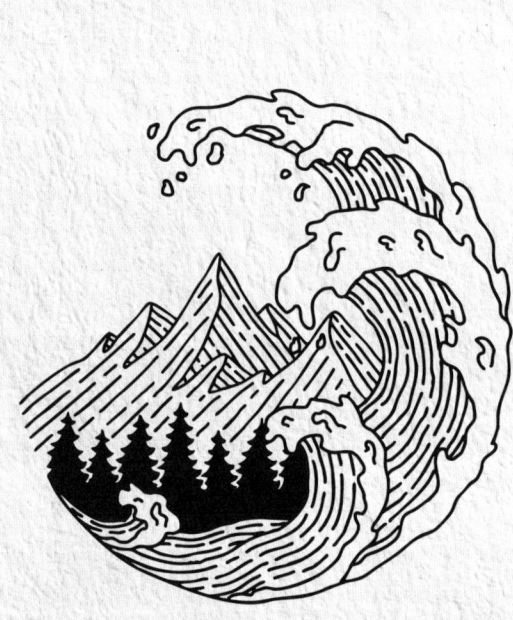

SHORE MEETS SKY

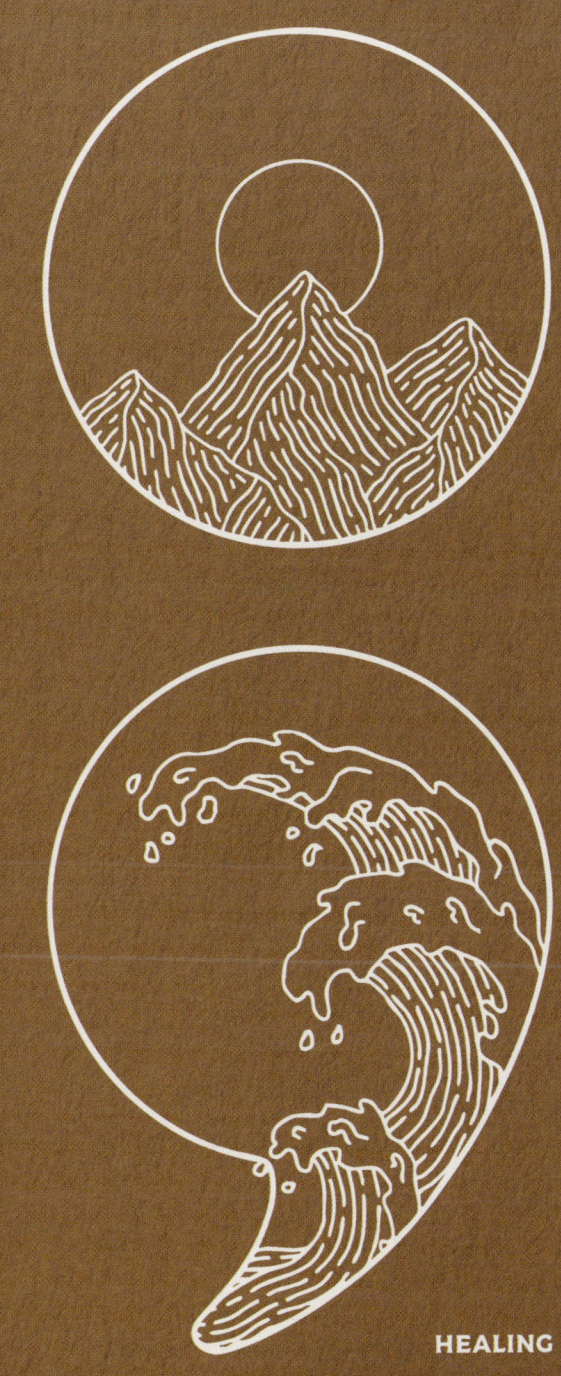

HEALING

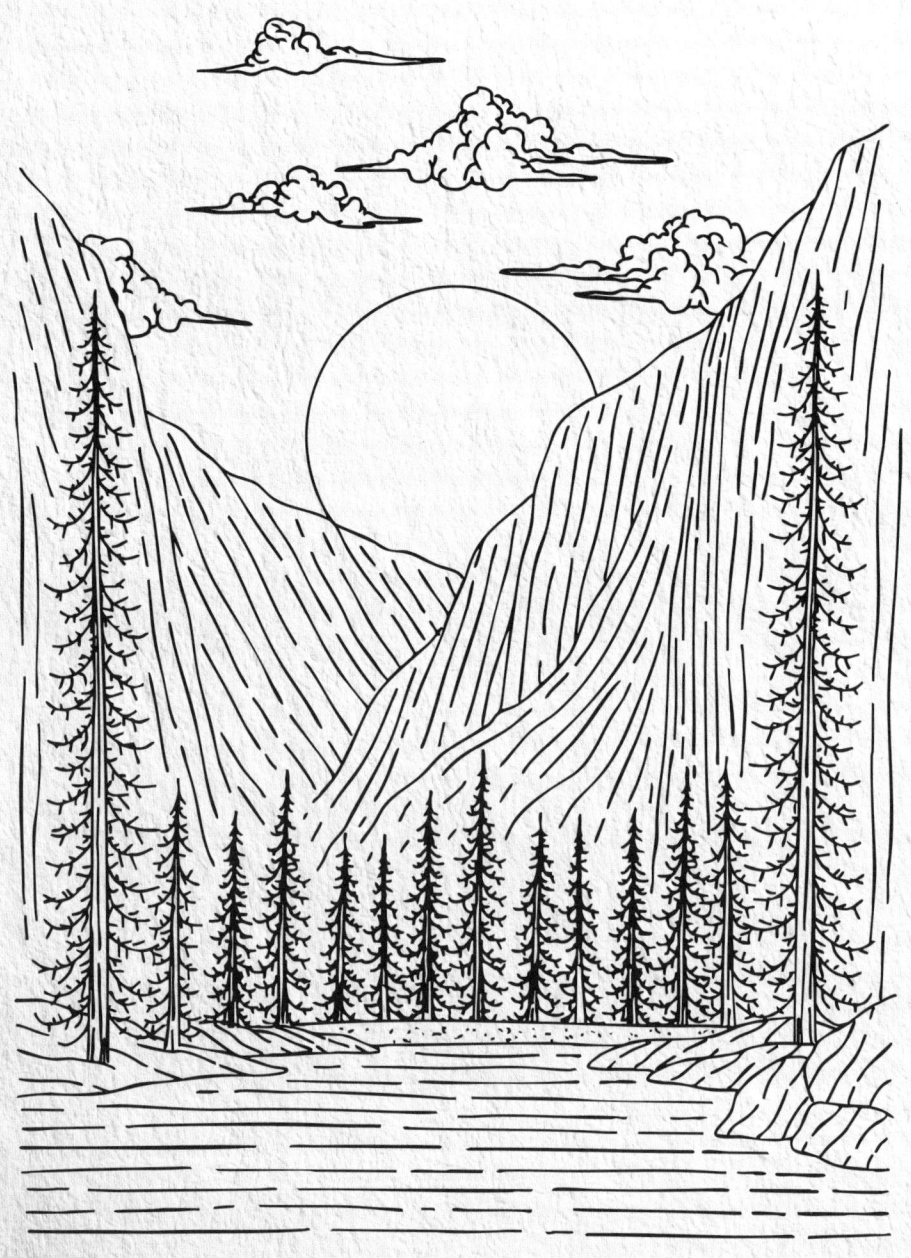

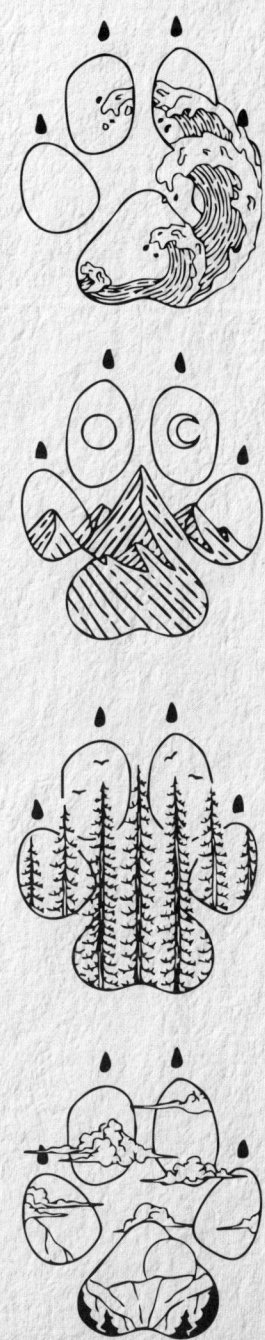

IMPRINTS

Four paw prints tell a story. One filled with waves, another with trees, another with mountains, another with skies. Each print is a reminder of your companion, the dog at your side, who walks with you through every element.

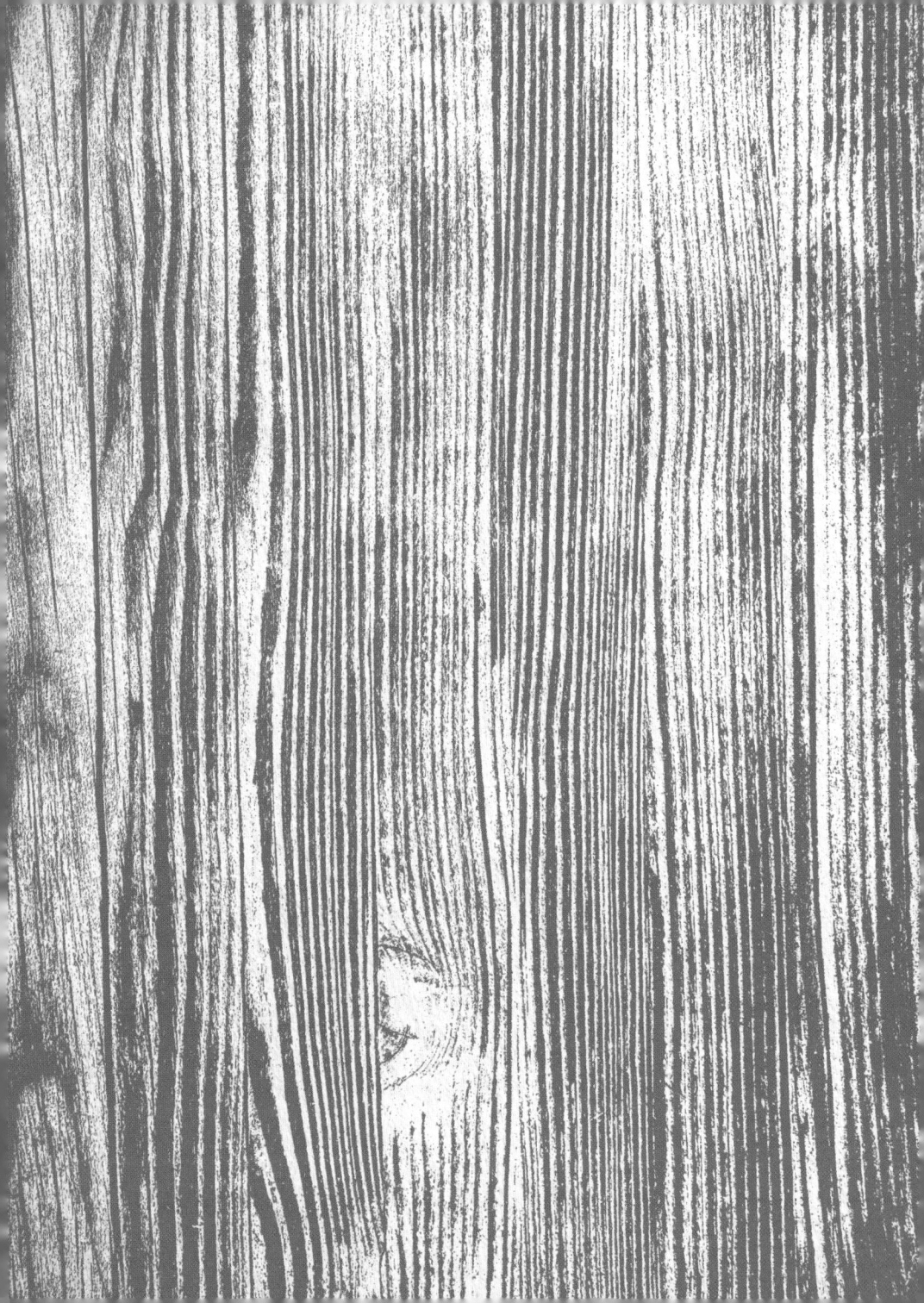

CHAPTER 6

WILD KIN

I've always loved animals, and they've always been a part of my journeys—whether in the form of my dog or an animal I've seen on a trail while hiking. This chapter is all about those experiences and a celebration of our pawed and feathered friends.

It was so hard to choose which creatures to include. Some animals reflect real encounters, spotted while on my adventures. Others live in my imagination, built from bits of memory and emotion—I'd love to see a bear one day. I drew these animals in an understated, organic way, with just enough line to bring them to life. And just enough whimsy to suggest the hidden lives we like to envision playing out when we're not looking and the commonalities we share as living, thinking, feeling beings.

This chapter is for the animal lovers. The ones who talk to their dogs and get excited when they see one in the wild. I hope you find your favorite animal here and that you feel the spirit of the amazing animal kingdom that we should all be so grateful for.

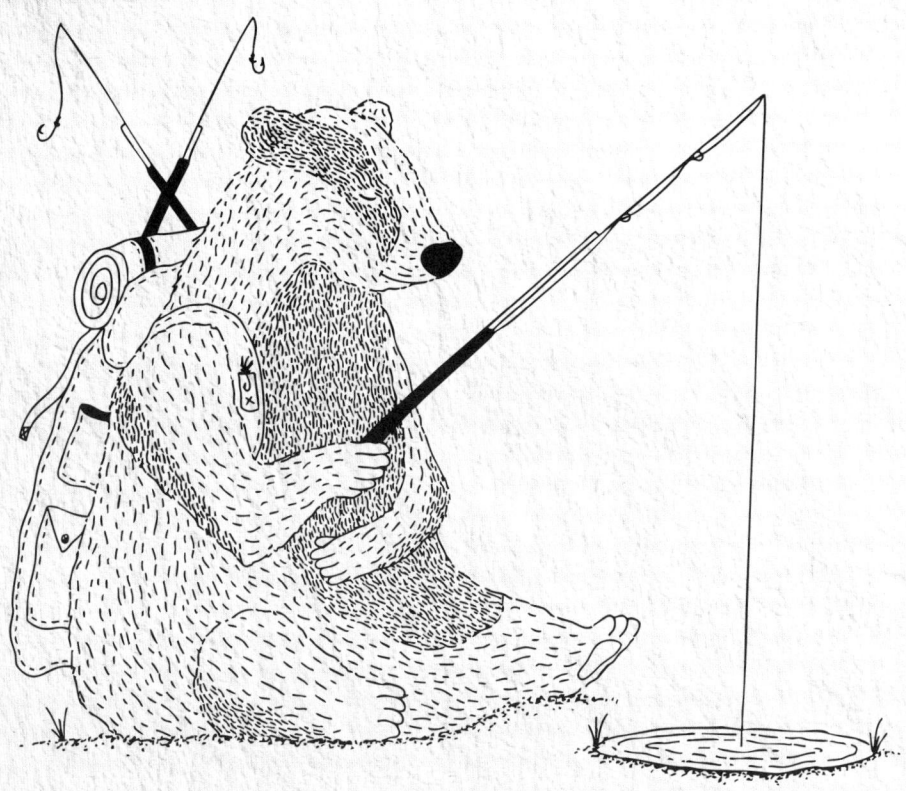

ANGLER

A badger sits patiently by a hole in the ice, backpack behind him, fishing line in hand. Eyes closed, he's round, calm, and meditative. In his stillness, there's joy and peace.

"THE LOVE FOR ALL LIVING CREATURES IS THE MOST NOBLE ATTRIBUTE OF MAN."

– CHARLES DARWIN

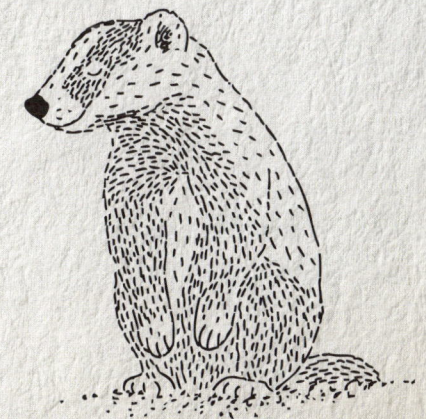

BADGER

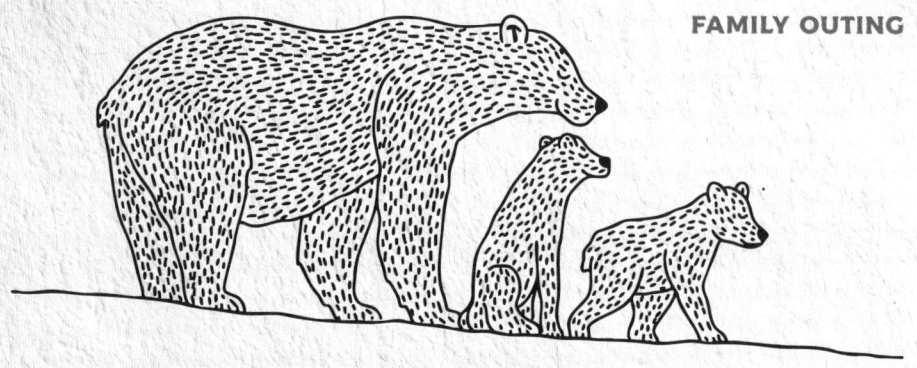

FAMILY OUTING

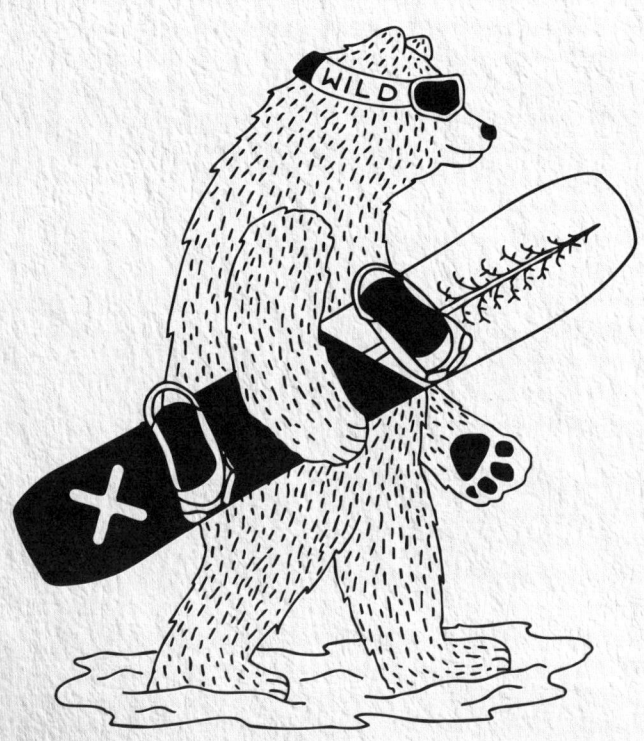

CUB CARVER

BEAR

A bear faces forward, etched in soft detail, belly round, smile gentle. He looks content, one with the woods, carrying the quiet joy of a life lived simply. He feels like a friend both mighty and endlessly at home in the forest.

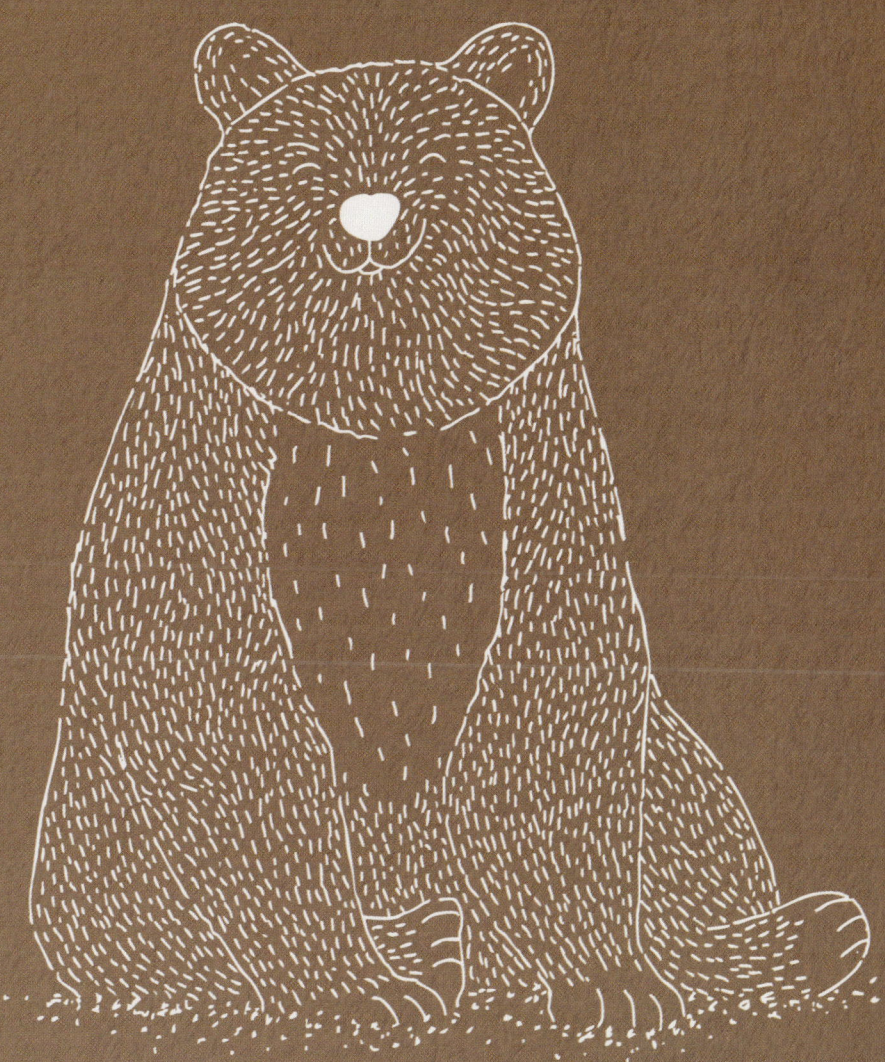

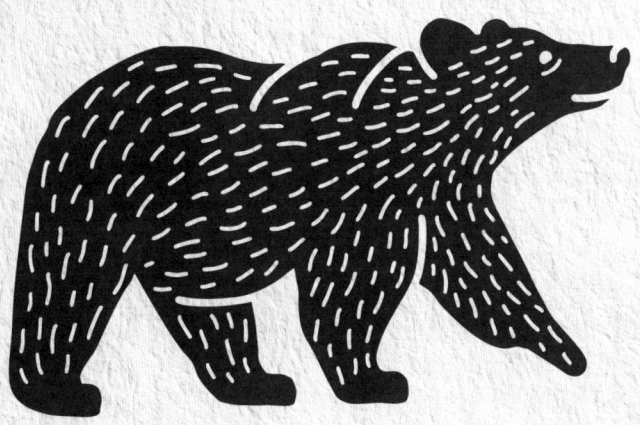

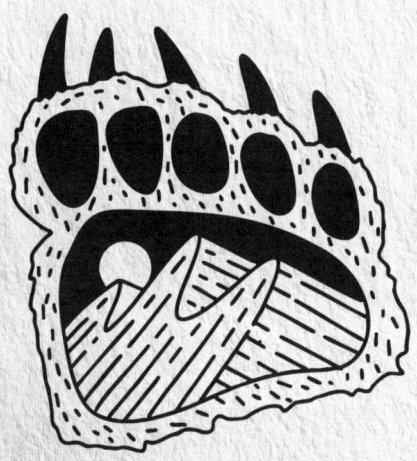

CLAW MARK

A bear's mark reveals more than tracks—within it lies a mountain range. These peaks are their domain, wild and vast, reminding us of the bear who belongs wholly to the land. Every claw mark left behind feels like a boundary line of wilderness itself.

BEAR HUG

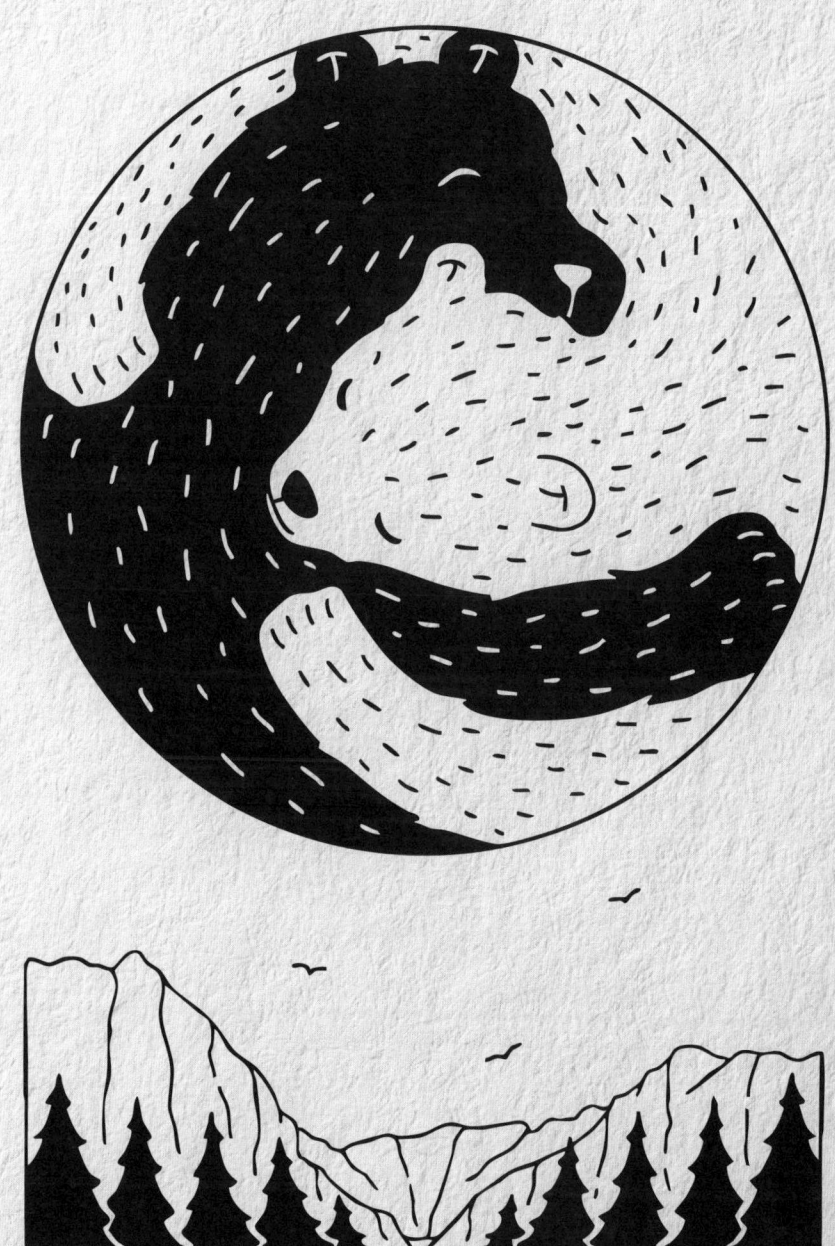

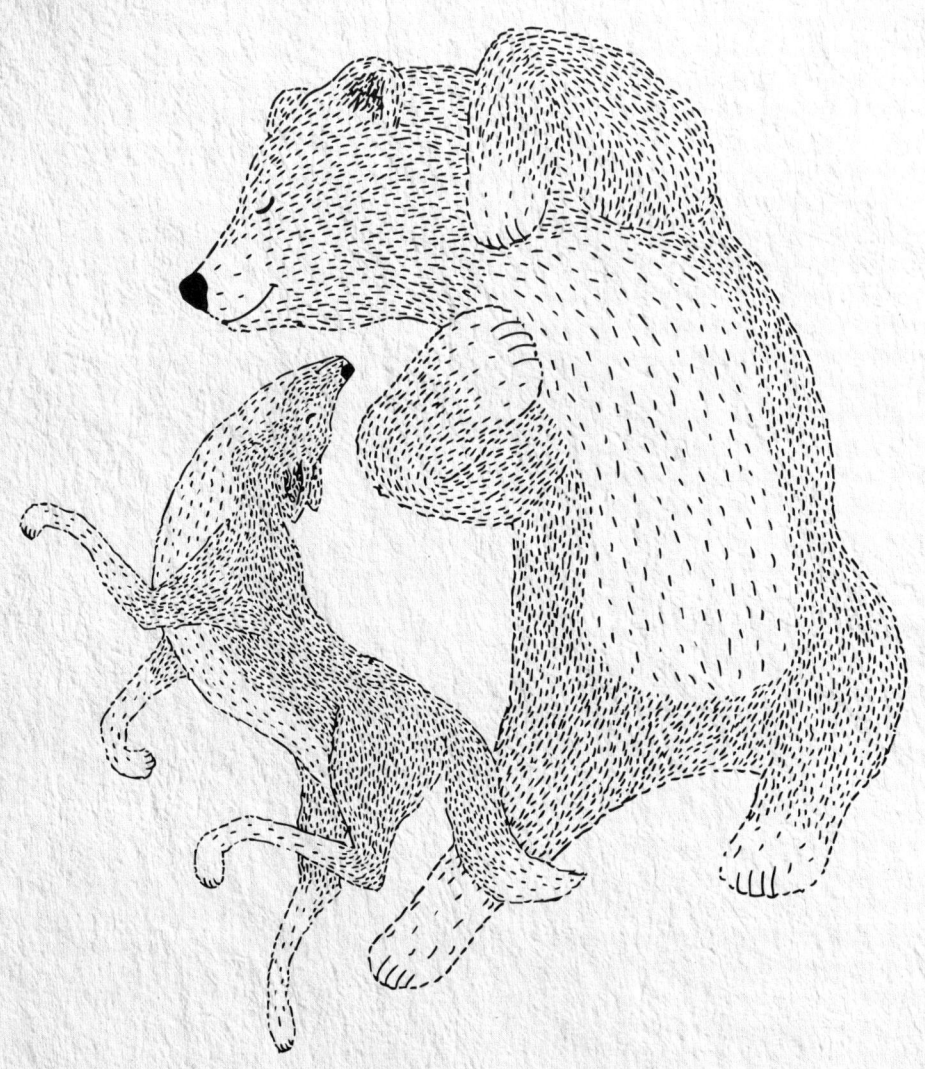

HARMONY

LITTLE JOYS

A bear sits by the fire, marshmallow in paw, roasting with delight. His fox friend sits nearby, sipping tea cross-legged on a stump. It feels like a scene from my childhood imagination, where animals share secrets when no one is watching.

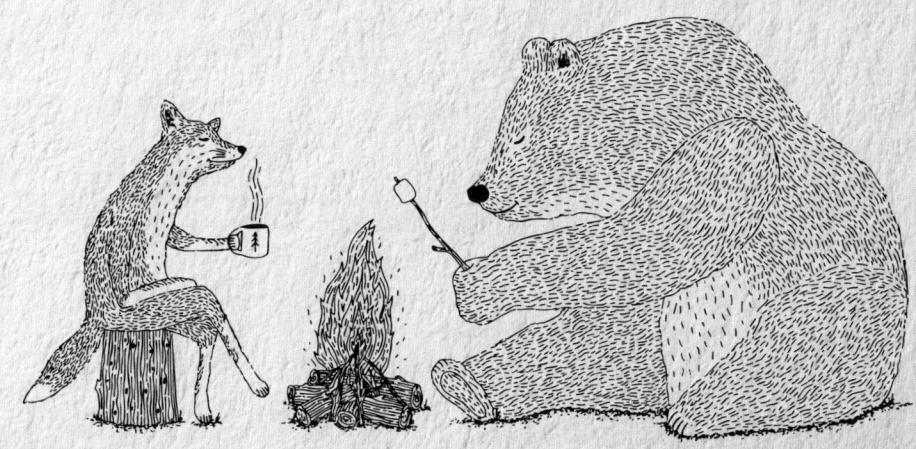

"STUDY NATURE, LOVE NATURE, STAY CLOSE TO NATURE. IT WILL NEVER FAIL YOU."

– FRANK LLOYD WRIGHT

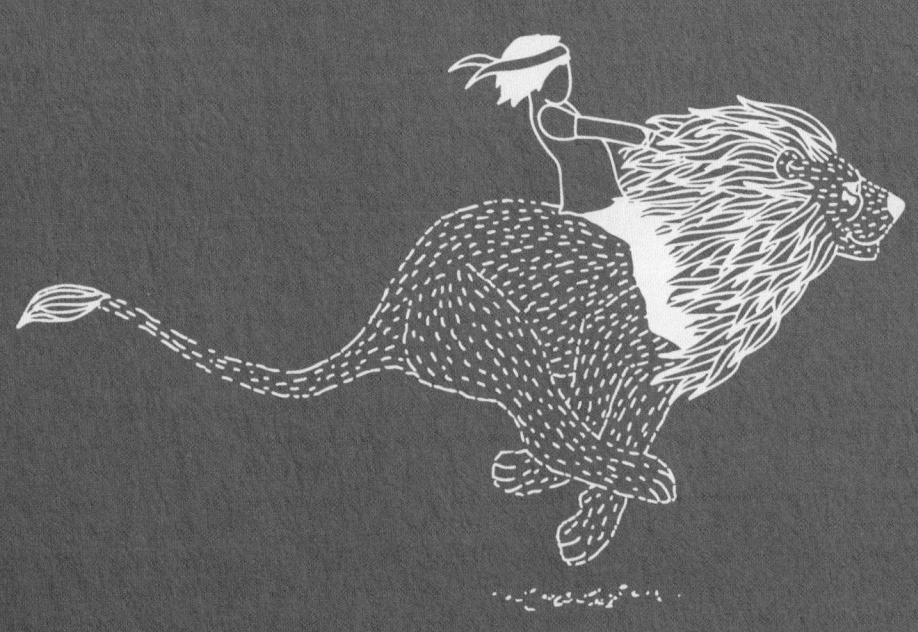

WILD RIDE

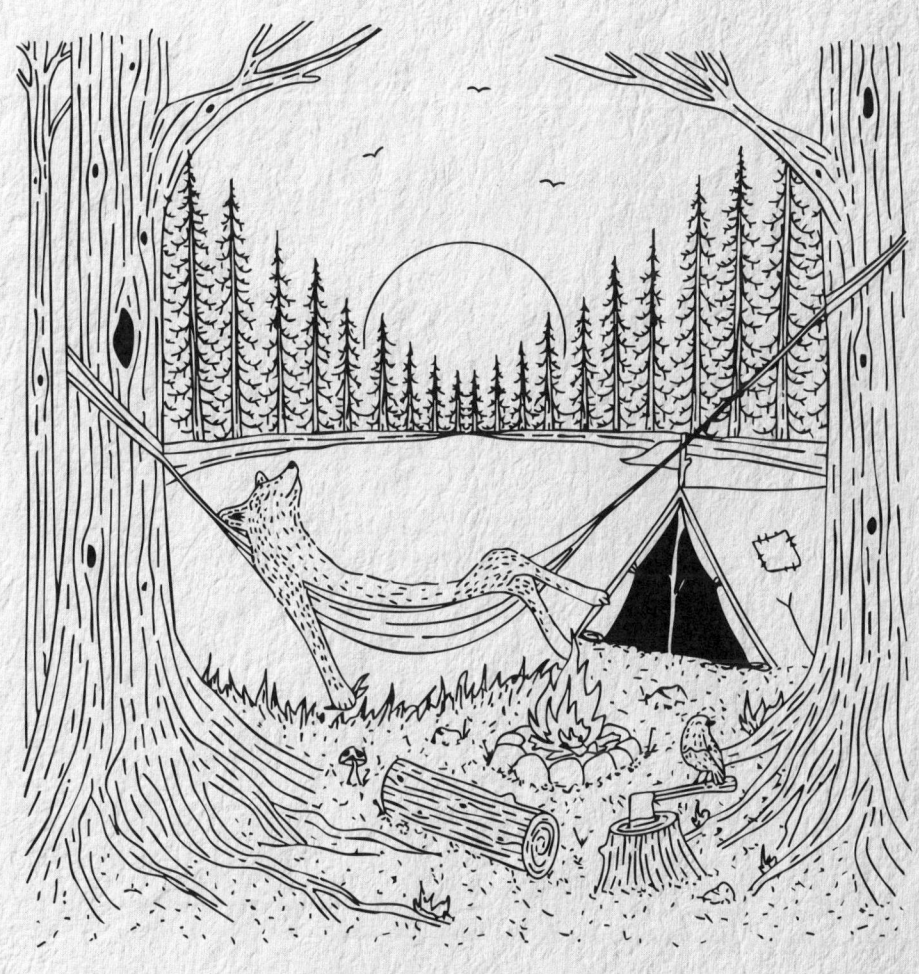

FIRESIDE DREAMS

DOE

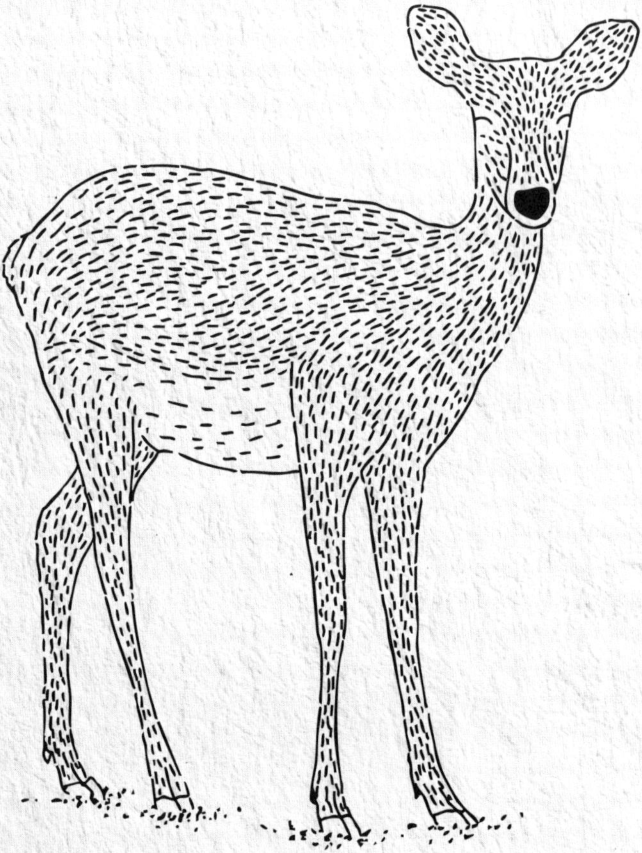

MOUSE

A tiny mouse peeks from beneath a flower's leaf, nibbling a nut in warm sun. Watching from the shadows, he adds sweetness to the woods, reminding you the forest is alive with gentle, unseen friends.

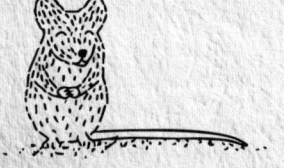

HARE

A hare pauses, ears tall, nose twitching.
Always listening, always alert, he
feels like the forest's eyes and ears.
Someone small is keeping watch, ready
to dart, leap, and survive.

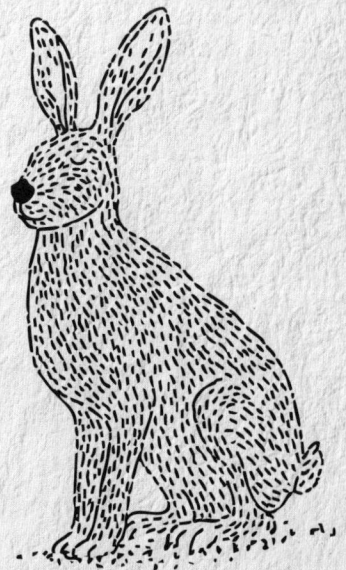

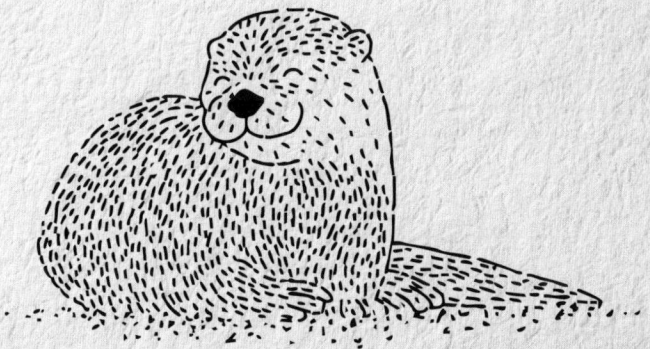

OTTER

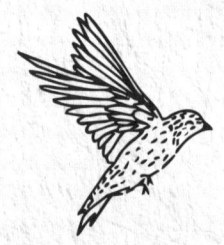

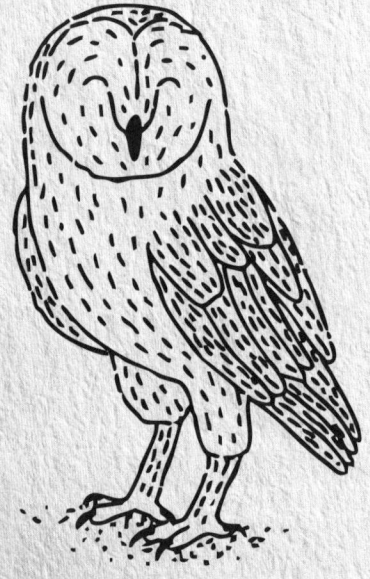

OWL

A barn owl rests, eyes closed, a faint smile soft on its beak. Etched in quiet charm, it feels like a magical companion of the night forest. To glimpse such a creature is to be reminded: the world still holds mystery, and some guardians only wake in the darkness.

RUGGED RETRIEVER

A golden retriever's form carries whole landscapes in its fur mountains, forests, and sunrise. Spirit and nature bound together, he looks like both guardian and guide. Loyal, happy, and at one with the earth, he's the kind of companion who makes the forest feel like home.

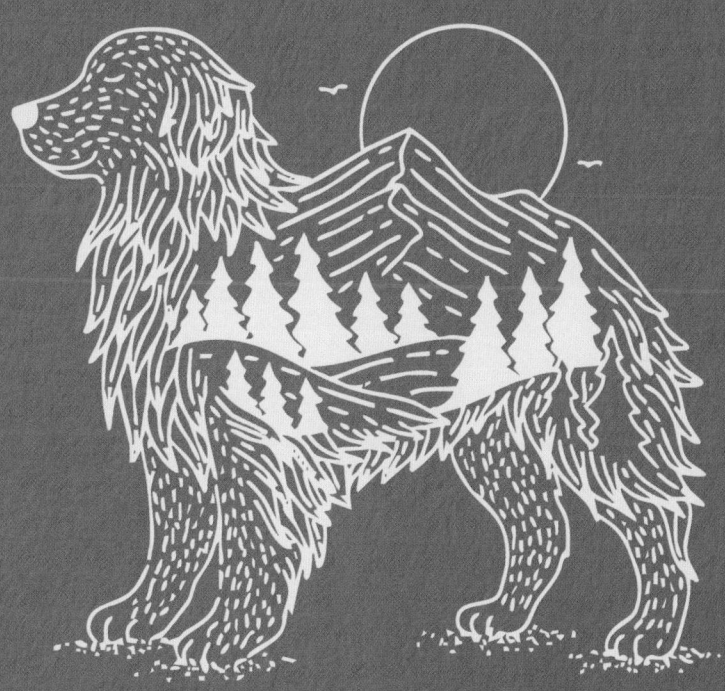

POUNCE

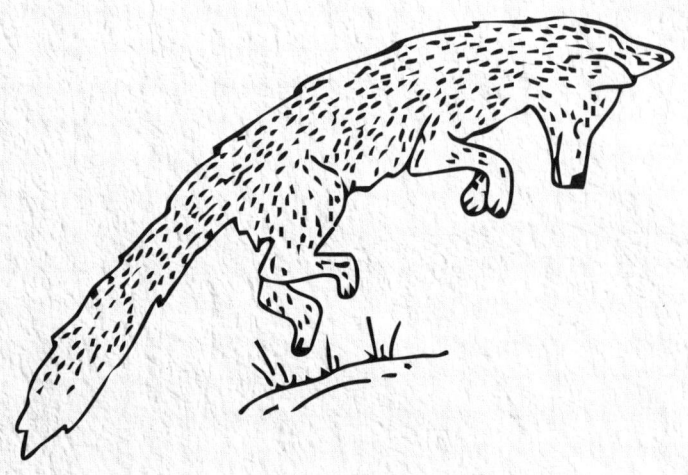

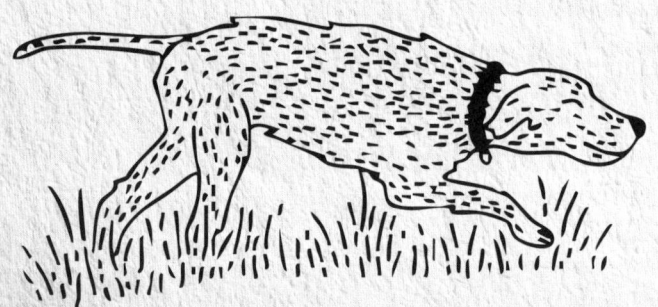

POINTER

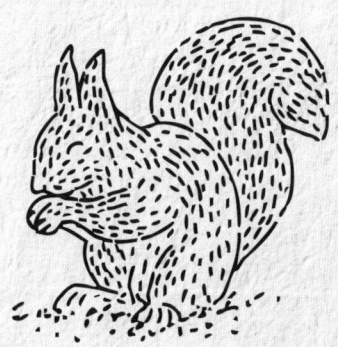

SQUIRREL

The squirrel is everywhere, darting, climbing, leaping between trees. Playful yet determined, he lives with wild energy, always in motion. A forest companion, he reminds us that life in the woods is never still, always alive.

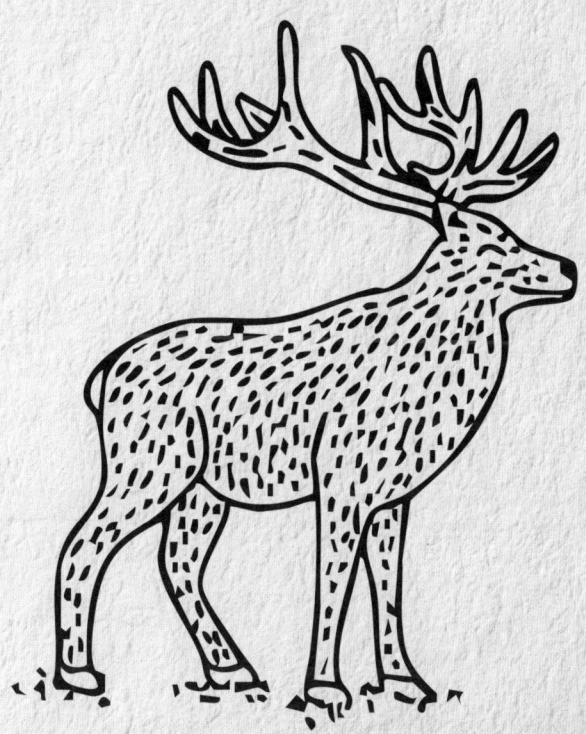

STAG

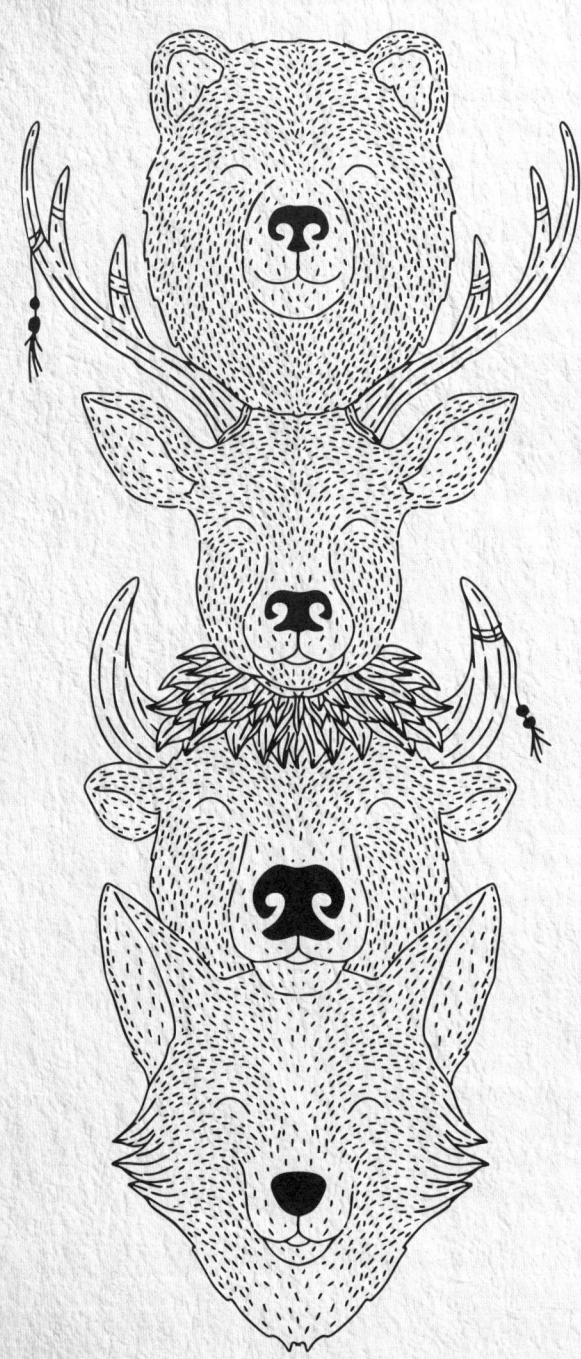

WILD NEIGHBORS

"TO SIT IN THE SHADE ON A FINE DAY IS THE PERFECT REFRESHMENT."

— JANE AUSTEN

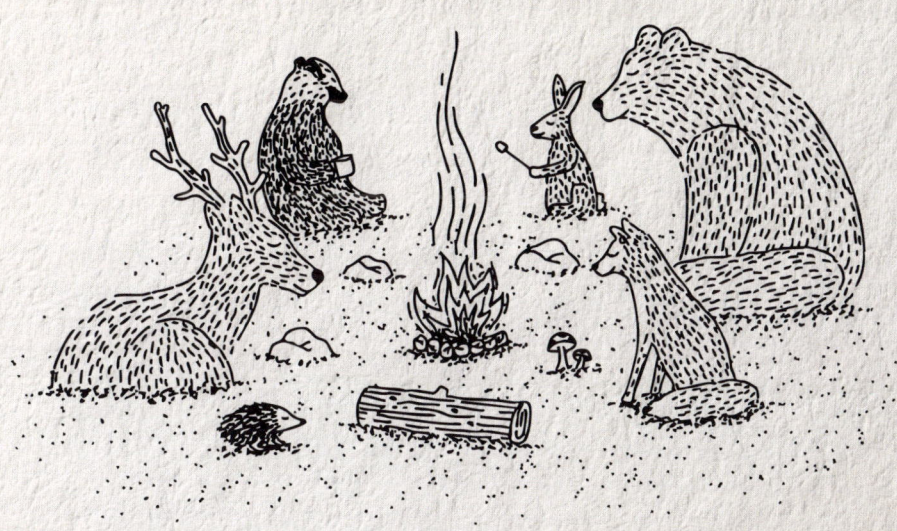

S'MORES TO SHARE

CAMPING
AND
CABINS

I've always loved camping. I love the idea that you can make a home anywhere—pitch up and create your own space away from the world. I also love the look and shelter of a log cabin. You just can't beat them; little retreats tucked away in the forest or in the mountains.

From campfires with friends and hammocks swaying in the trees to cozy days in lodges and tiny tents, this chapter reminds you that you don't need that much to feel at home and comfortable in the wilderness. These pieces are meant to take you back to moments when you've slowed down and felt grounded there.

They're for those who love waking up surrounded by the birds and the smell of last night's fire. They recall shared stories. If you know the joy of cooking breakfast over a fire or gazing up at the stars from your sleeping bag, these images are for you.

CABIN COMPANY

Tucked beneath the pines, the cabin is warm and inviting. Smoke curls from the chimney, fire flickers inside, and conversation drifts across the trees. Here, time slows. With friends nearby and the woods all around, home is as simple as this.

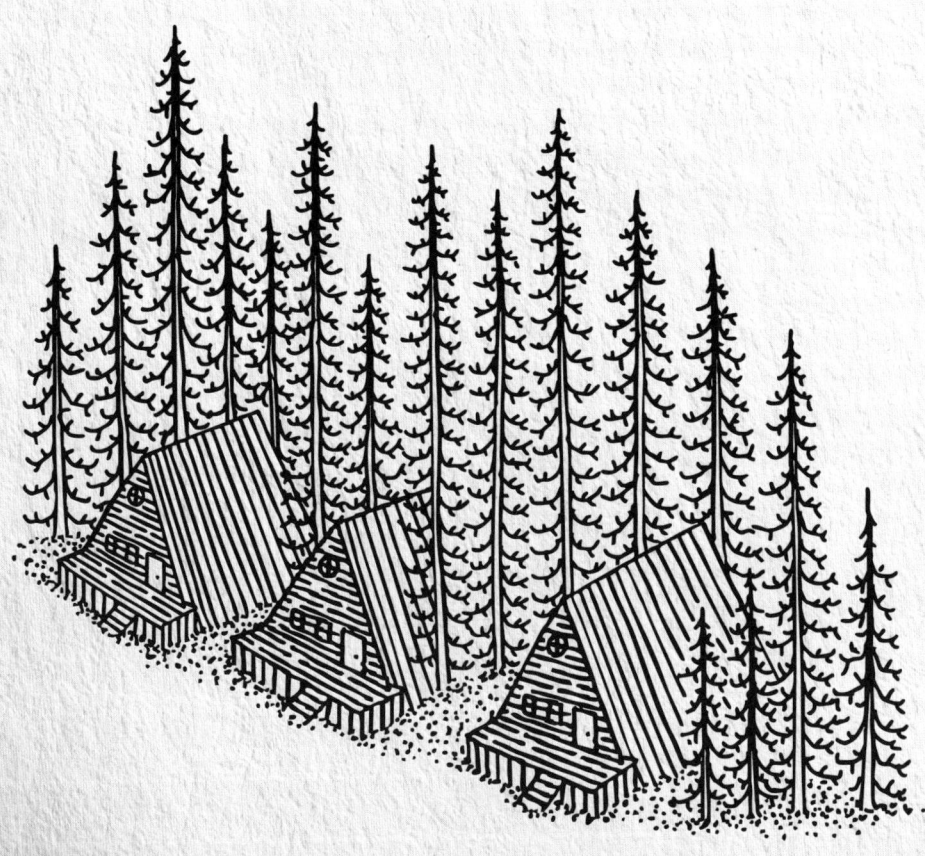

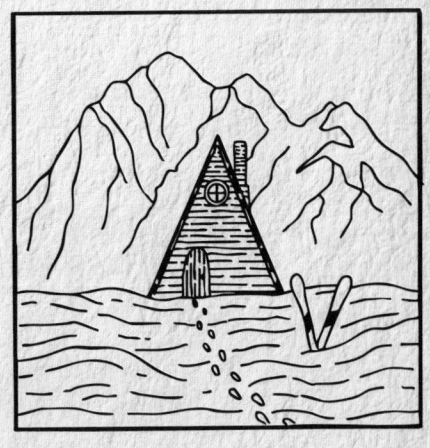

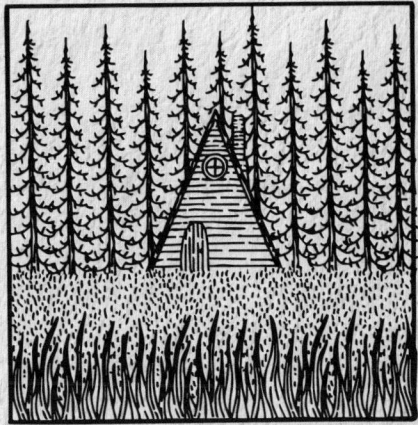

CABIN SNAPSHOTS

Snow hushes the forest, waves murmur
beyond the trees, and the cabin glows
like a lantern in the quiet. Boots dry
by the door. The scent of woodsmoke
lingers. Wrapped in blankets, you listen
to winter settle and the tide breathe, at
once remote and deeply at home.

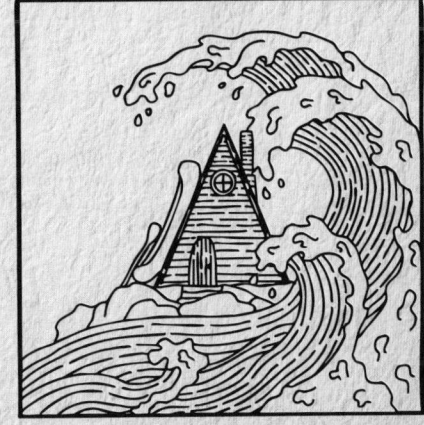

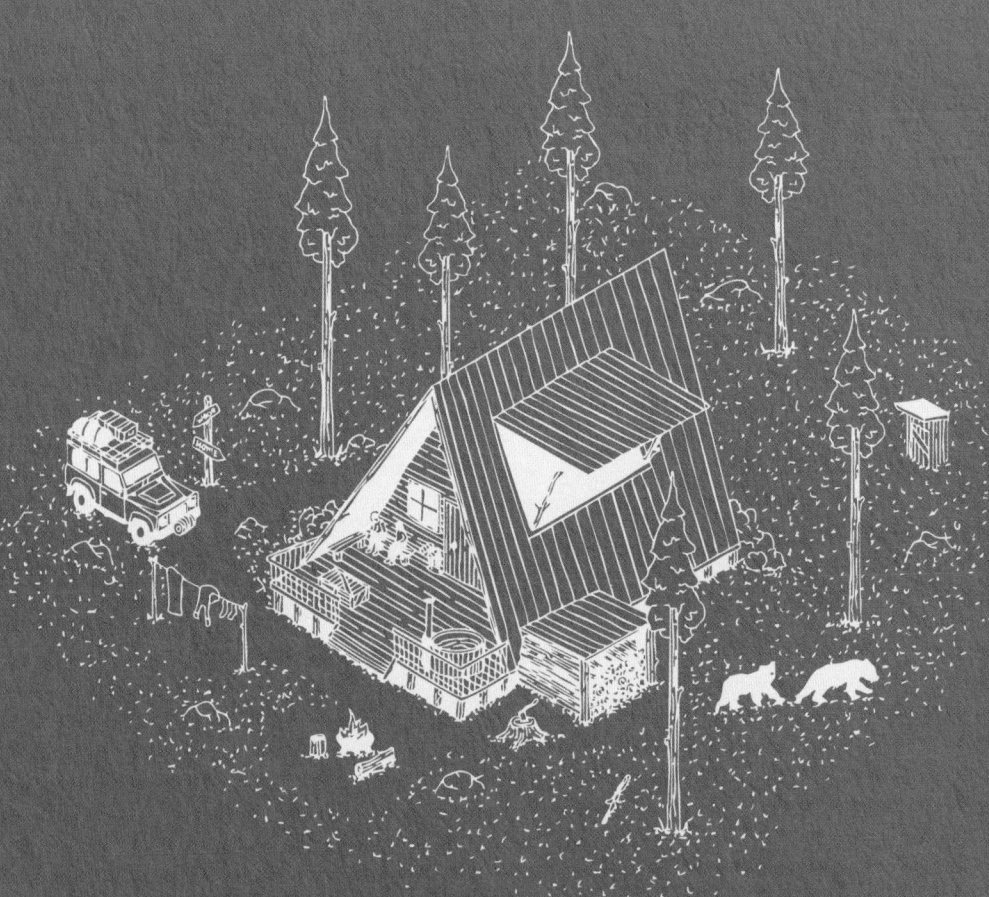

A-FRAME HAVEN

"ALL GOOD THINGS ARE WILD AND FREE."
– HENRY DAVID THOREAU

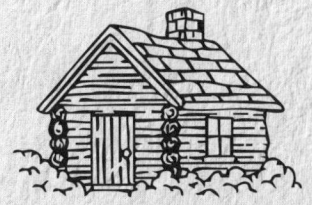

COZY CABIN

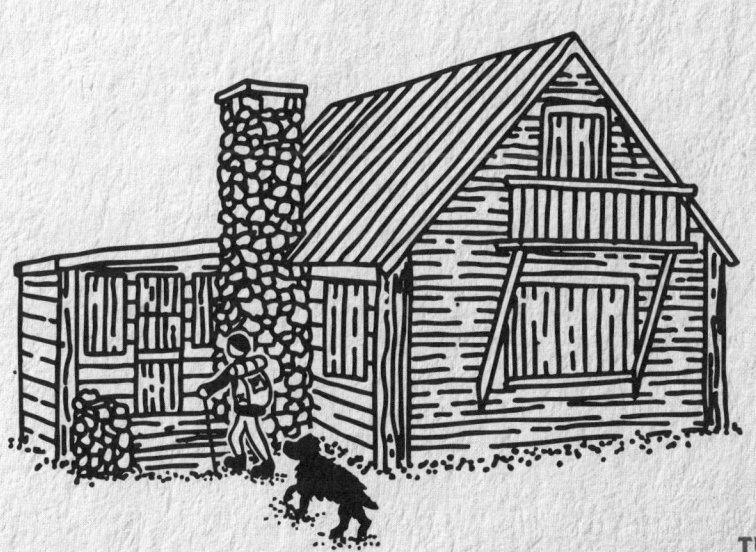

TUCKING IN

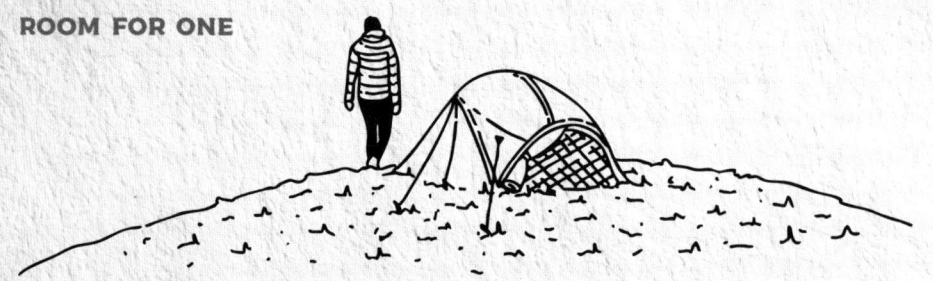

ROOM FOR ONE

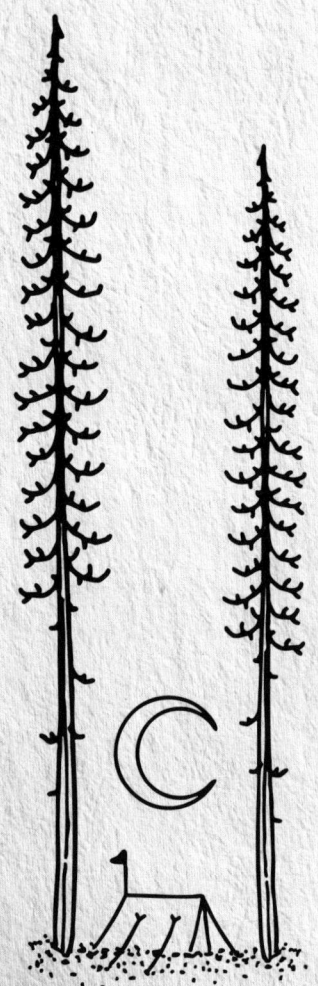

WANDERER'S REST

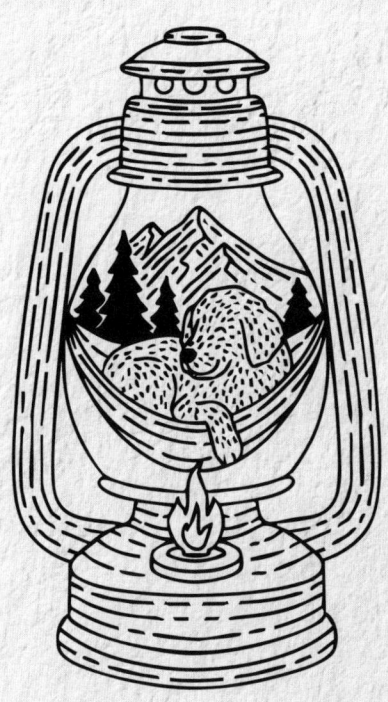

ILLUMINATED

A classic lantern glows softly, a
mountain range and pine forest alive
within its glass, a small flame flickering
below. It feels like carrying the whole
wilderness in your hand's warmth,
shelter, light.

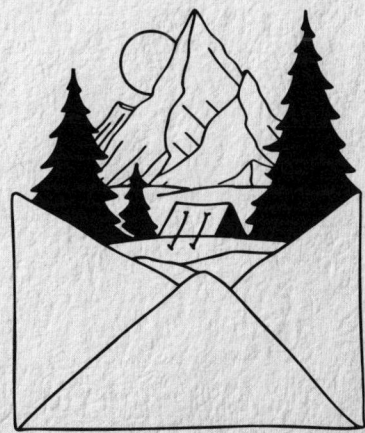

INVITATION

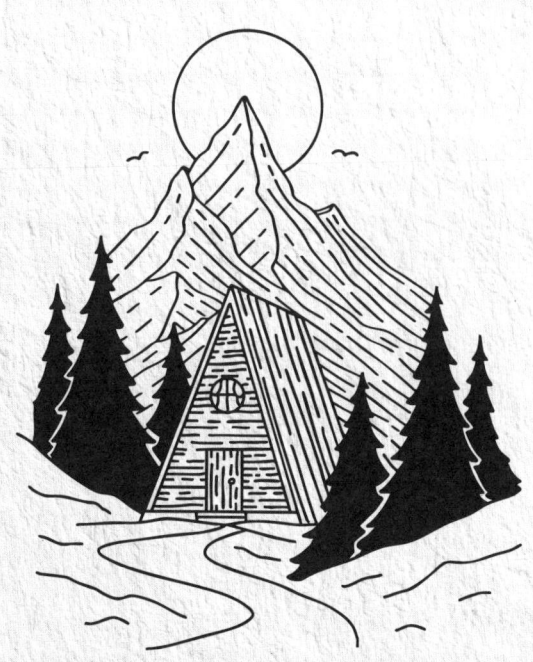

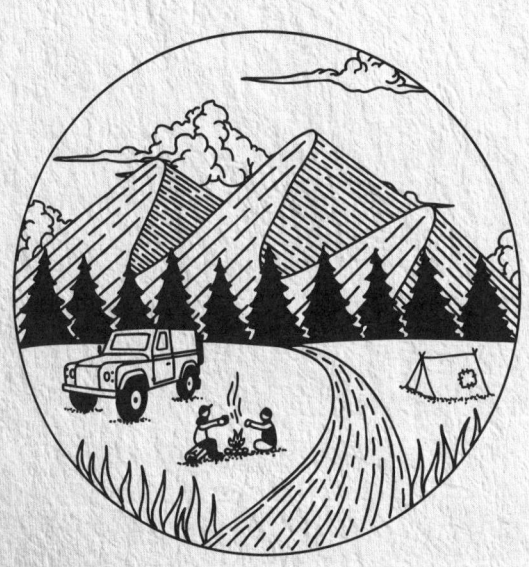

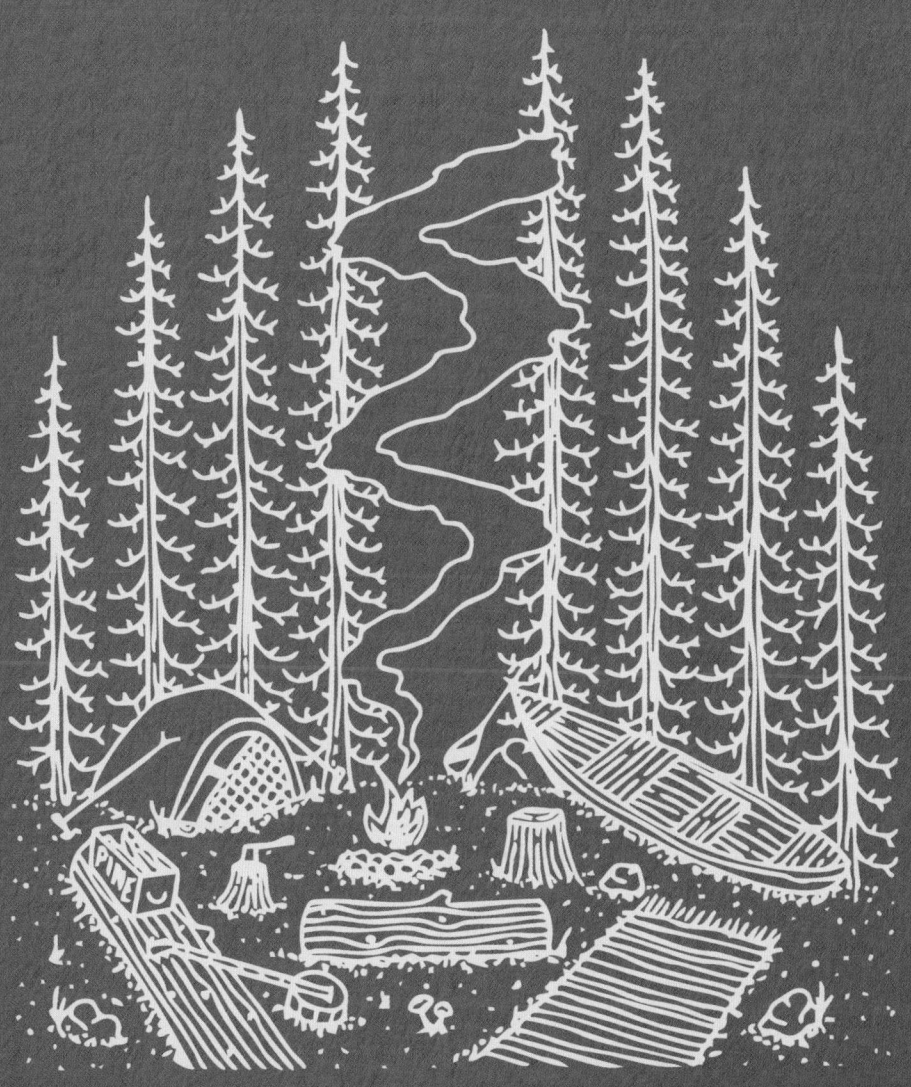

HAMMOCK HAPPY

A hammock sways gently between two tall trees. A dog curls nearby as stars scatter across the sky. The night hums with quiet comfort, and the fire's glow lingers. Here, the simplest moments—wind through the trees, hum of the insects, and birds chirping—remind you how little it takes to feel complete.

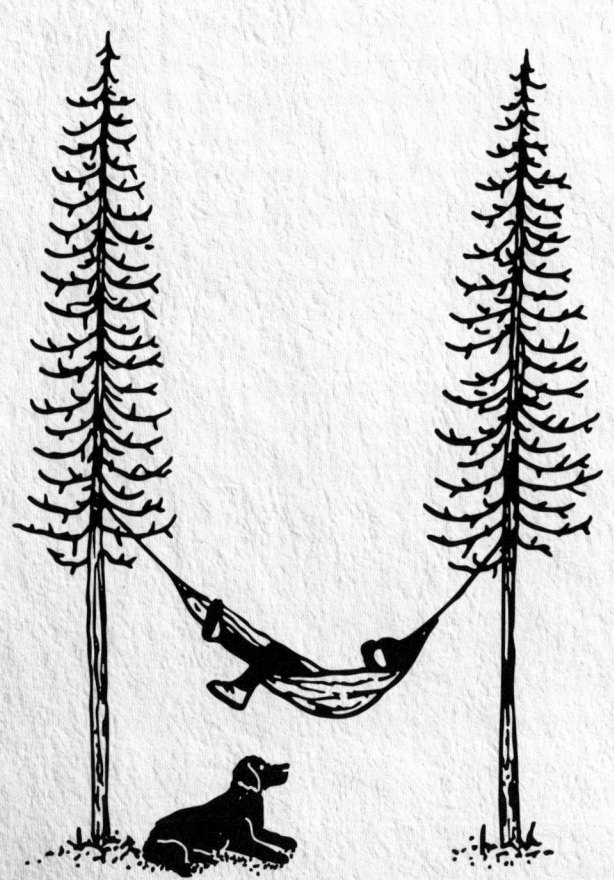

UNDER THE PINES

A small cabin glows softly in the deep woods, chimney smoke drifting into the night sky. In front, a fire crackles, and a camper roasts a marshmallow on a stick. The forest is quiet, and it feels like home.

"THE CLEAREST WAY INTO THE UNIVERSE IS THROUGH A FOREST WILDERNESS."

– JOHN MUIR

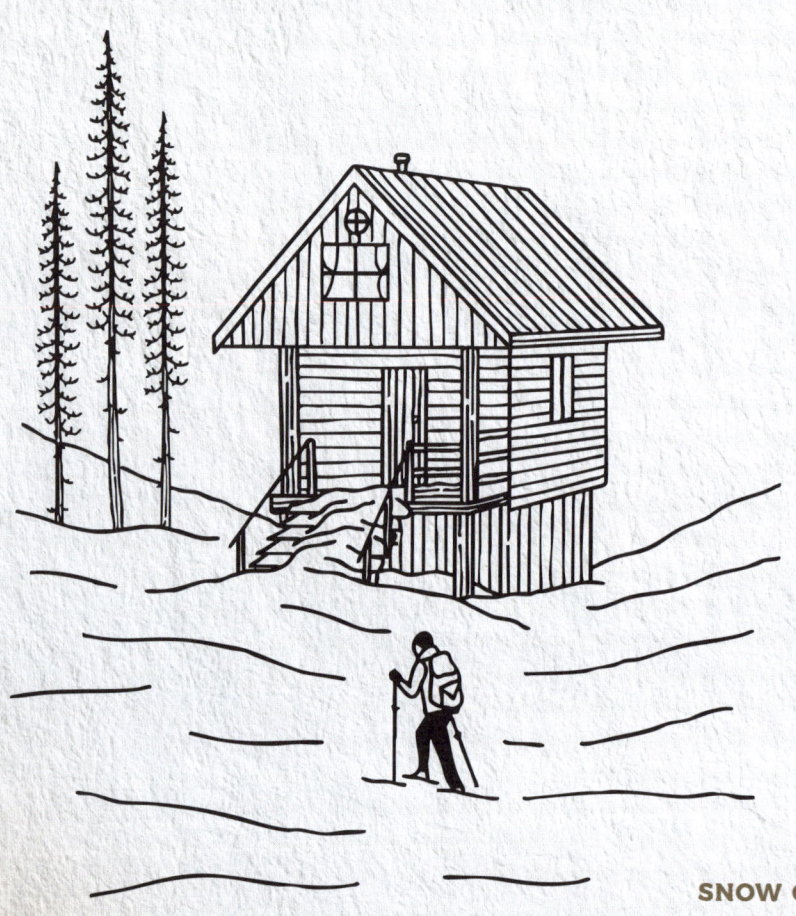

SNOW CHALET

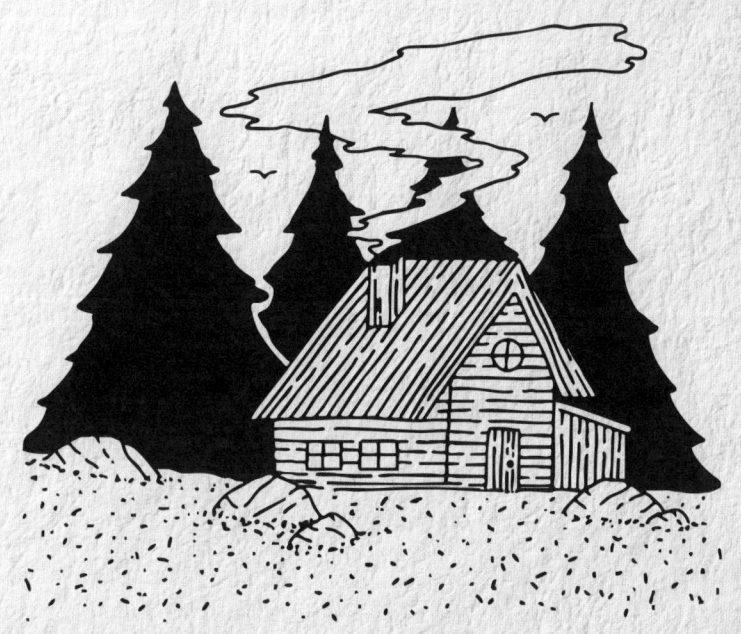

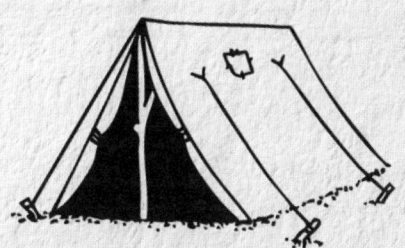

CAMPING CREW

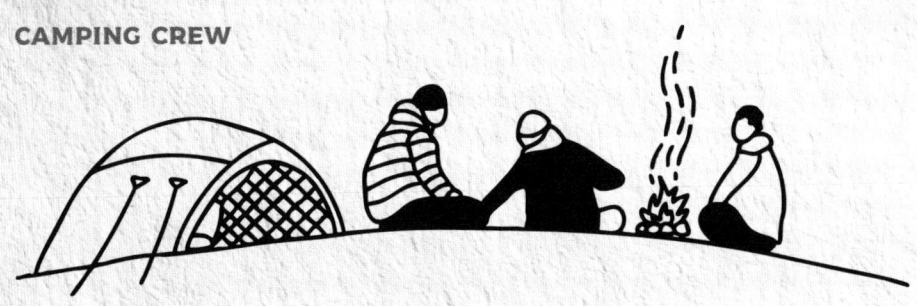

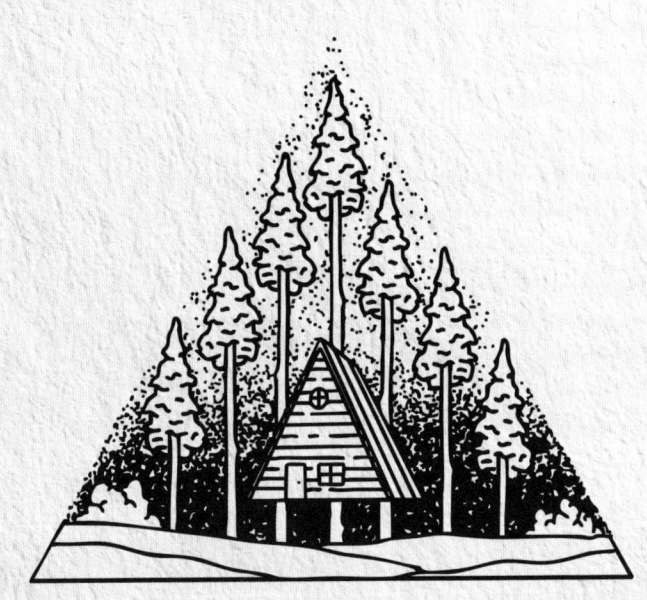

UP AND OUTPOST

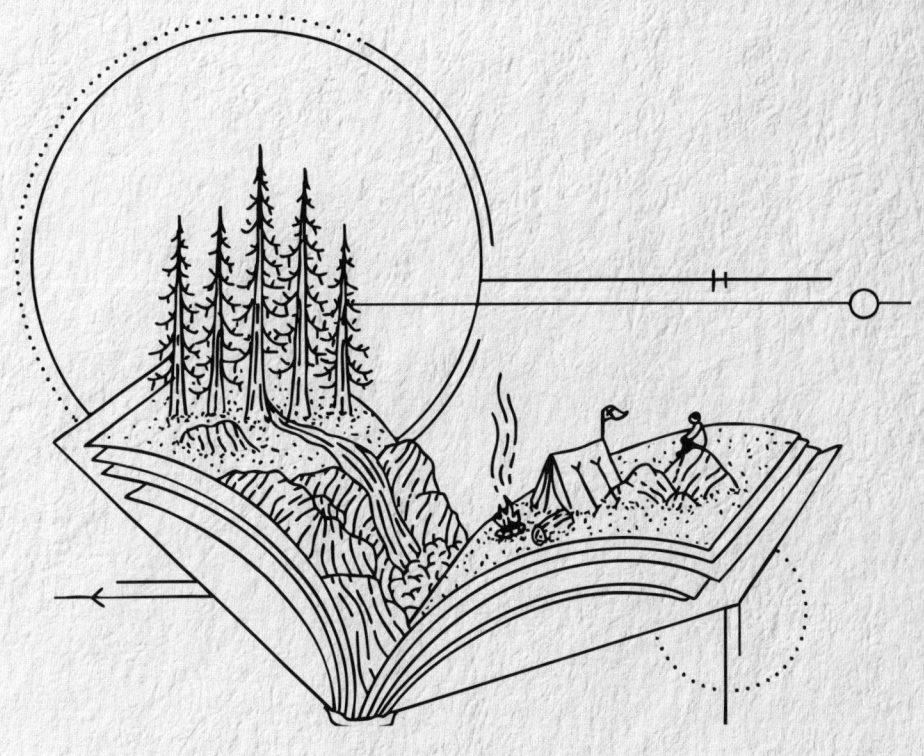

CAMPFIRE TALE

An open book becomes a landscape
page unfolding into pine trees, a tiny
tent, a fire burning quietly before it.
A lone camper sits nearby, wrapped
in stillness. It's a reminder that stories
live not just in words, but in the nights
we spend under stars listening and
remembering.

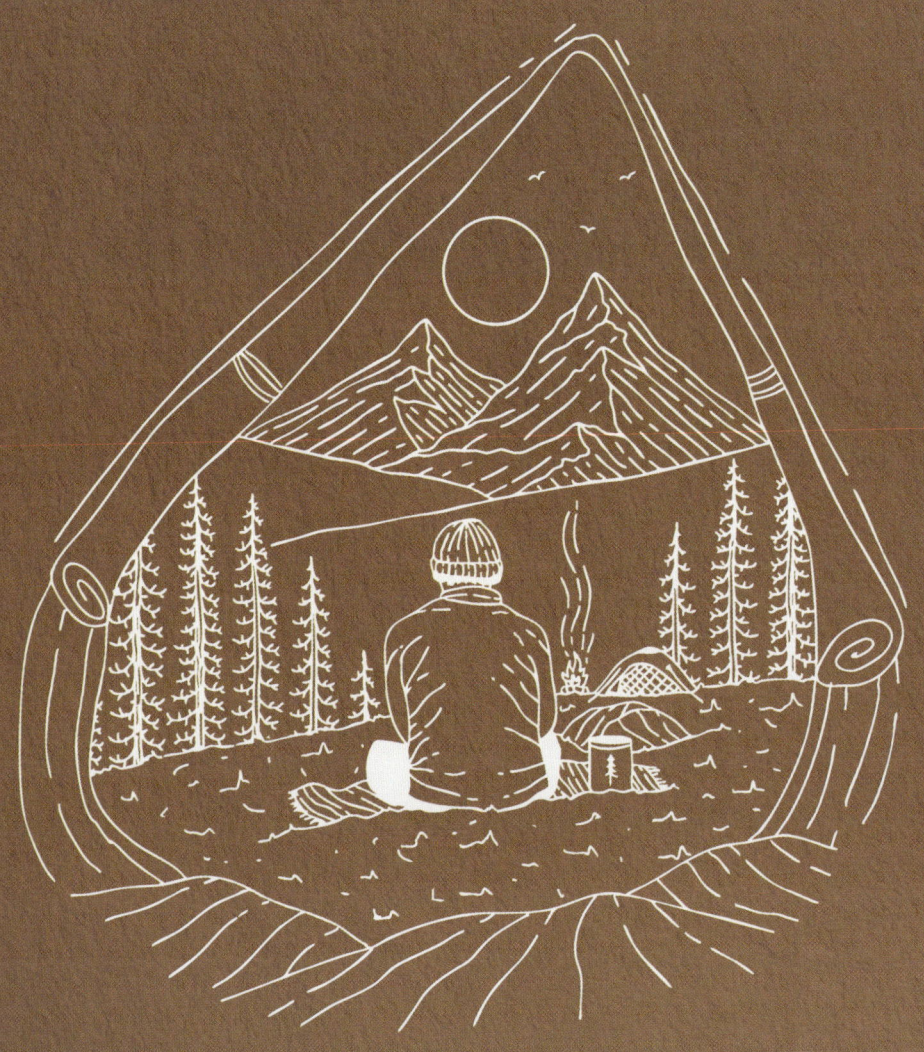

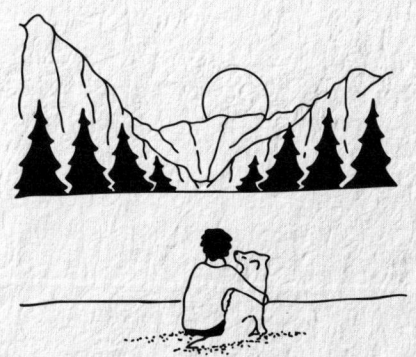

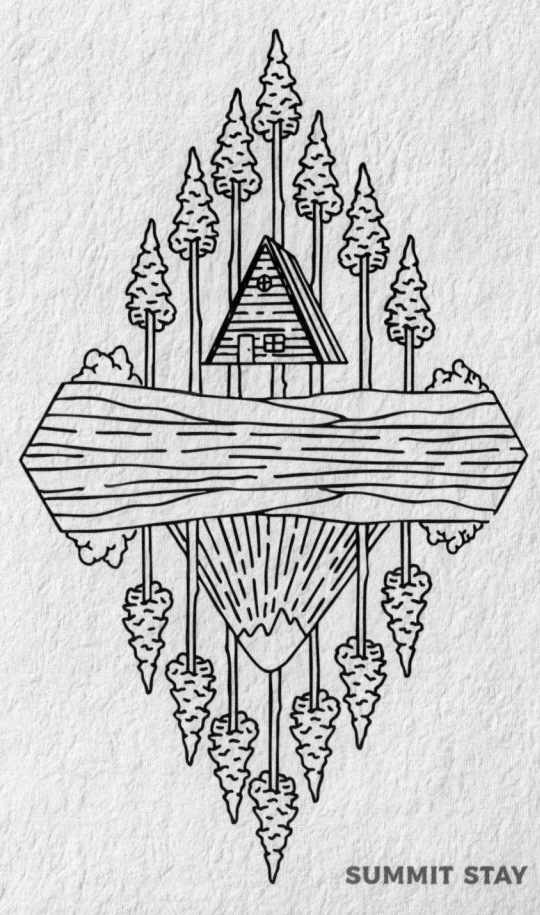

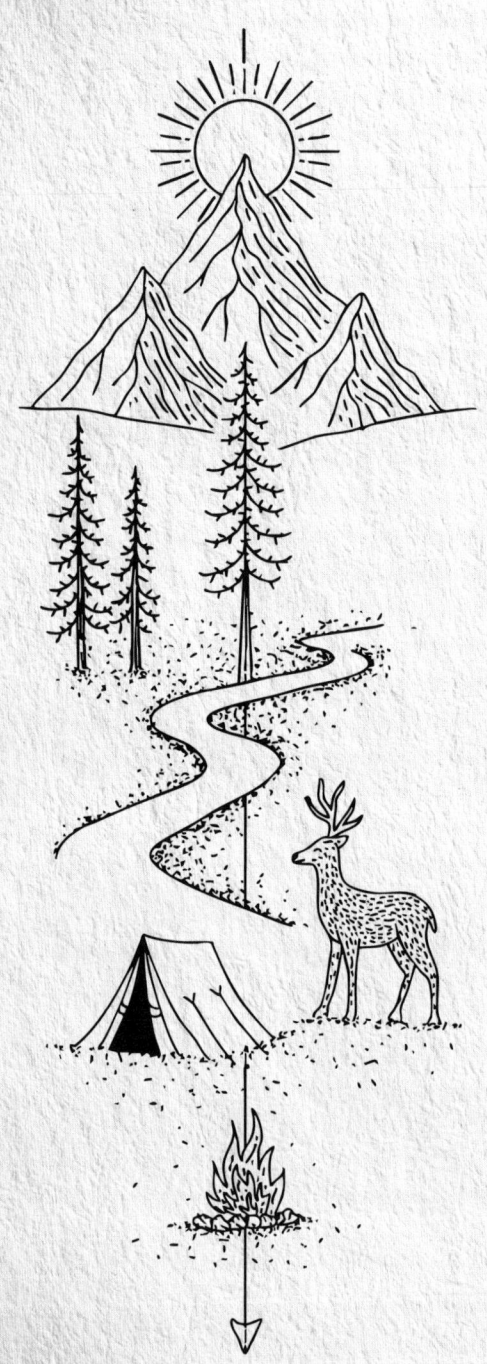

TRAILHEAD TRANQUILITY

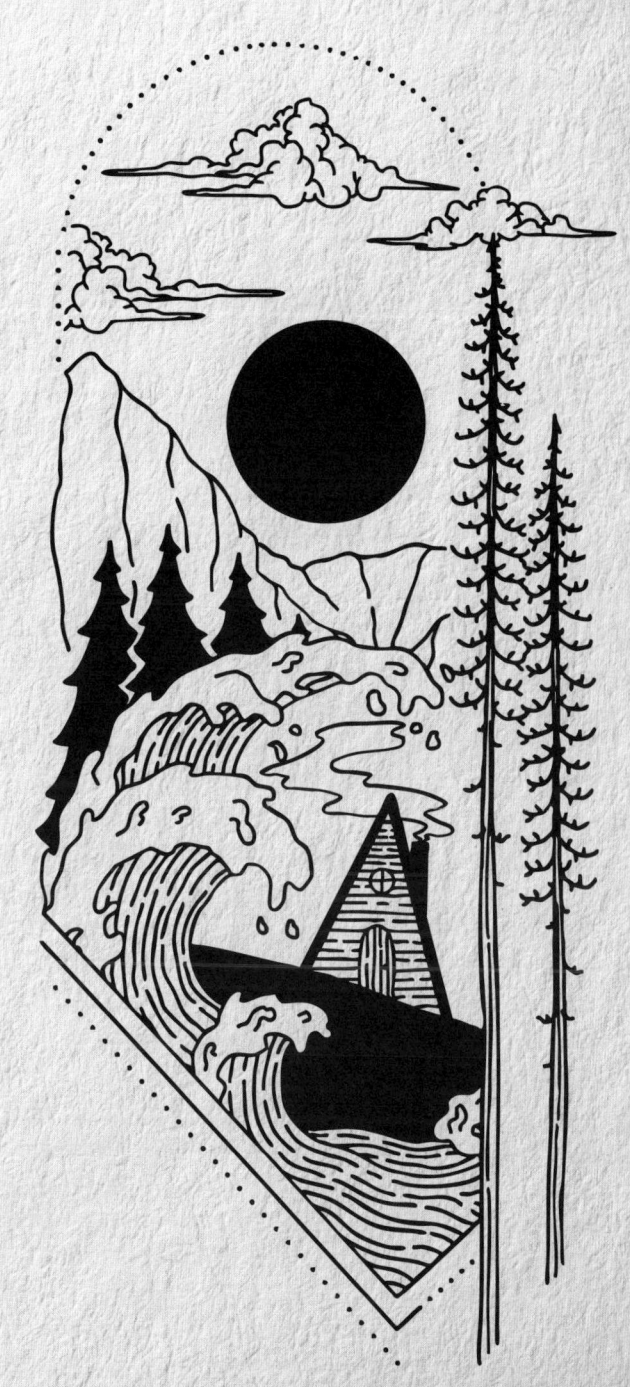

WILD HOME

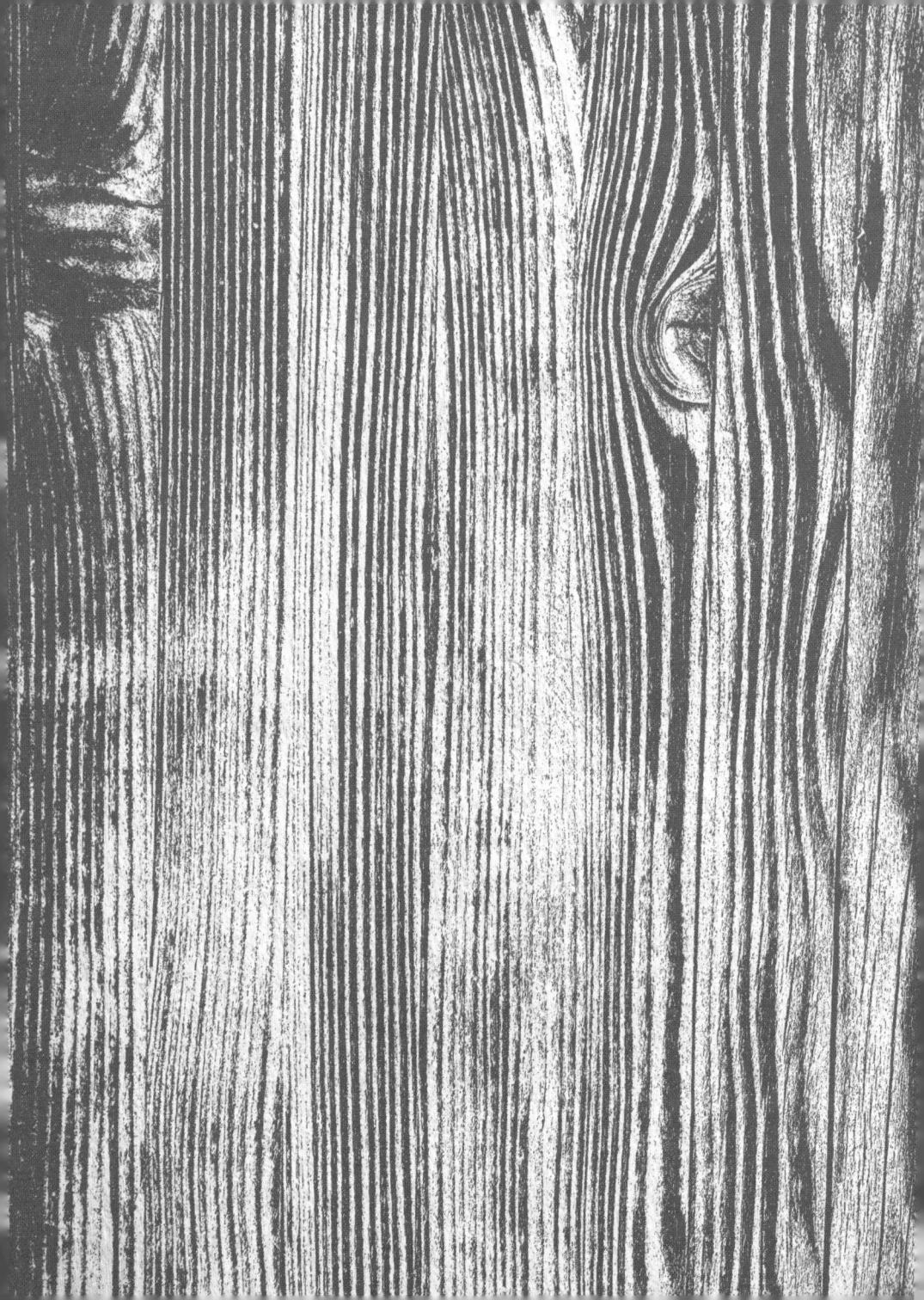

CHAPTER 8

ALL-NATURAL DIVERSIONS

Not every illustration has to have a deep meaning behind it. Sometimes, I just draw for fun. Some art is, in fact, just meant to make you smile.

This chapter is filled with a selection of small, playful designs that have often stemmed from lighthearted ideas and moments of my own joy while on the road. They might not convey a big story, but they arise from, and hopefully spark, a bit of fun.

These types of designs usually come to me during quiet breaks in my outdoor excursions or downtime in between more serious drawings. They let my imagination run wild. I find freedom in that kind of artistic expression, spilling my random thoughts onto the page and seeing where my pen takes me.

These designs are for people who see the lighthearted side of life—or who need a reminder of it. They're for the moments that feel good for absolutely no reason. They show that not everything has to be serious in life. You can simply enjoy its randomness and spontaneity, and see where the road takes you.

FLORAL FLUTTER

A butterfly unfurls with a bouquet blooming from its wings. Roses and tiny wildflowers in flight. It feels like spring captured mid-motion, beauty without effort or reason.

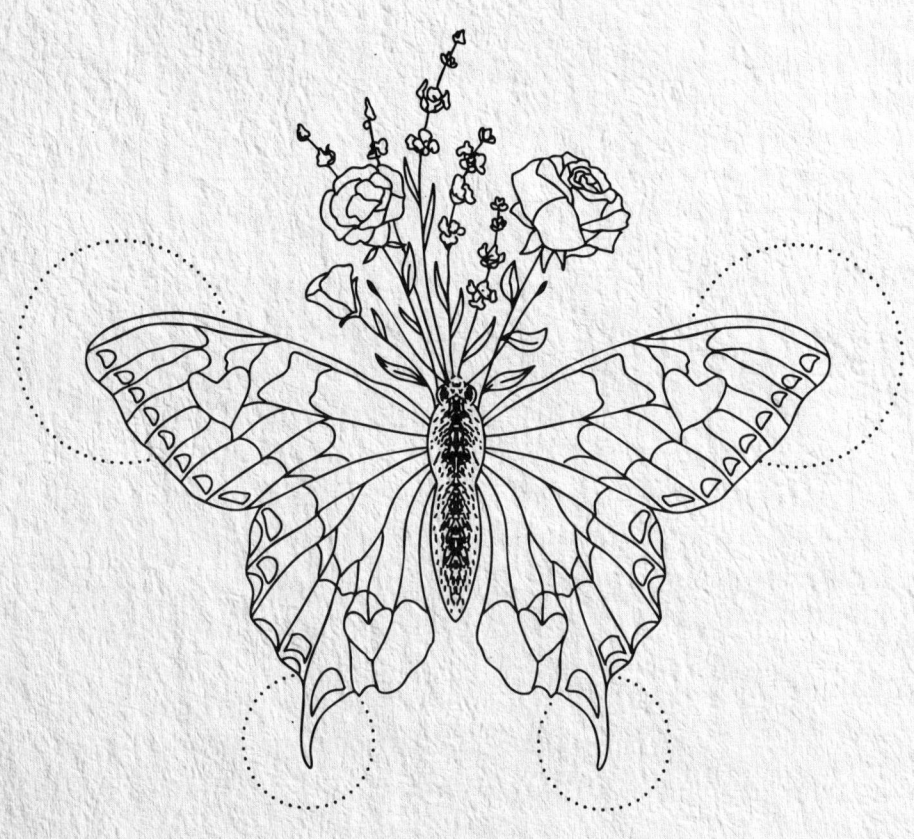

"ONE TOUCH OF NATURE MAKES THE WHOLE WORLD KIN."

– WILLIAM SHAKESPEARE

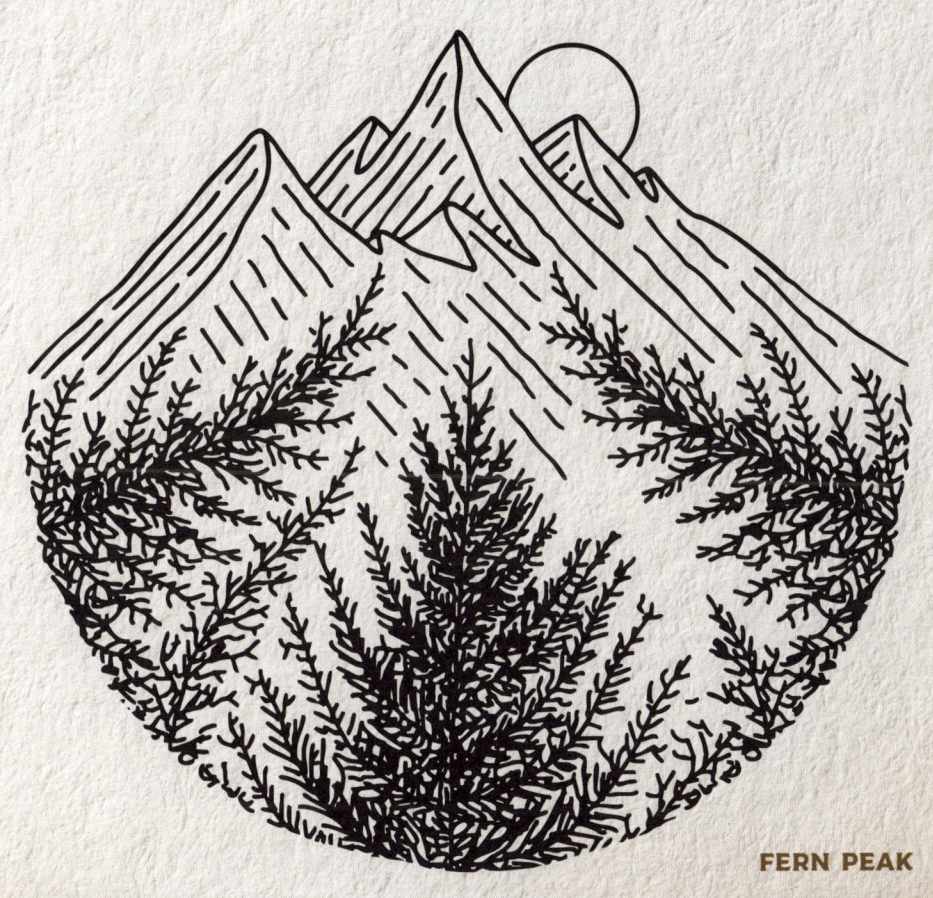

FERN PEAK

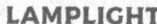

LAMPLIGHT

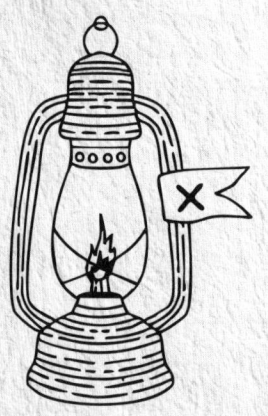

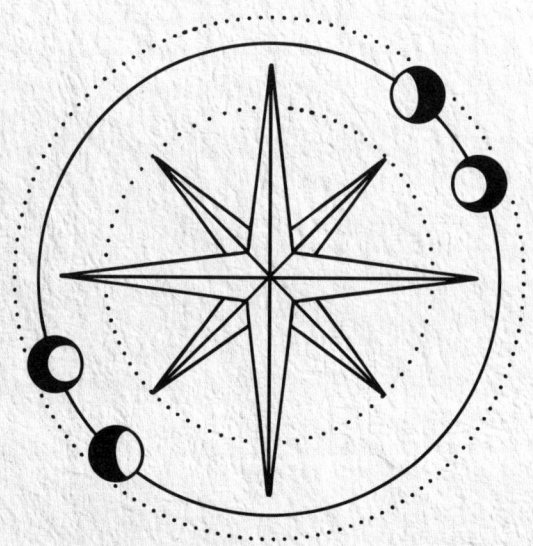

GUIDING LIGHT

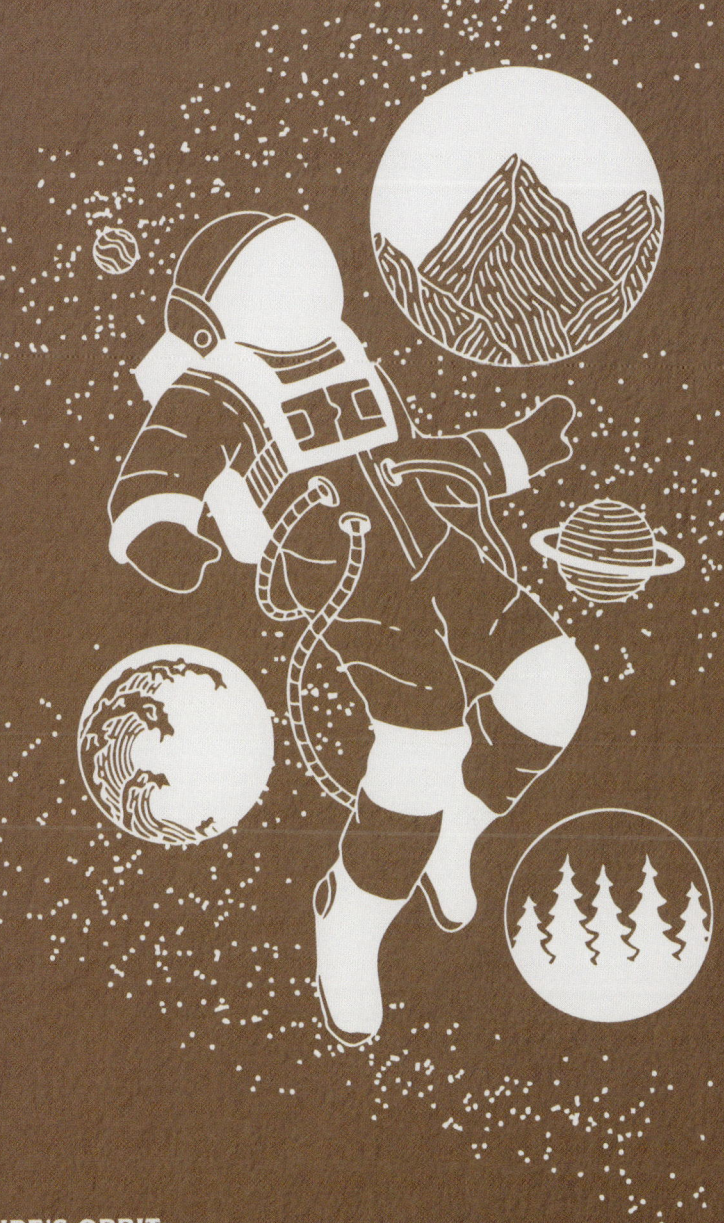

NATURE'S ORBIT

SURF'S UP

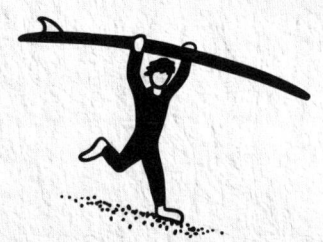

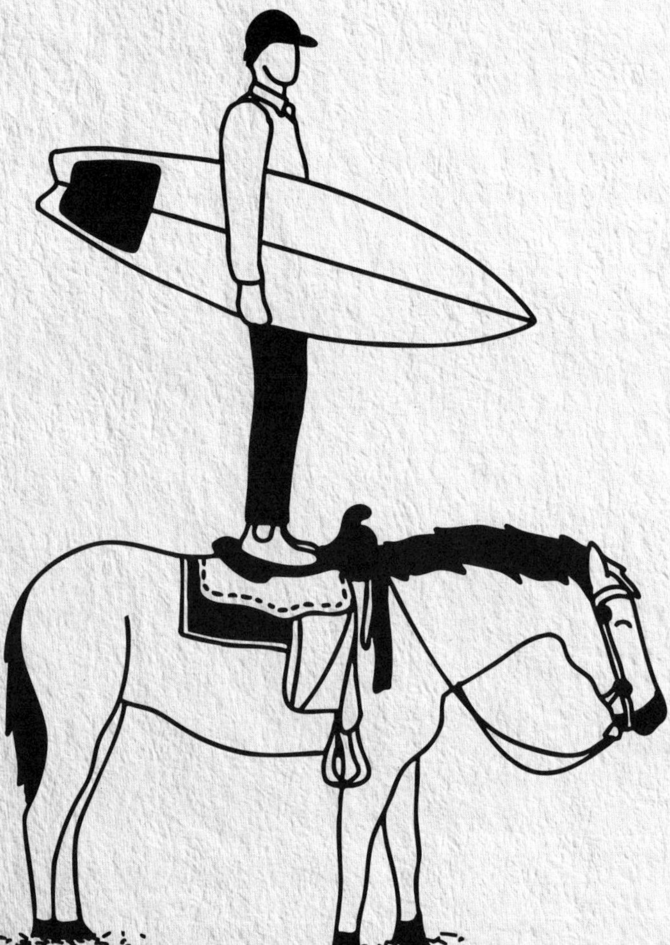

SURF STEED

CROSS STEP

A lone surfer stands poised on calm water, the sun just rising. Legs crossed, balanced and unhurried, they glide with quiet confidence.

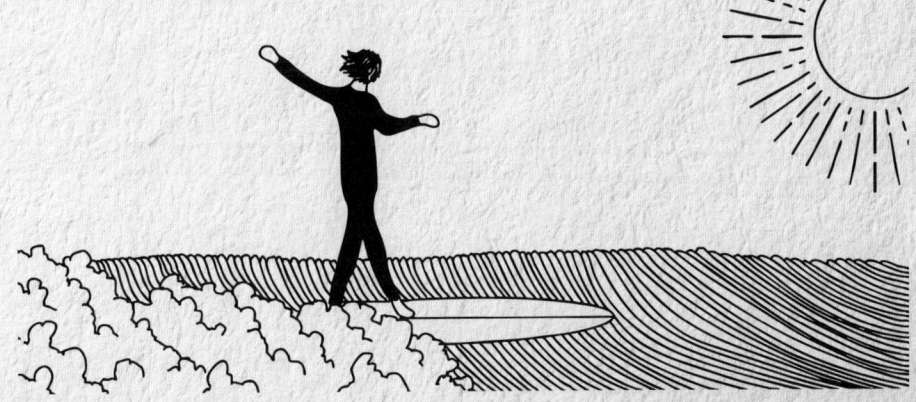

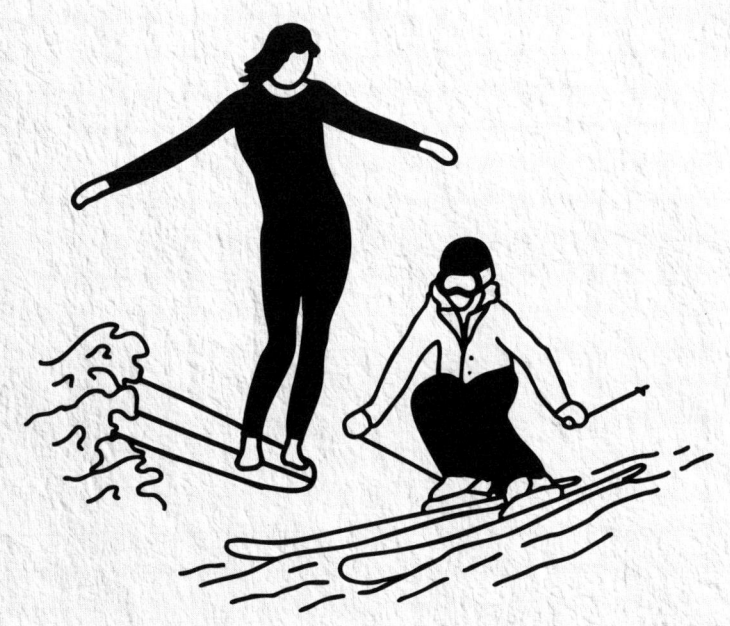

GLIDE

A surfer skims the sea while a skier carves the mountain. Two souls chasing the same thrill through water in different forms. Whether liquid or frozen, motion feels the same: freedom, balance, joy.

"THE GOAL OF LIFE IS LIVING IN AGREEMENT WITH NATURE."

– ZENO OF CITIUM

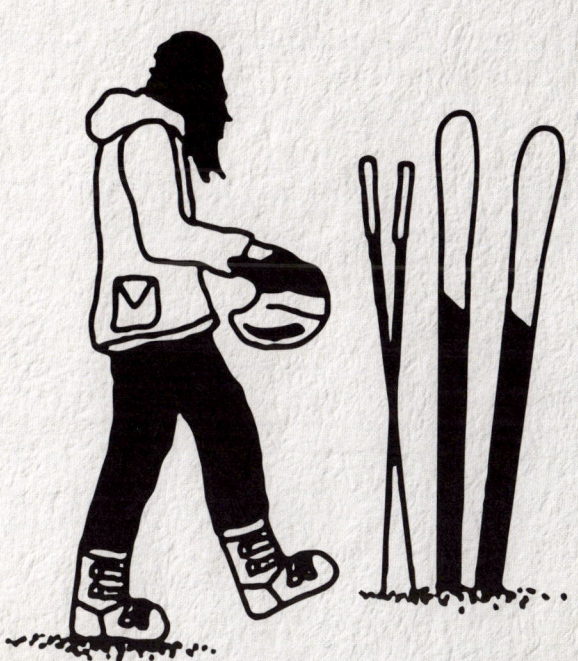

SKI SEASON

SUN SUMMONER

Two hands stretch toward the sun:
hands open to its warmth. It's as if the
light itself leans down to greet them. A
small moment of connection; simple,
grounding, alive.

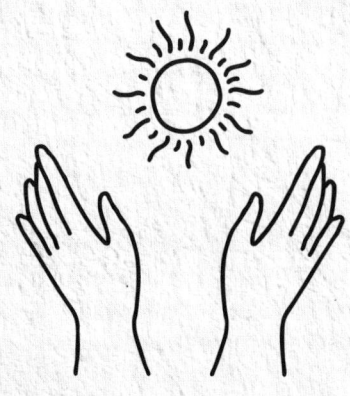

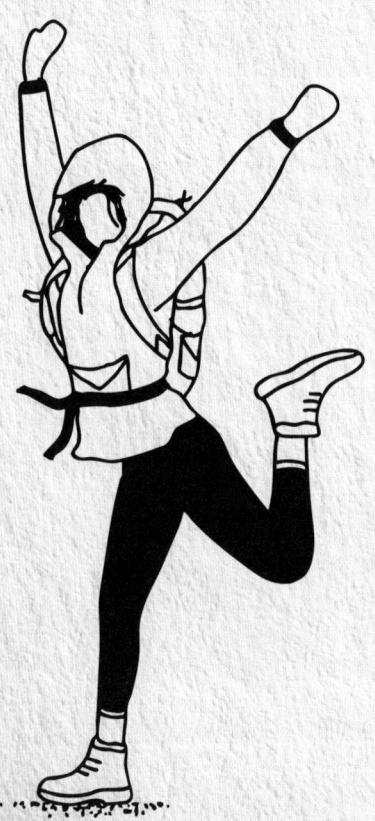

REACH FOR THE SKY

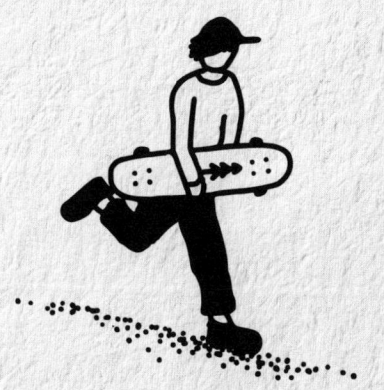

SKATE ON

A skater walks through the city, board under arm, cap pulled low . . . Pavement becomes playground, and every street has a new path. It's about movement for the sake of joy, just rolling with wherever the day leads.

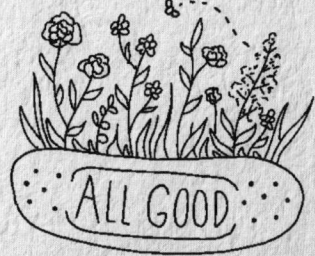

ALL GOOD

"NATURE NEVER DID
BETRAY THE HEART
THAT LOVED HER."
– WILLIAM WORDSWORTH

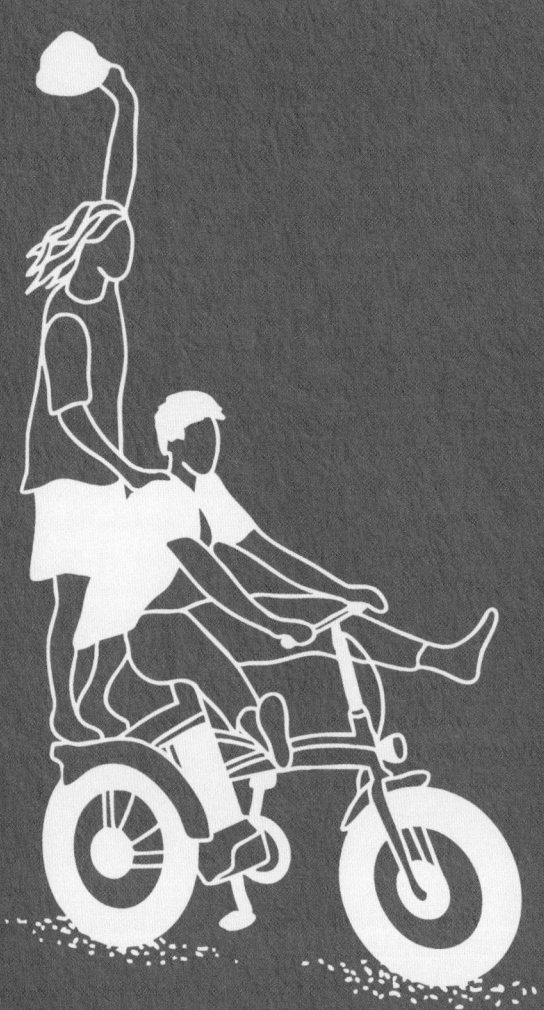

LIVE LIFE

SCOUT DAYS

Two friends sit by a fire, one roasting a marshmallow, the other smiling from a stump. Sparks rise, laughter lingers, and the night feels endless. It's a simple kind of happiness: warmth, friendship, and the soft comfort of knowing you're exactly where you're meant to be.

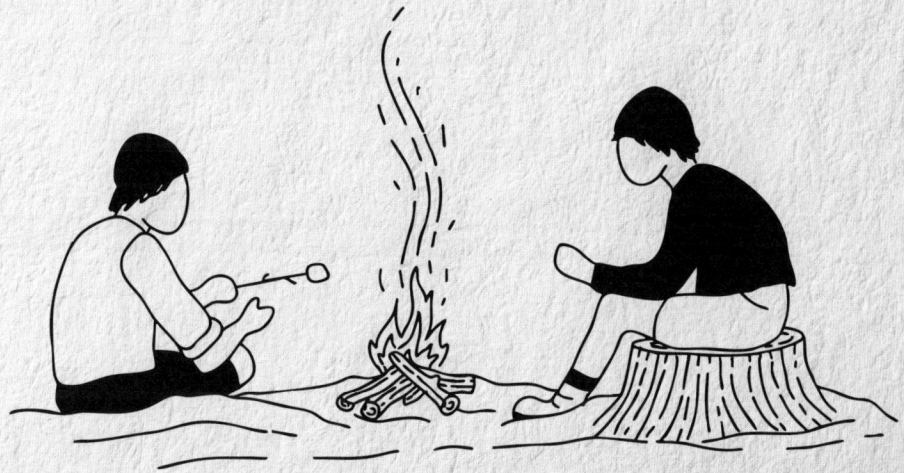

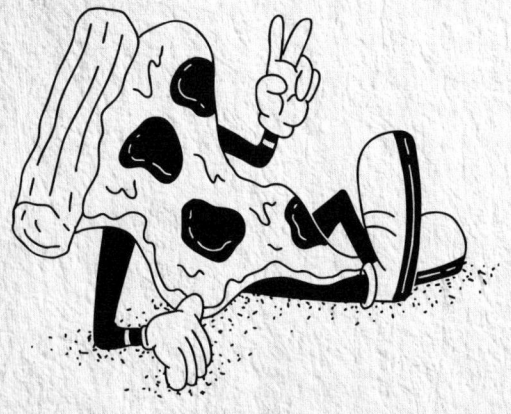

NICE SLICE

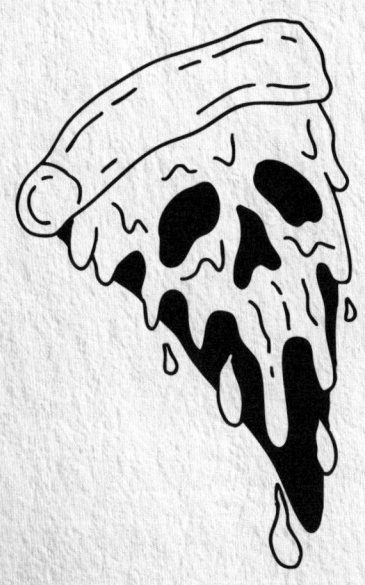

SLICE OF DOOM

WHITTLE DOWN

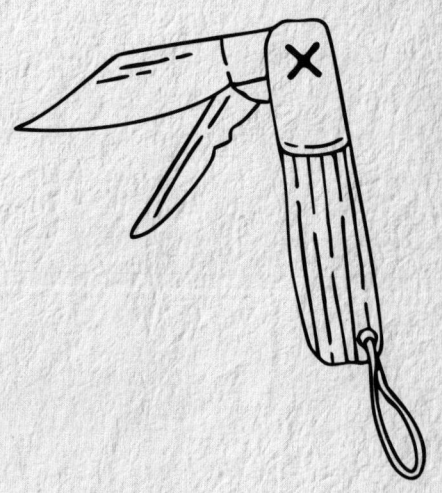

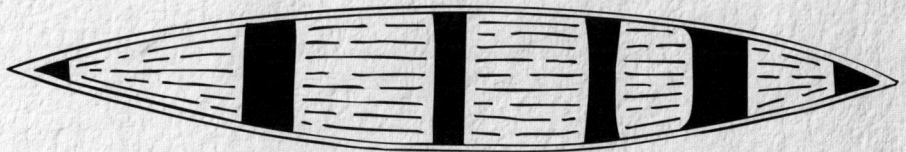

VOYAGER

From above, a wooden canoe drifts on still water detailed and sturdy, built for slow adventure. Four seats, endless possibilities.

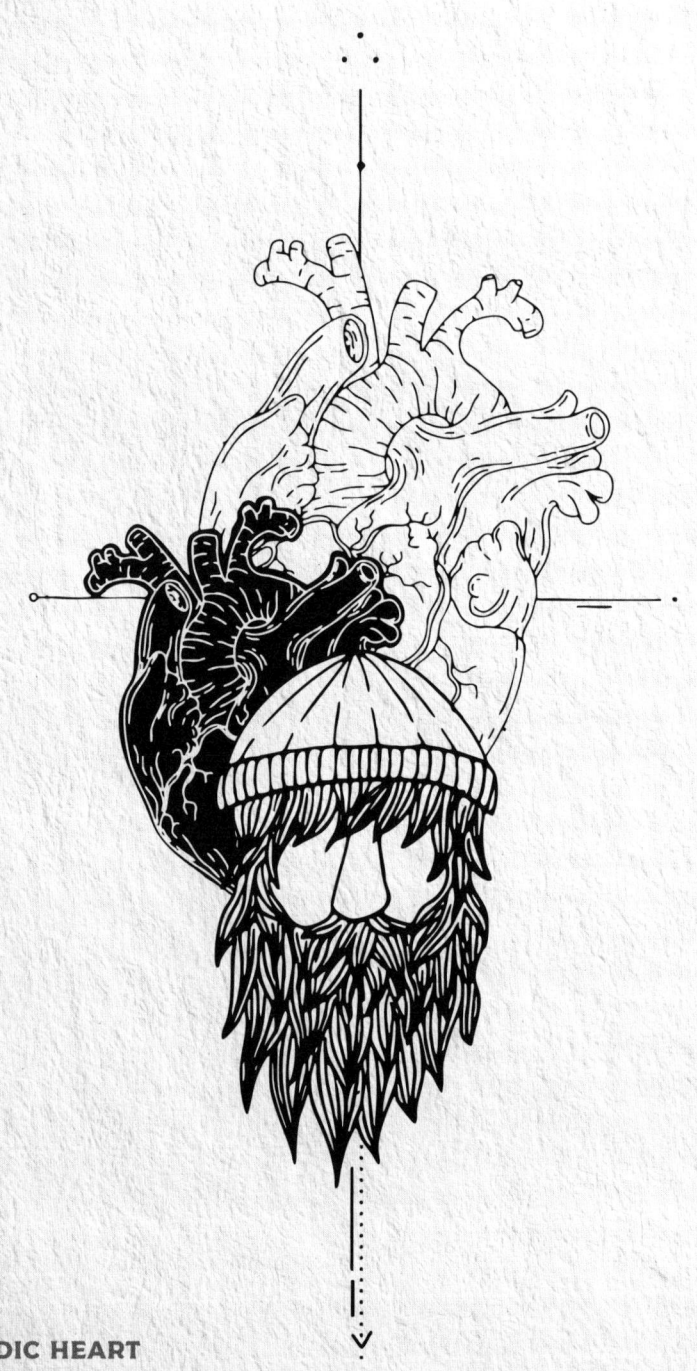

NOMADIC HEART

"IN ALL THINGS OF NATURE THERE IS SOMETHING OF THE MARVELOUS."

– ARISTOTLE

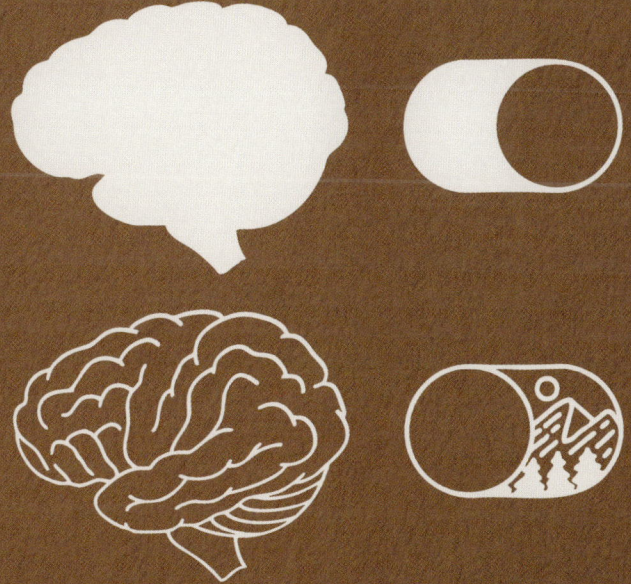

SWITCH ON

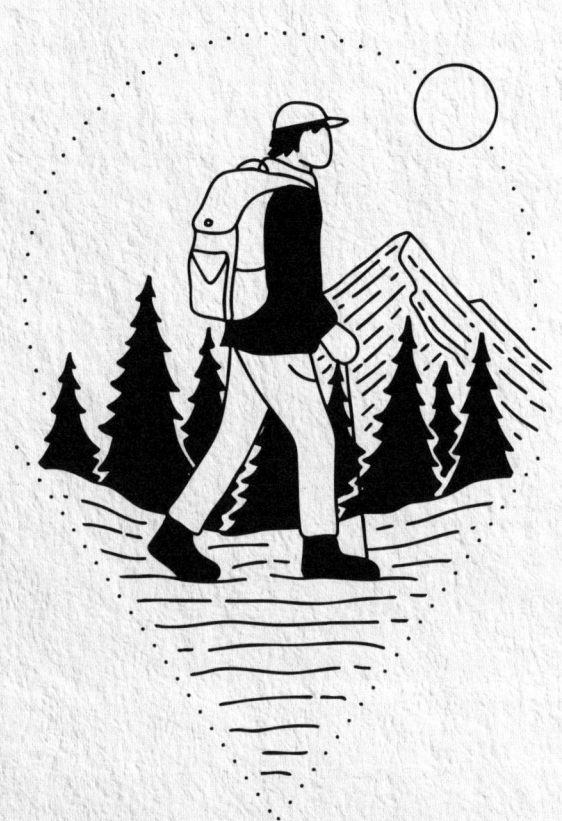

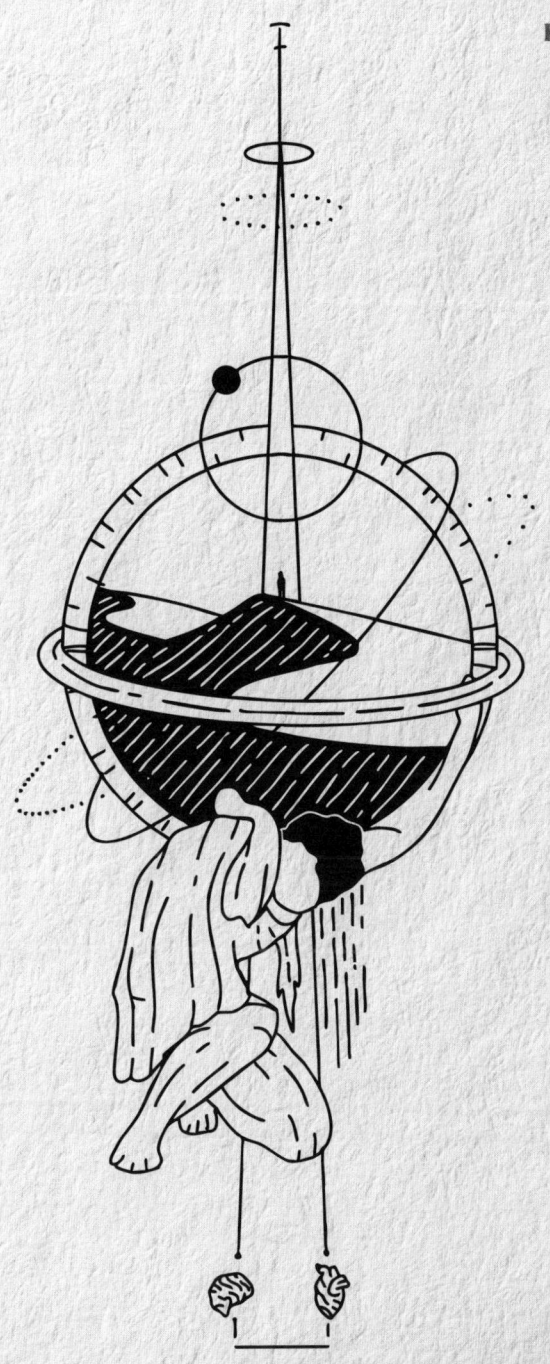

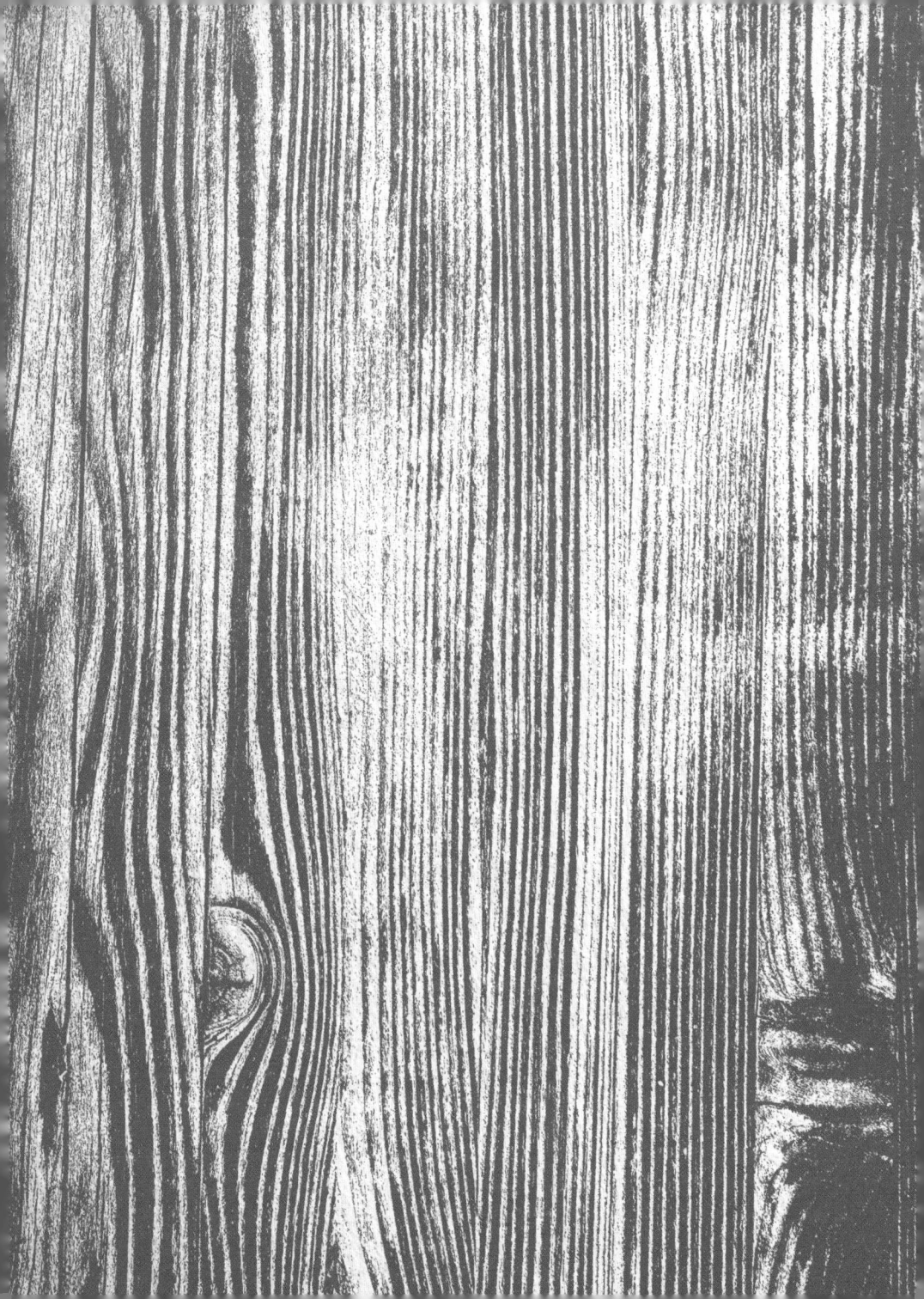

CHAPTER 9

PEAKS
AND
PATHS

Mountains have an amazing way of reminding us how small we are. Whether you've stood at the top of one or admired them from below, there's no doubt that you'll have felt the strength that they carry.

They're solid, steady, constant, and powerful. Their longevity is mind-boggling. This chapter grew from that feeling of quiet power we feel in their presence.

Most of these sketches were created during pauses in my hiking trips: art of single-peak outlines, stacked ridgelines, trails, or simple peaks with simple points and gentle curves that capture the landscape and terrain. But the lines of the mountains have always drawn me in—how they rise and fall, jagged or smooth, endlessly varied. These designs are for people who love the view from the top and don't mind the climb to get there.

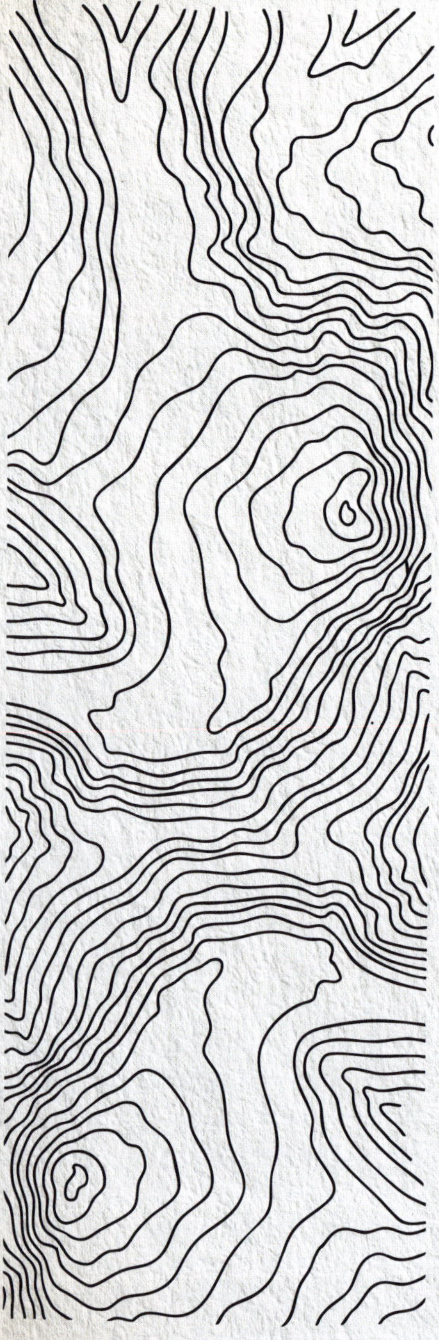

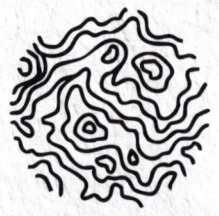

CRESTING CONTOURS

TYPOGRAPHIC TRAILS

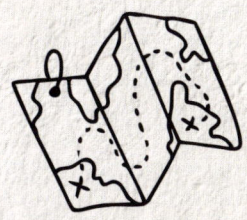

CARTOGRAPHER

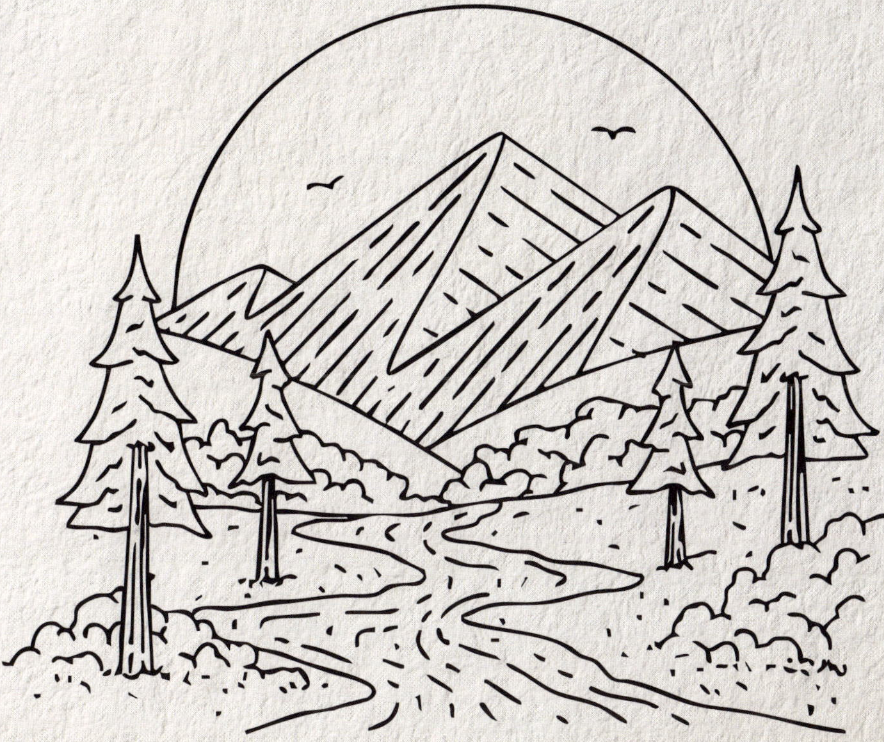

WINDING ROADS

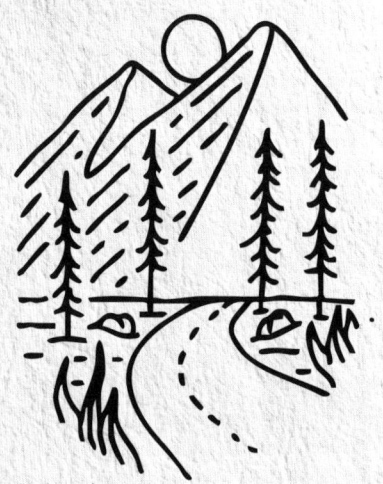

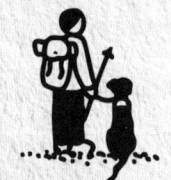

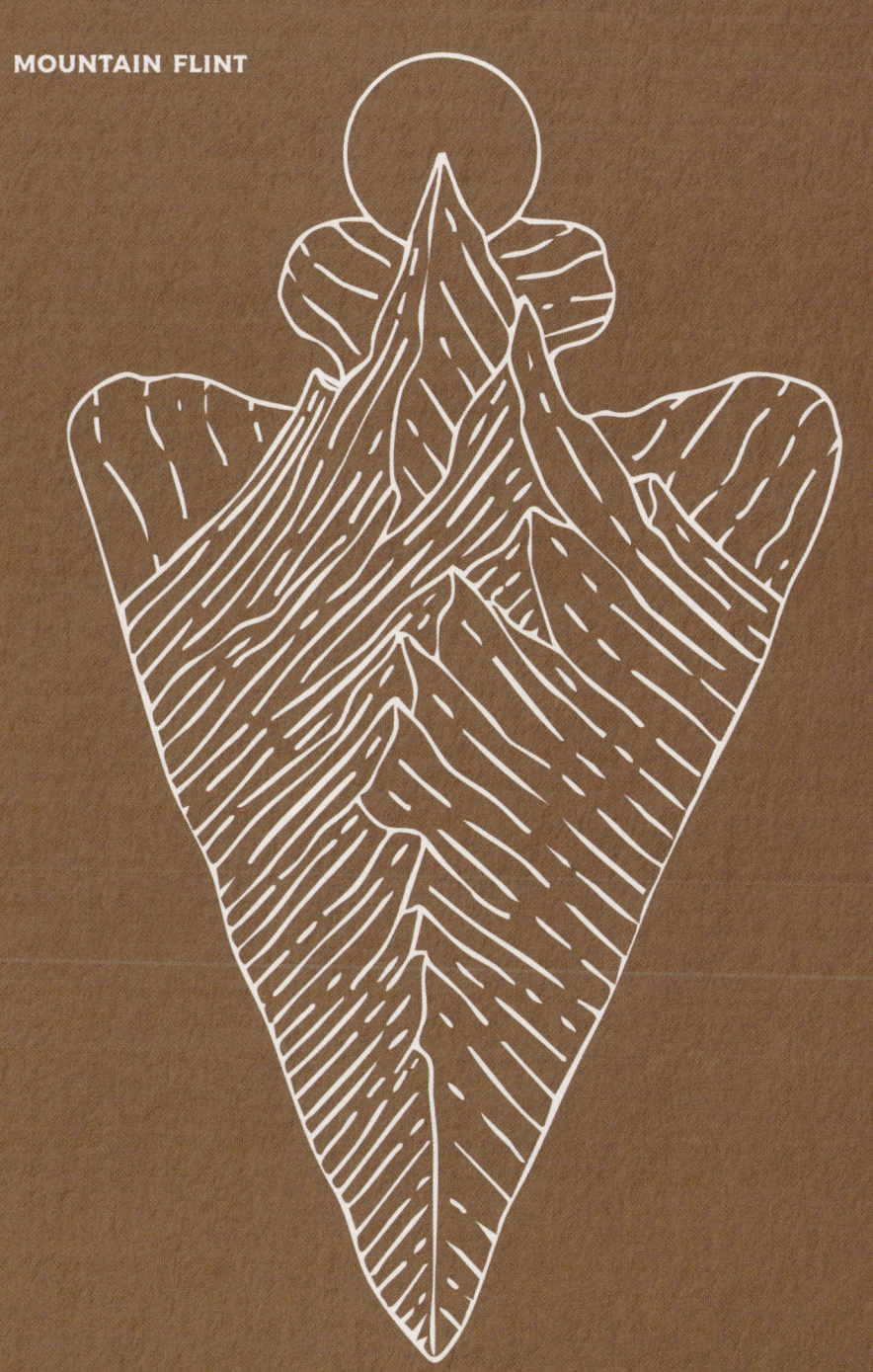

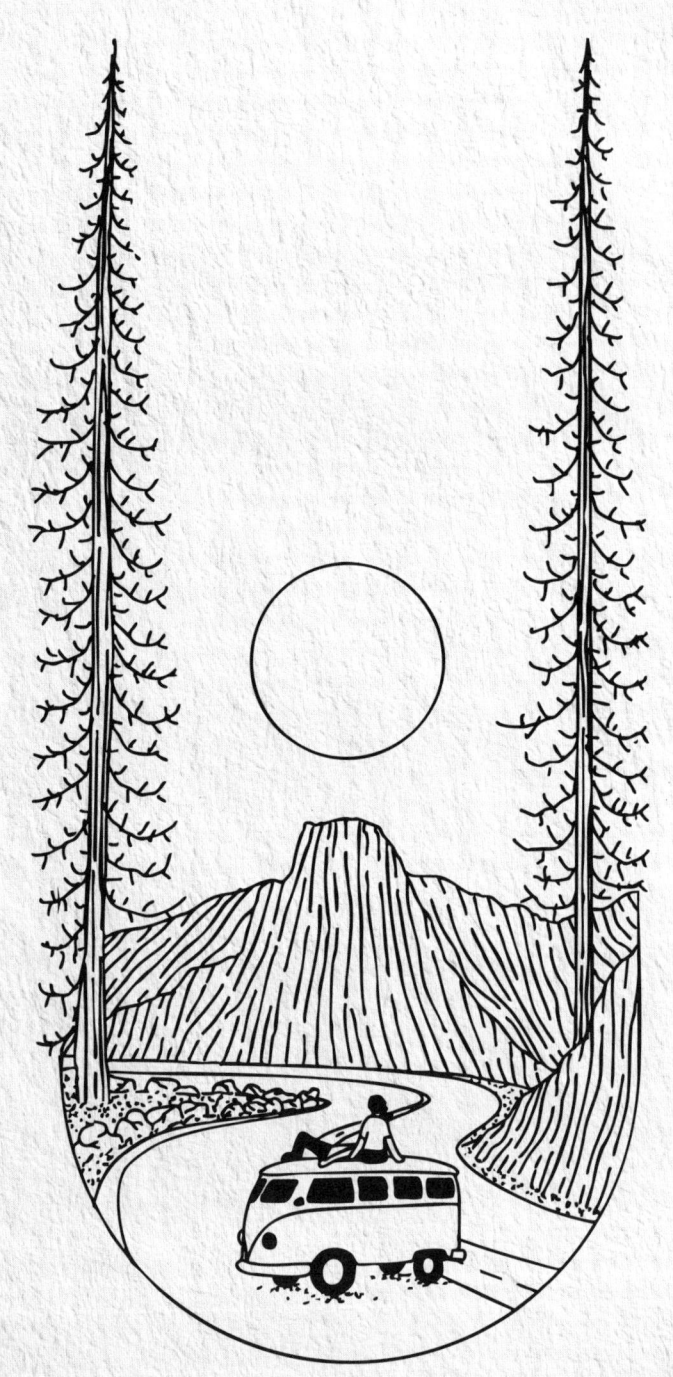

LOOKING AHEAD

"AFOOT AND
LIGHT-HEARTED
I TAKE TO THE OPEN
ROAD, HEALTHY, FREE,
THE WORLD BEFORE ME."

– WALT WHITMAN

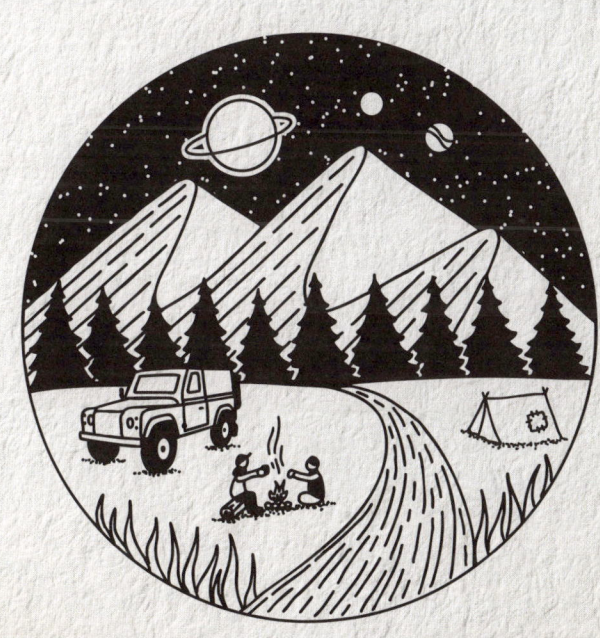

COSMIC CAMPOUT

SKYWARD

Geometric peaks and distant moons form a landscape that feels both alien and familiar. These summits remind us that adventure doesn't stop at the horizon, it continues wherever imagination dares to wander.

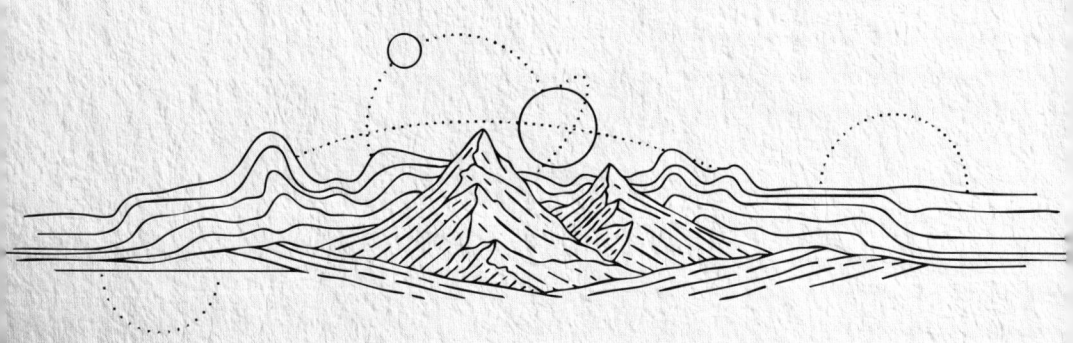

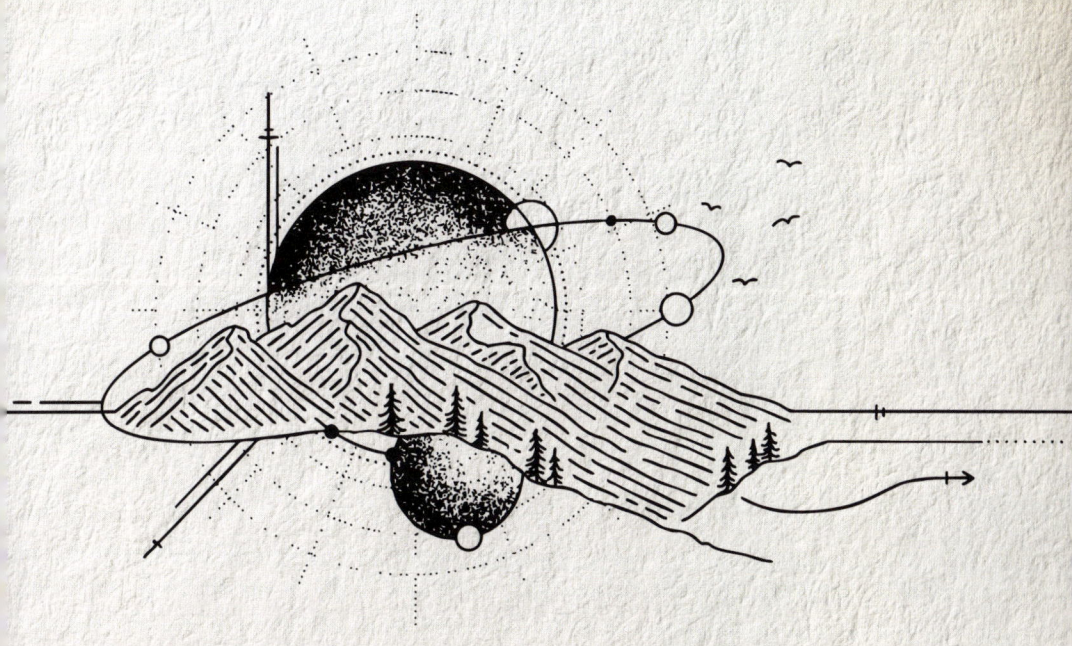

STARRY SUMMITS

A surfboard drifts through the cosmos, mountains and planets intersecting across its form. It's a meeting of worlds. This piece feels like ascent itself: the endless pull to rise, explore, and find balance between grounded paths and endless skies.

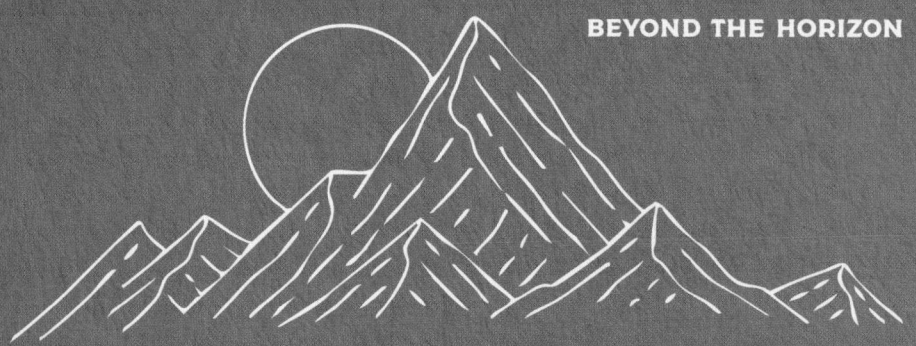

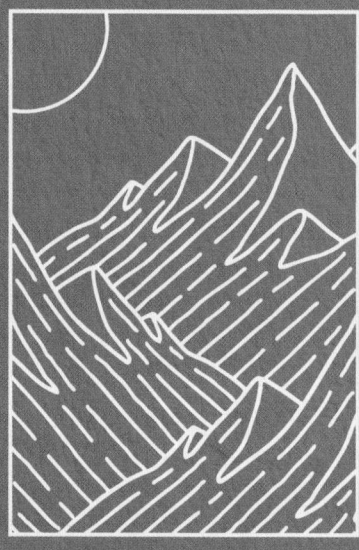

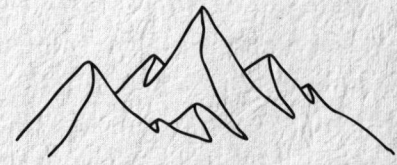

RIDGELINES

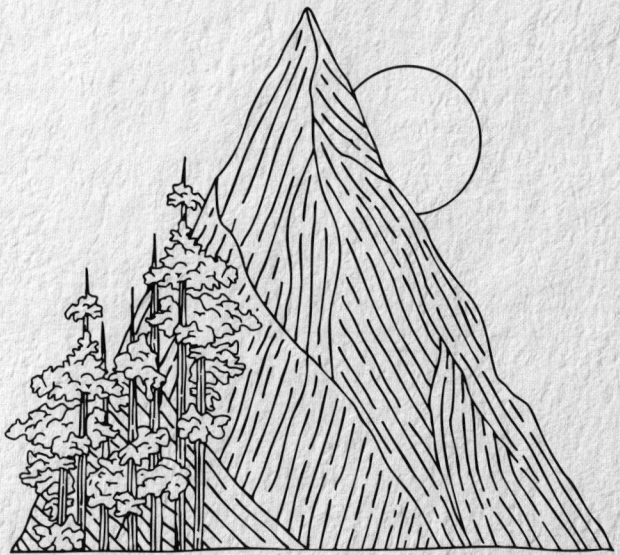

PEAK AND PINE

"THE CLEAREST WAY INTO THE UNIVERSE IS THROUGH A FOREST WILDERNESS."

– JOHN MUIR

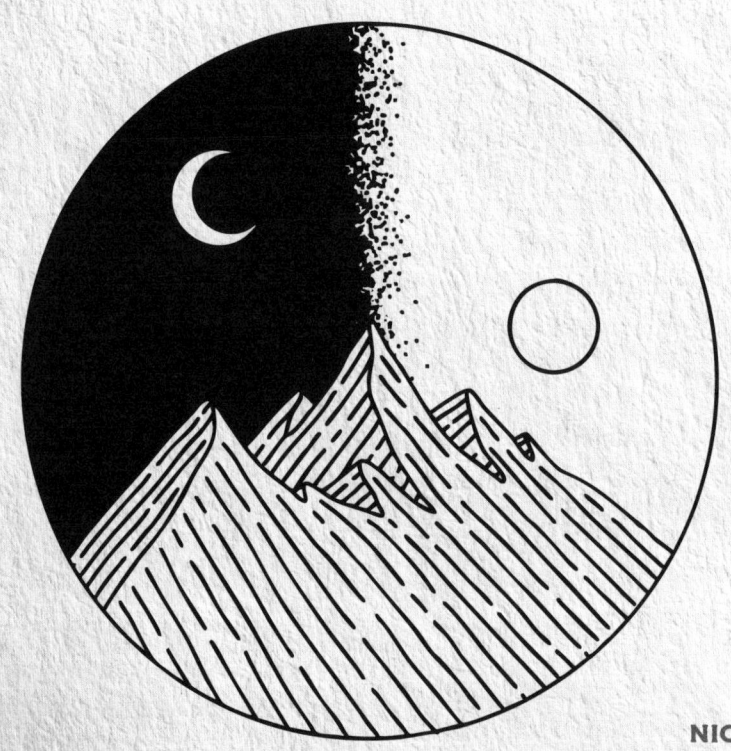

NIGHT AND DAY

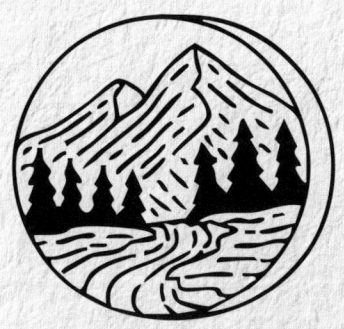

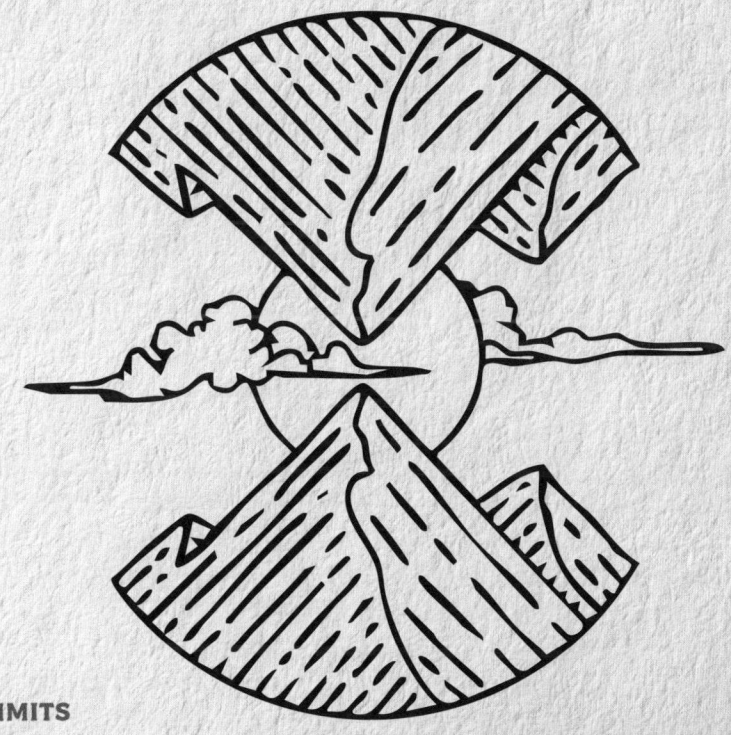

RADIAL SUMMITS

EVER AGLOW

A jagged range rises beneath a
radiant cloud, light spiking in all
directions. The mountains seem alive,
shimmering with quiet power. Their
glow feels eternal, like dawn caught in
stillness. This piece captures that rare
moment when nature both humbles
and lifts you at once.

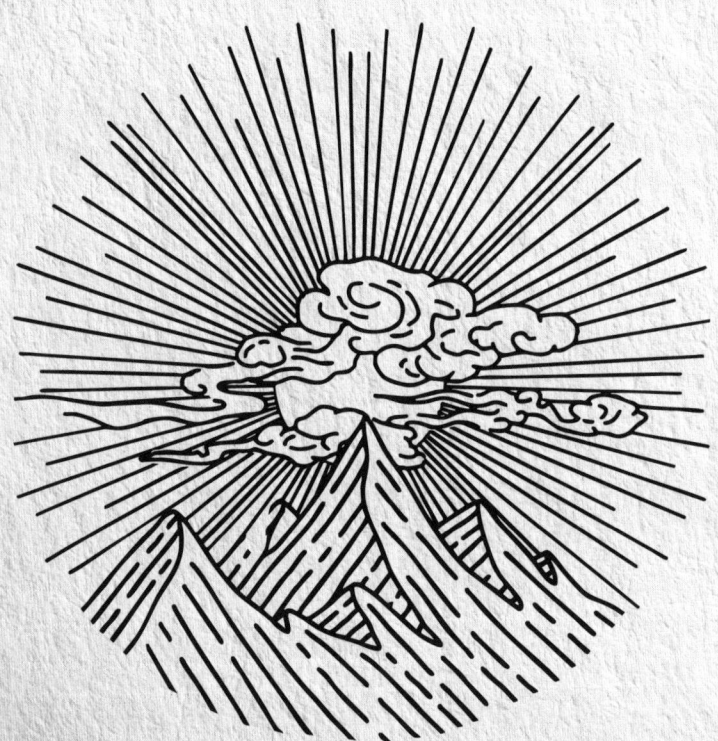

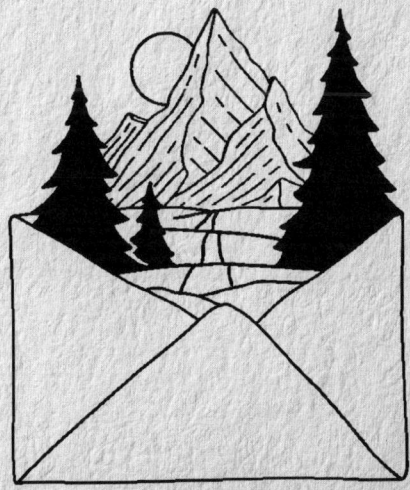

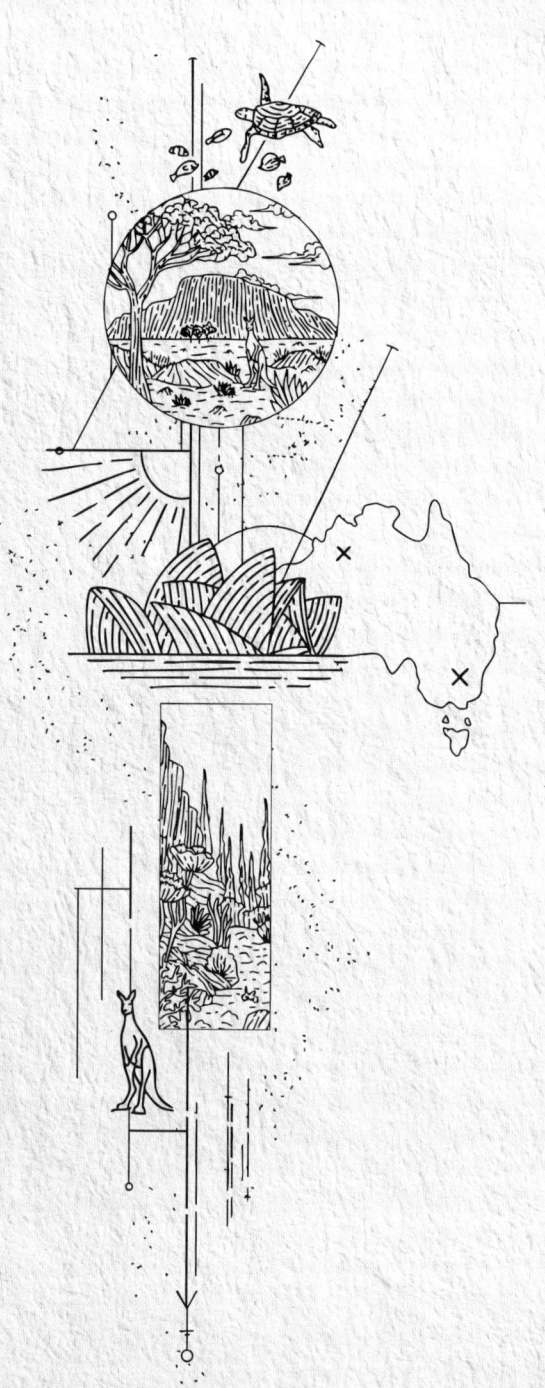

TRAVEL AUSTRALIA

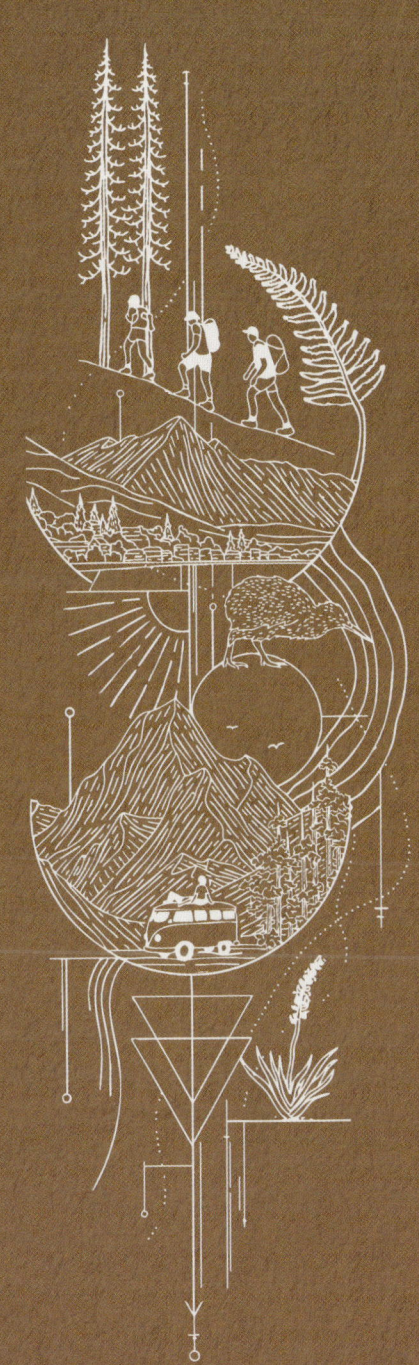

TRAVEL NEW ZEALAND

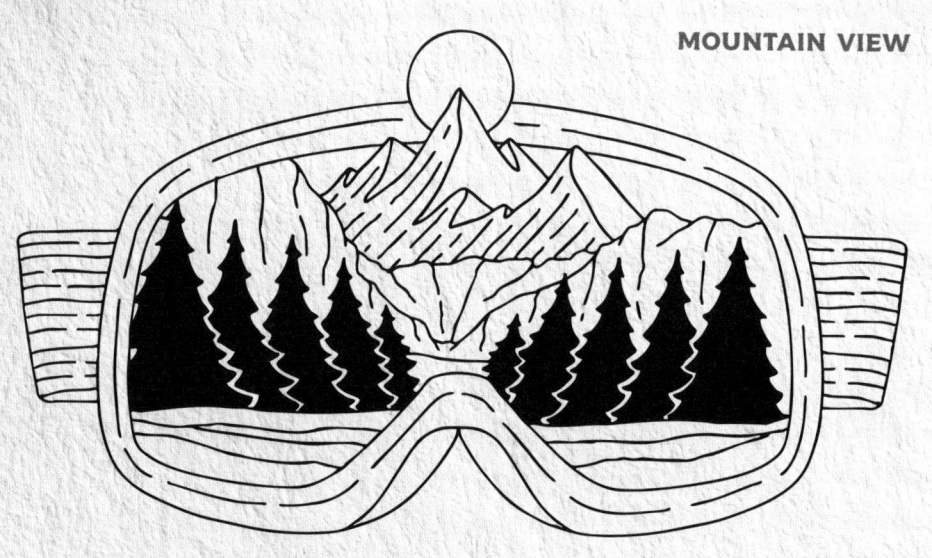

MOUNTAIN VIEW

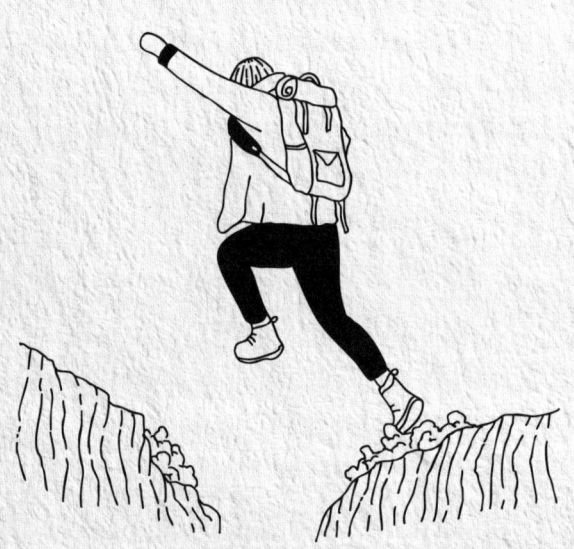

TAKE A LEAP

"DO NOT GO WHERE THE
PATH MAY LEAD,
GO INSTEAD WHERE
THERE IS NO PATH
AND LEAVE A TRAIL."

– RALPH WALDO EMERSON

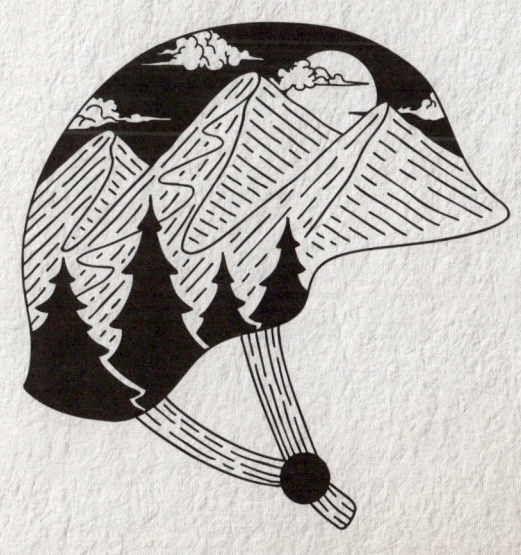

RIDGE RIDER

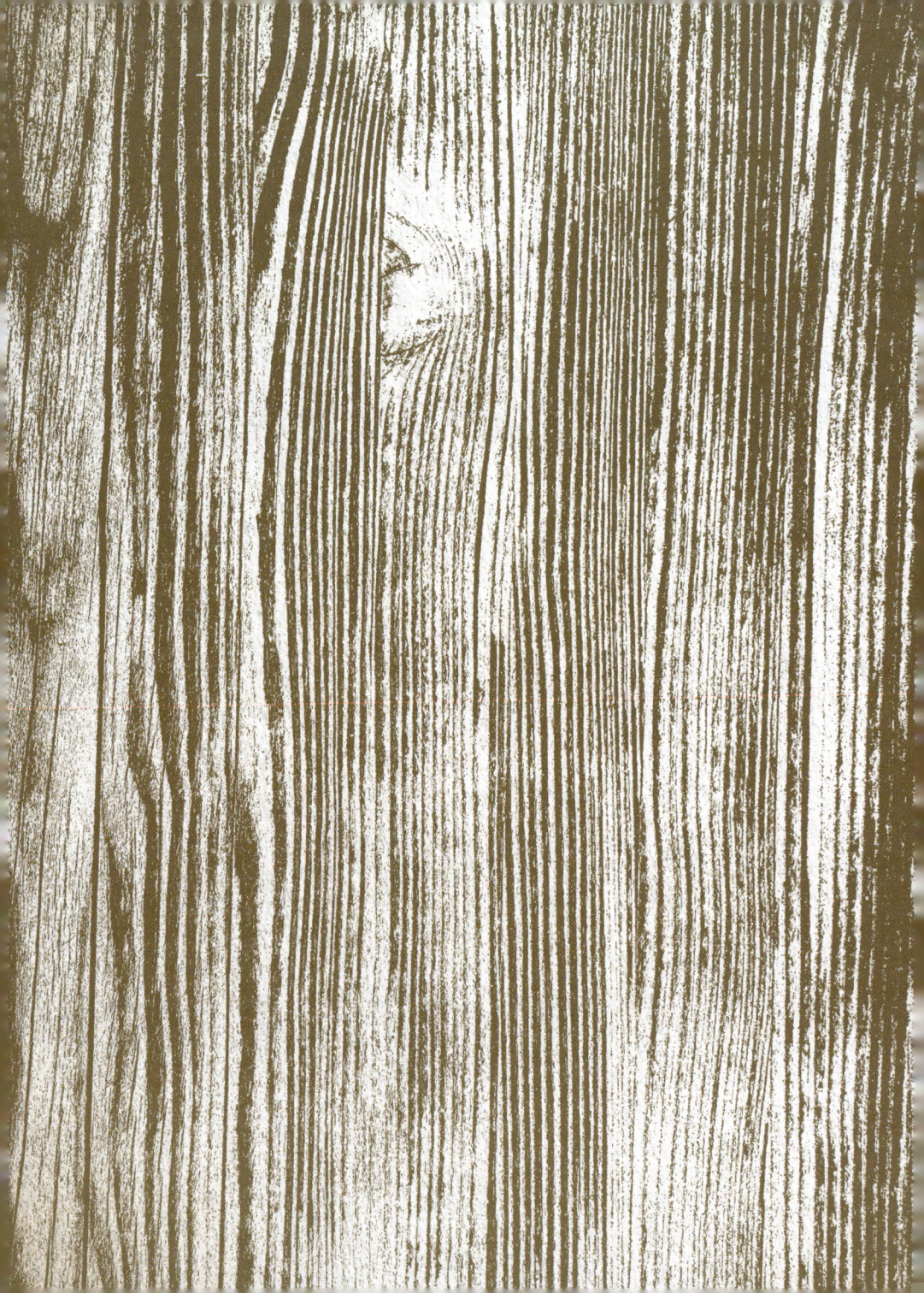

CHAPTER 10

WHEELS
AND
WANDERLUST

I spend a lot of time in the camper van, traveling around and collecting experiences and inspiration. Van life isn't always perfect. But even on the trickier days, there's something honest about it. The feeling of potential that they foster is unmatched.

Most of these designs were drawn along the road. I've sketched while parked in forests, under the shadow of mountains, and beside the sea. You'll find little details tucked into each one, from surfboard roof racks to little dogs and times with friends that the vans enable. These aren't just vehicles. They're homes. They're freedom.

You learn to go with the flow. I personally love having no destination, and when I don't, I tend to find the most adventures along my journey. That mindset is what I've tried to draw into these pieces. A sense of movement, of possibility, of being content with where you are.

This chapter is for the travelers. The ones who've built their own little moving homes or who dream of hitting the road one day. For anyone who's spent a night in a tin can tucked in the woods or pulled over beside a cliff with nowhere else to be. These drawings are about wanderlust, yes, but they're also about the comfort of carrying your home with you. They are about the love for the open road and the places it will take you.

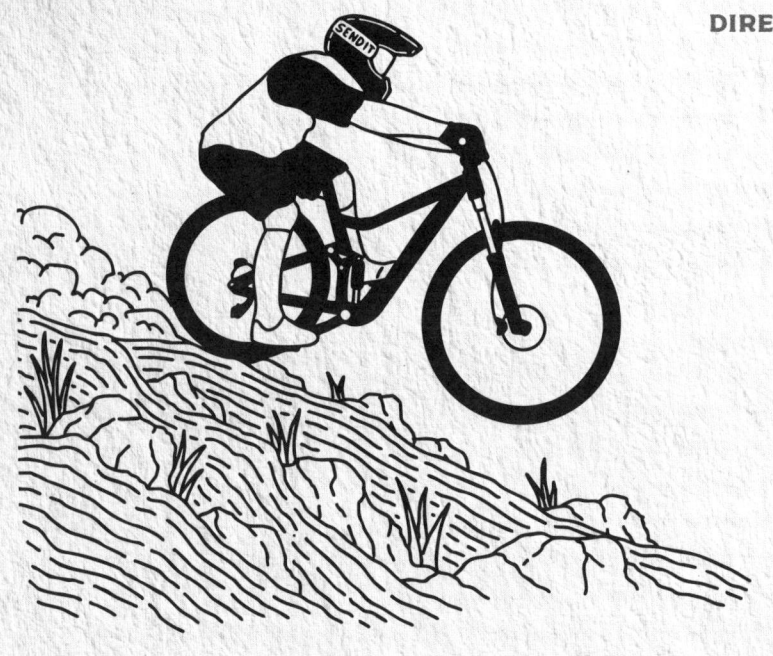

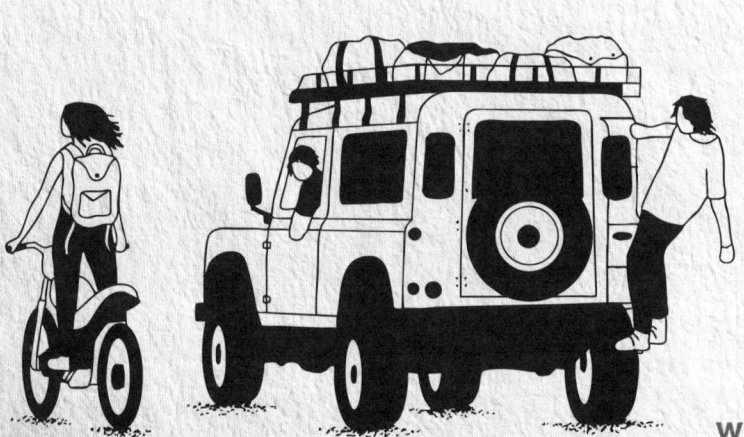

"NATURE ALWAYS WEARS THE COLORS OF THE SPIRIT."

– RALPH WALDO EMERSON

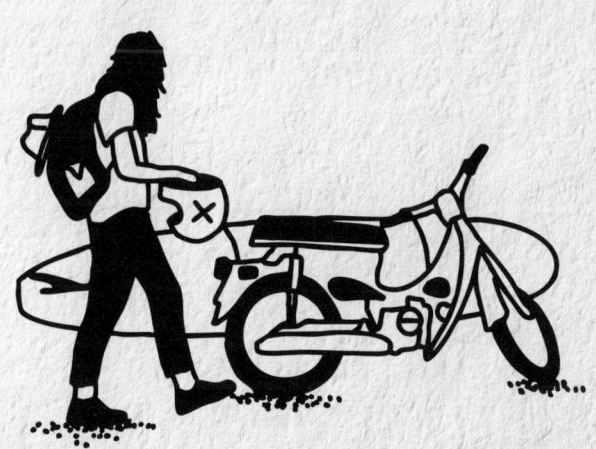

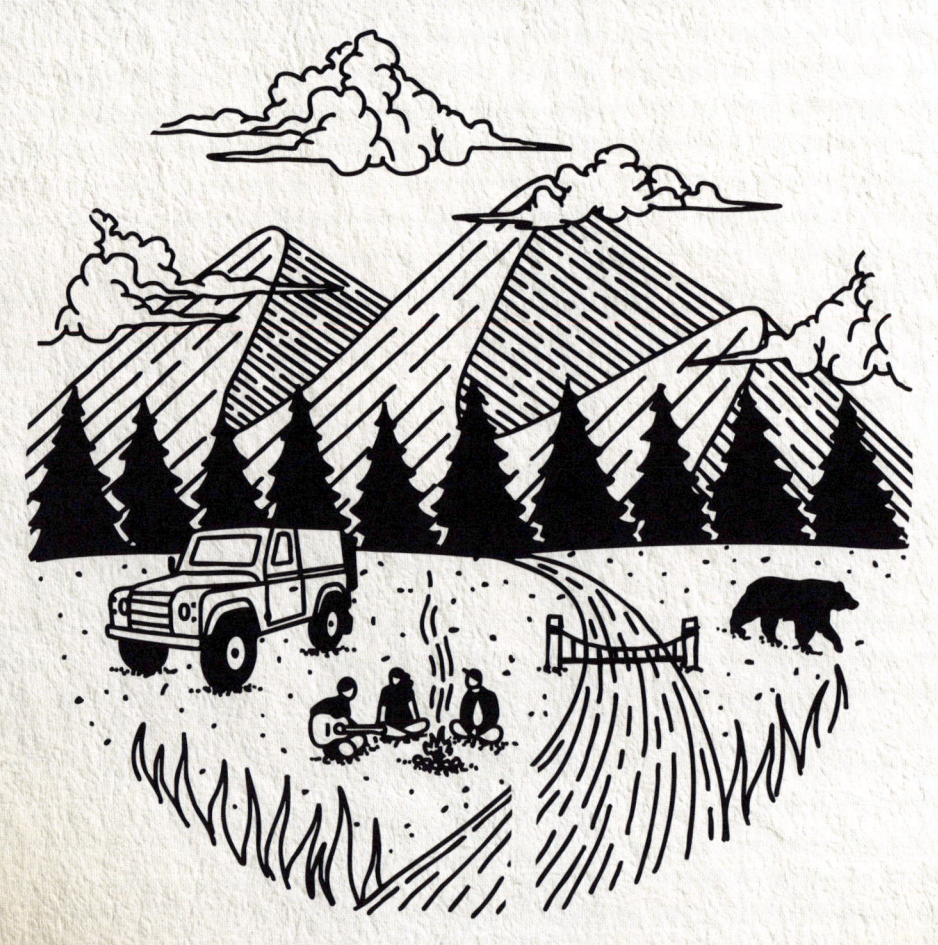

CAMPER CHILL

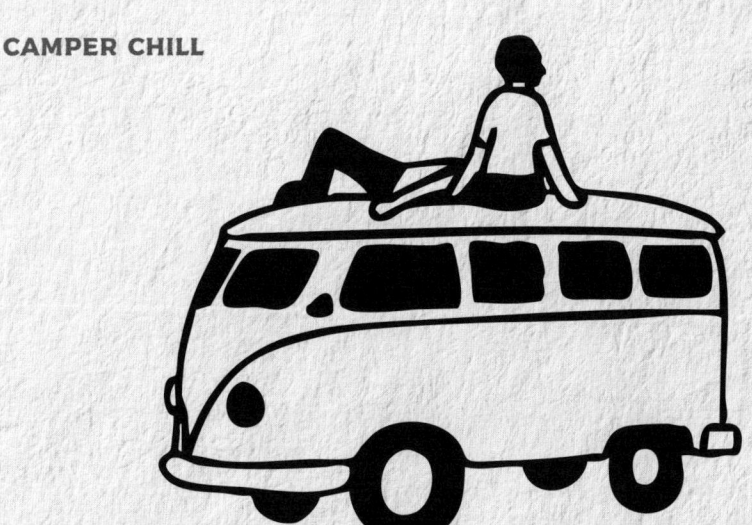

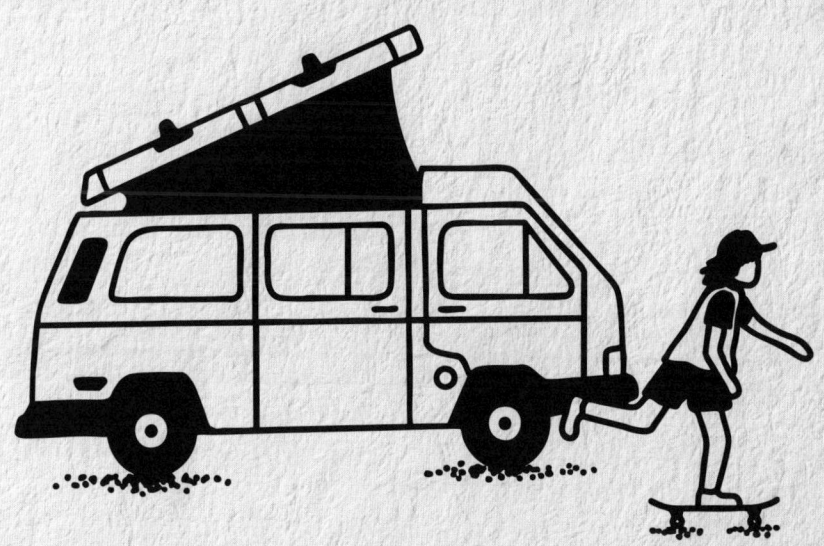

CAMPER CRUISER

KEEP PUSHIN'

The undercarriage of a skateboard—
scuffed, steady, and full of stories.
Skating feels like urban surfing, the
same rhythm as carving snow or riding
waves. You don't need a mountain or
an ocean to chase that feeling, just
pavement, patience, and a good push.

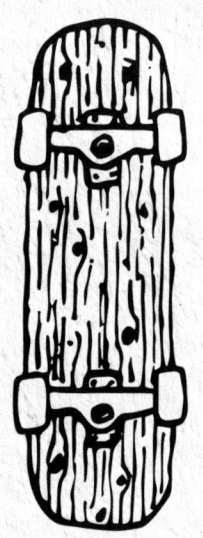

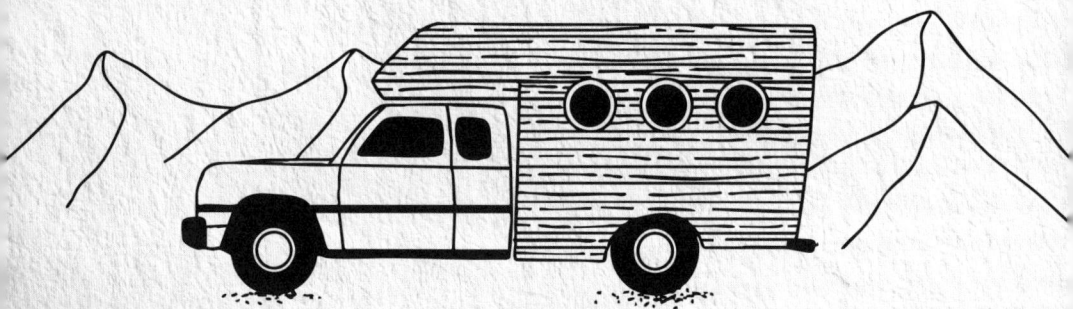

LONG-DISTANCE RANGE

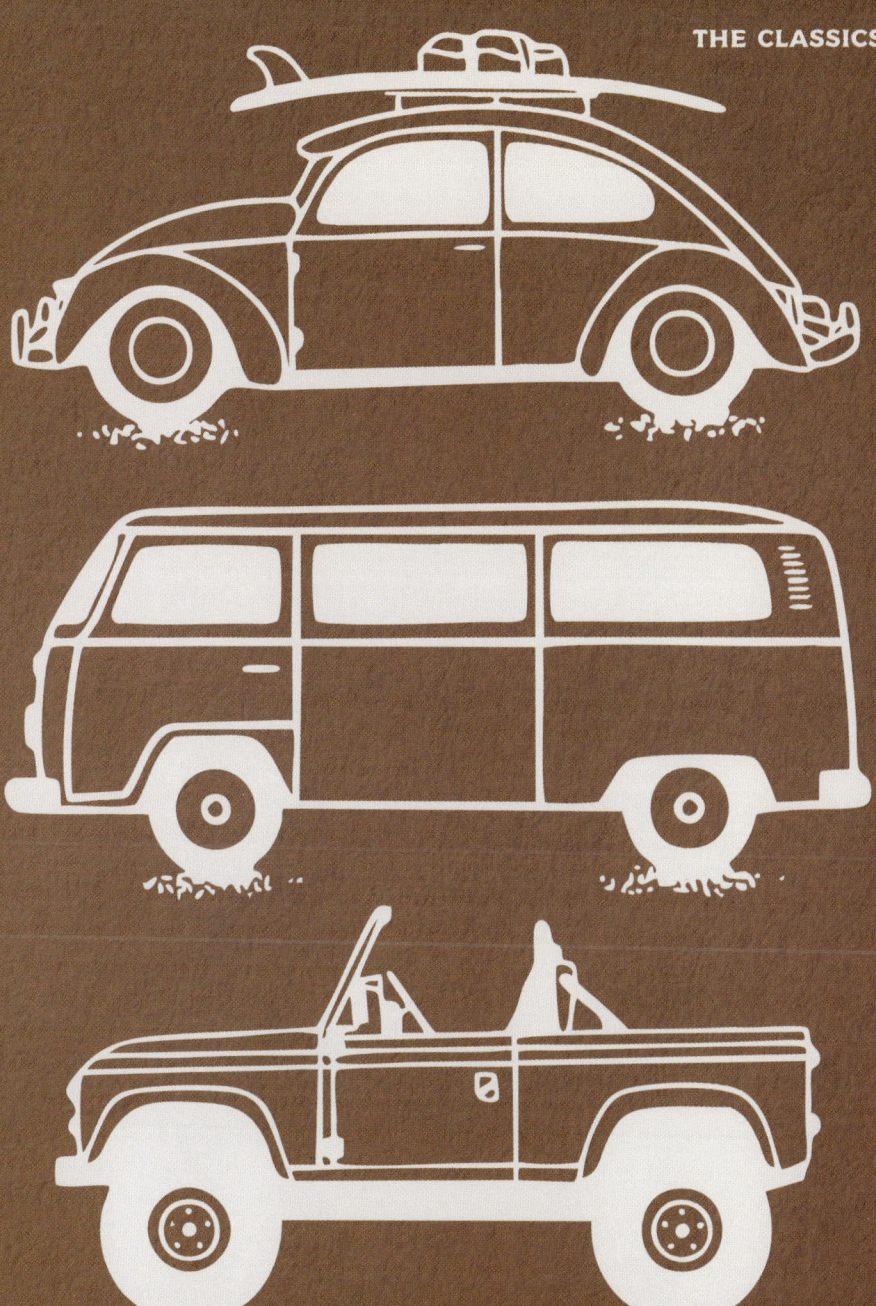

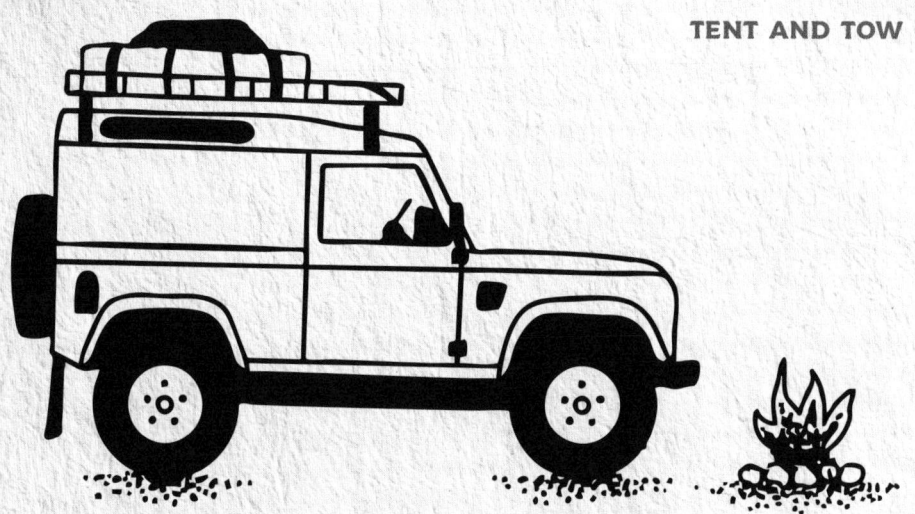

TENT AND TOW

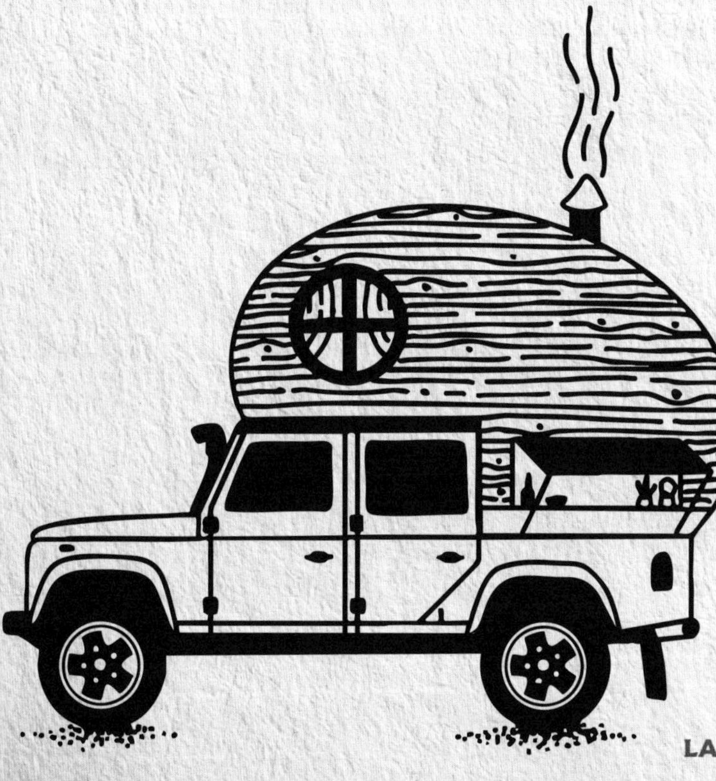

LANDY WAGON

POP TOP

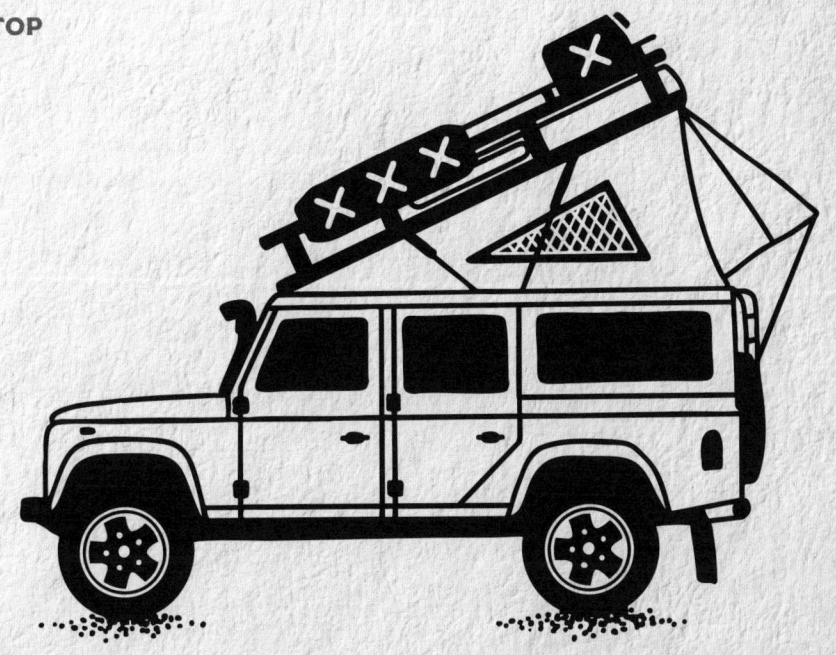

SURF BUS

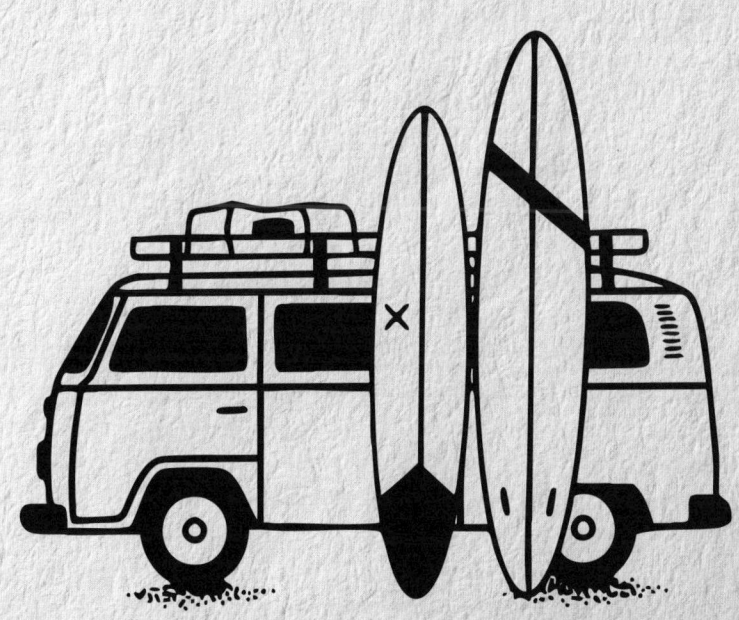

SURF BUG

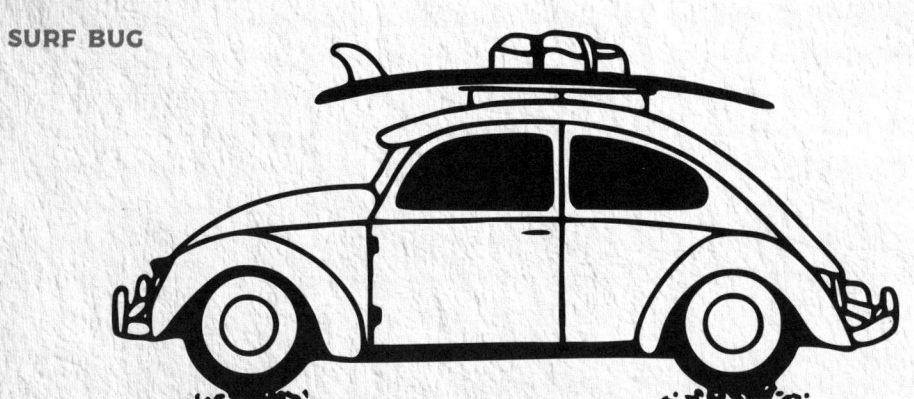

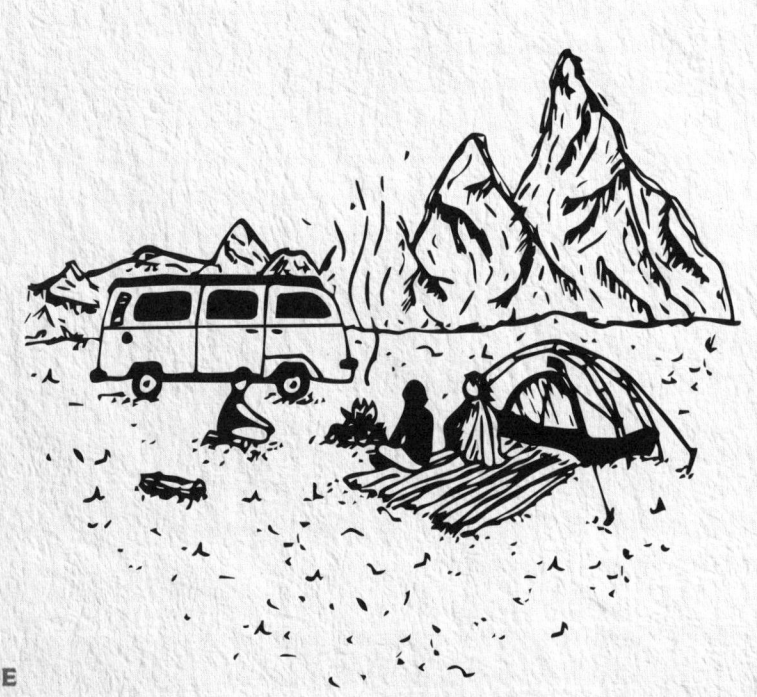

SUMMITSIDE

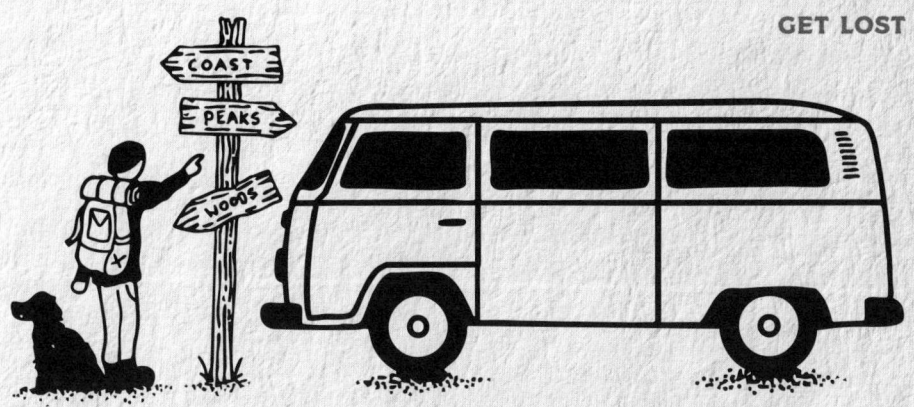

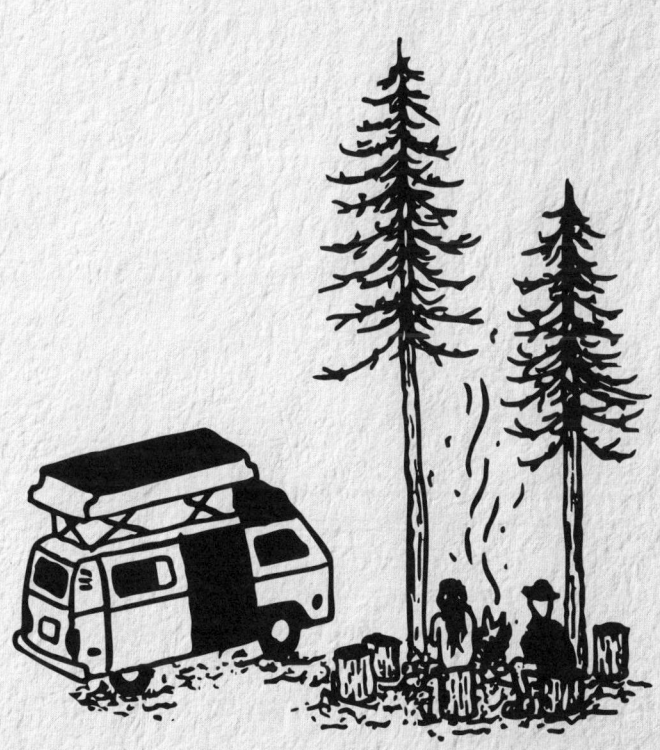

PINE PARKING

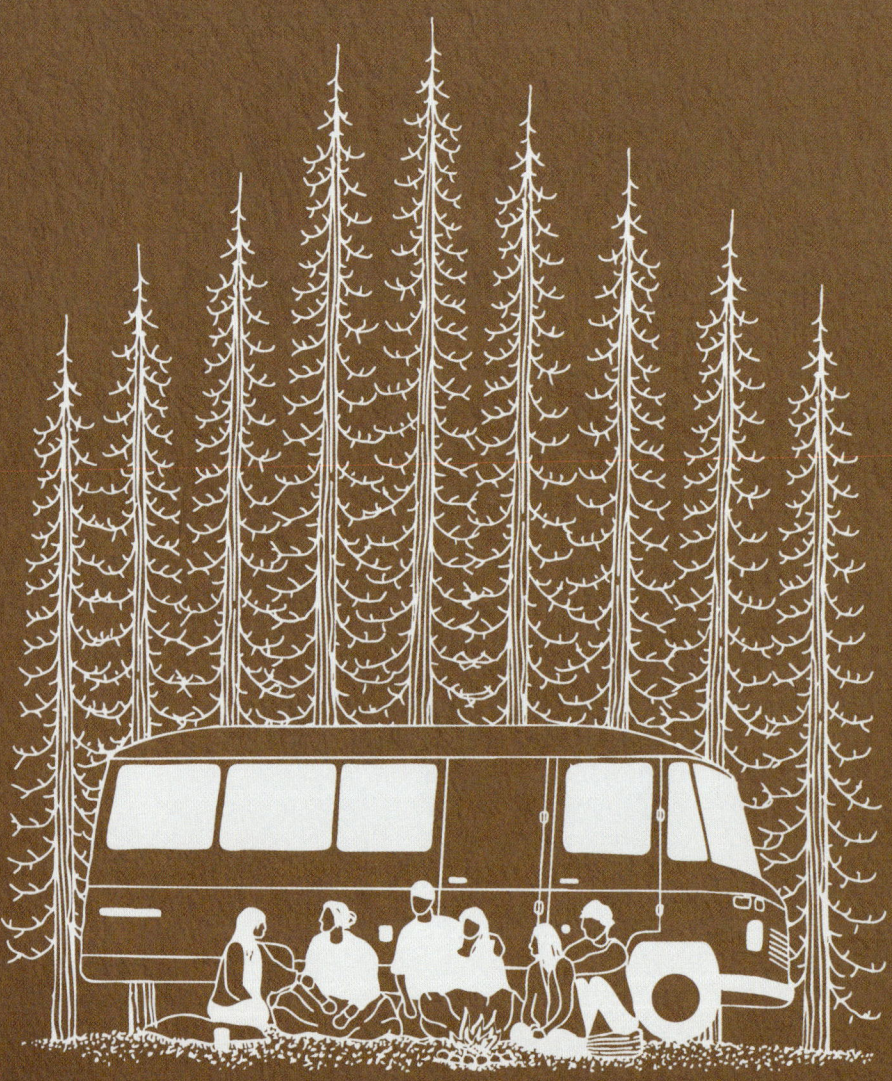

OVER NOOK

A van parked beneath the trees, roof popped up, campfire flickering nearby. Two friends stand chatting; one sits close to the flame. Blankets spill from the open door, an extra tire rests on the roof. It's a cozy home made of warmth and the road itself.

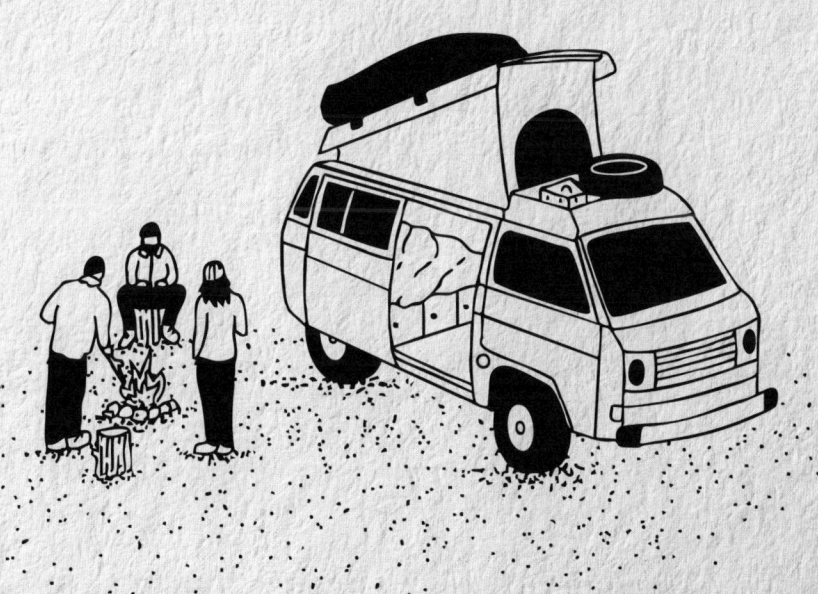

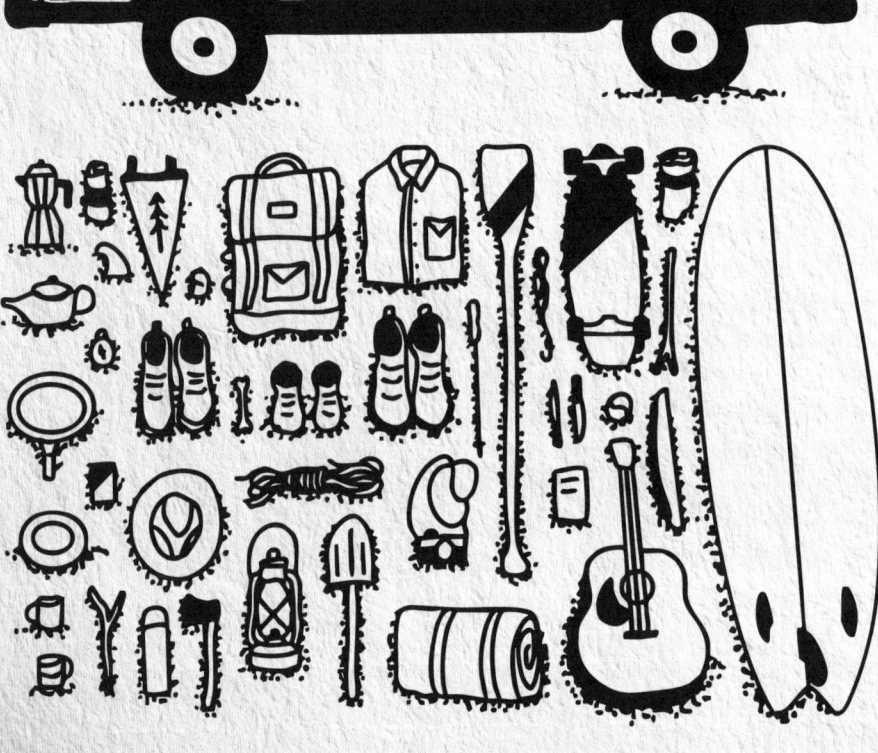

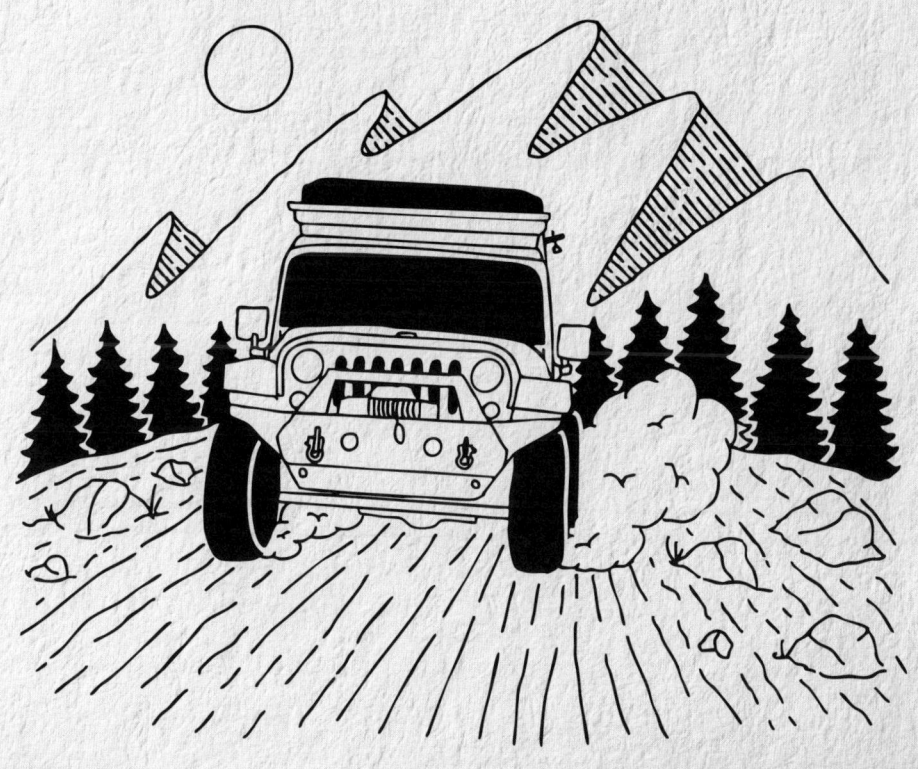

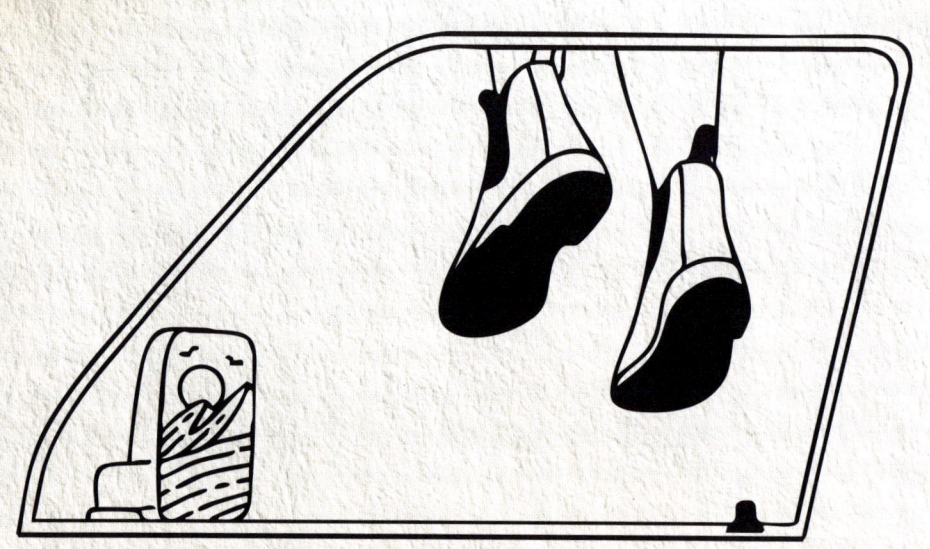

WINDOW SEAT

"BETWEEN EVERY TWO PINES IS A DOORWAY TO A NEW WORLD."

– JOHN MUIR

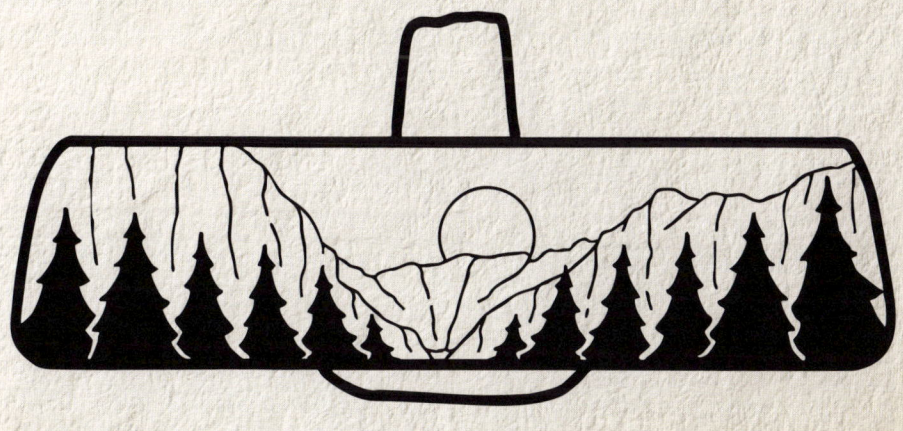

REAR VIEW

ROAD TRIP

The van doors swing wide, revealing a painted sunrise over mountains and a river that spills right out onto the earth. A surfboard leans nearby, ready for the next stop. It's the feeling of endless possibilities and the road unwinding before you.

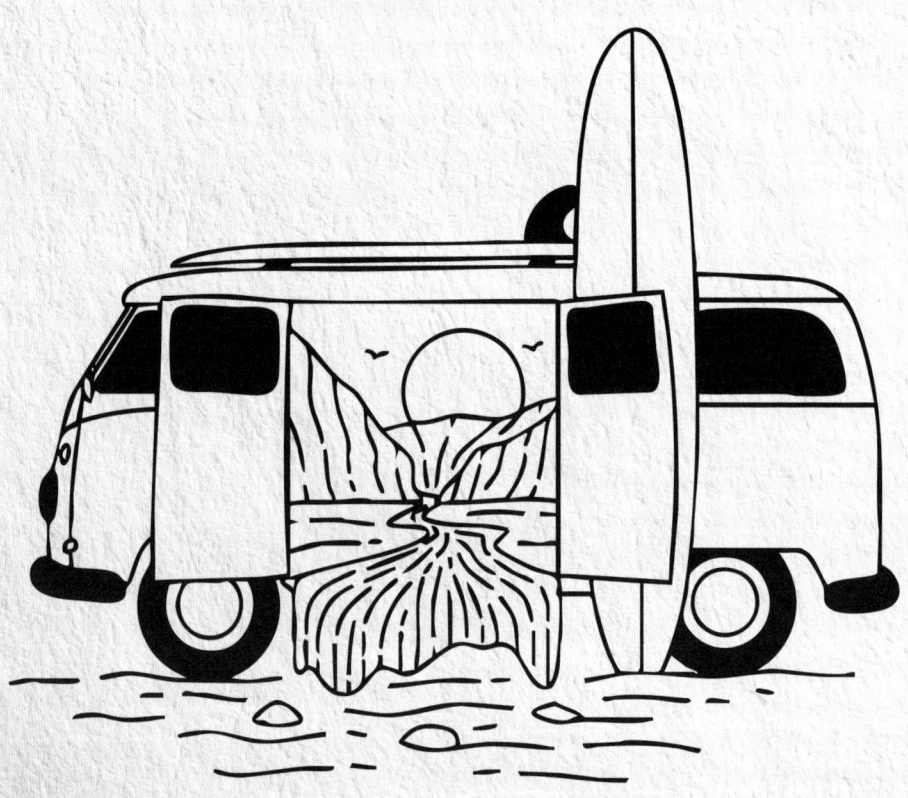

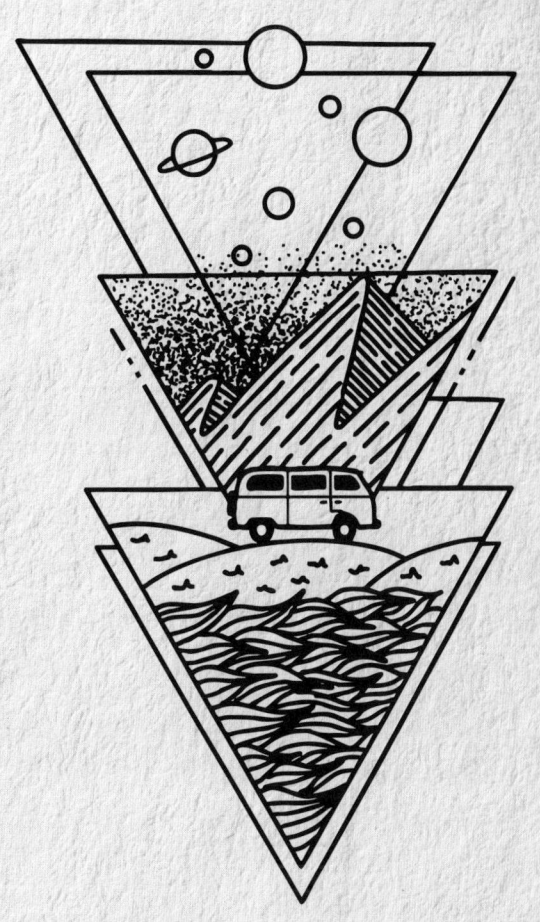

NOMADIQUE

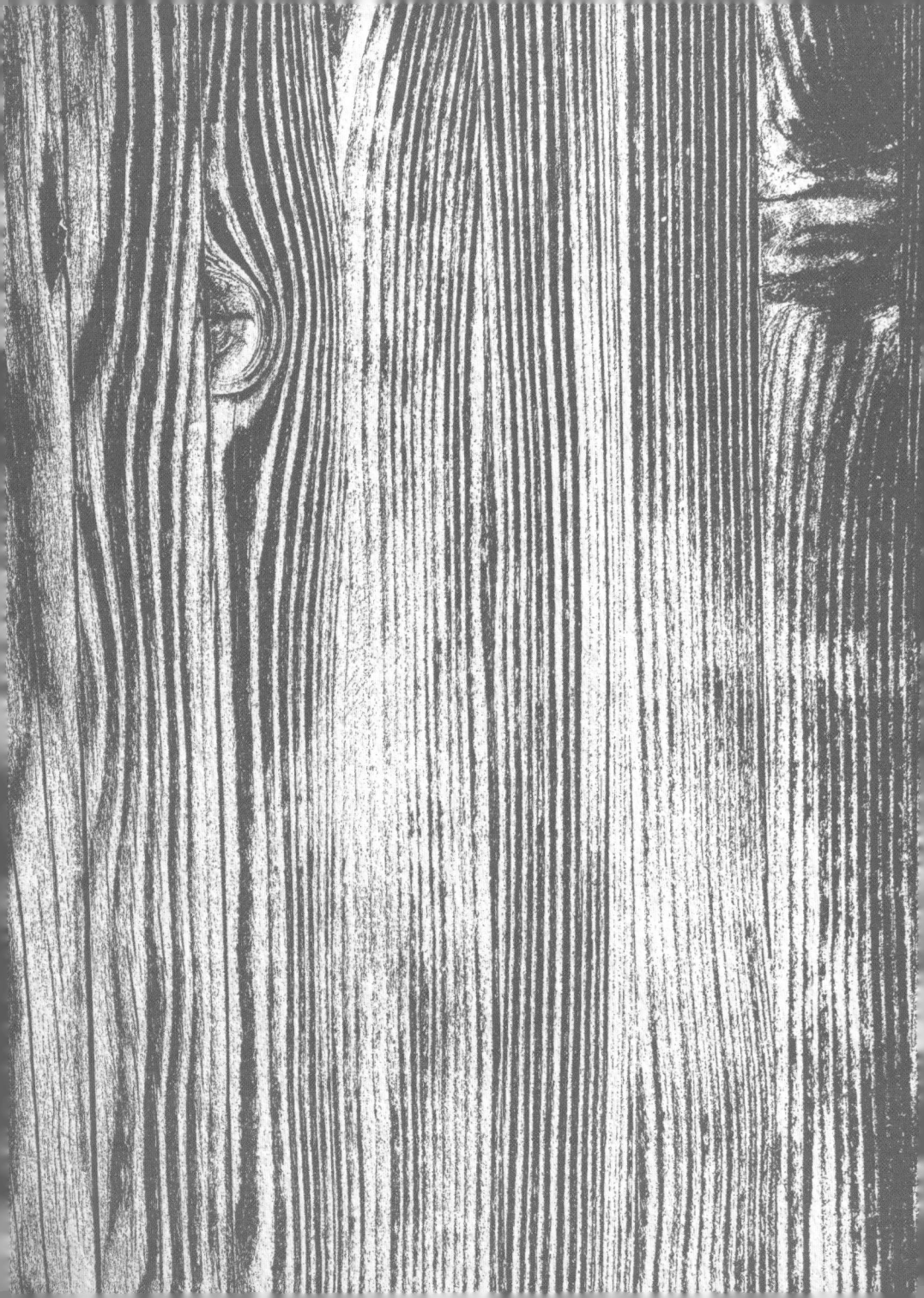

CHAPTER 11

TIDES
AND
TRANQUILITY

There's something about being in the water that clears my mind, whether I'm on a surfboard, swimming, or even just walking nearby. Whether it's a lake or the ocean, I've always loved it. This is one of the main reasons I was drawn to Devon.

Most of these pieces were drawn in my studio after a surf or a swim, or when I (often) find myself dreaming about surfing or throwing a ball into the sea for Tucker to chase. I recently got into diving, too, and there's something so calming about that experience. You'll see waves and shores of all kinds here: from beach breaks to calm lakes as well as items and activities you might enjoy near water. Some of the pieces are detailed and some are really simple. Just like the way water can take many forms. But whatever their subject or style, they all celebrate the intrinsic joy and renewal that it can provide.

This chapter is for the sea lovers. Whether you surf every day or just like the feeling of dipping your toes in the shallows, these designs are for you—a little tribute to one of my favorite elements.

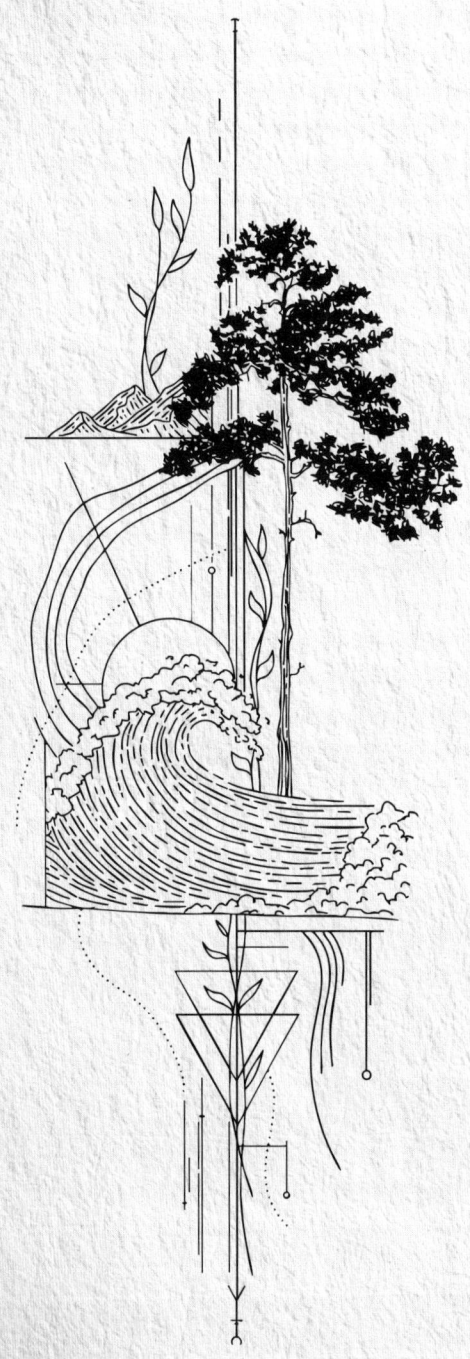

BOARD BREAK

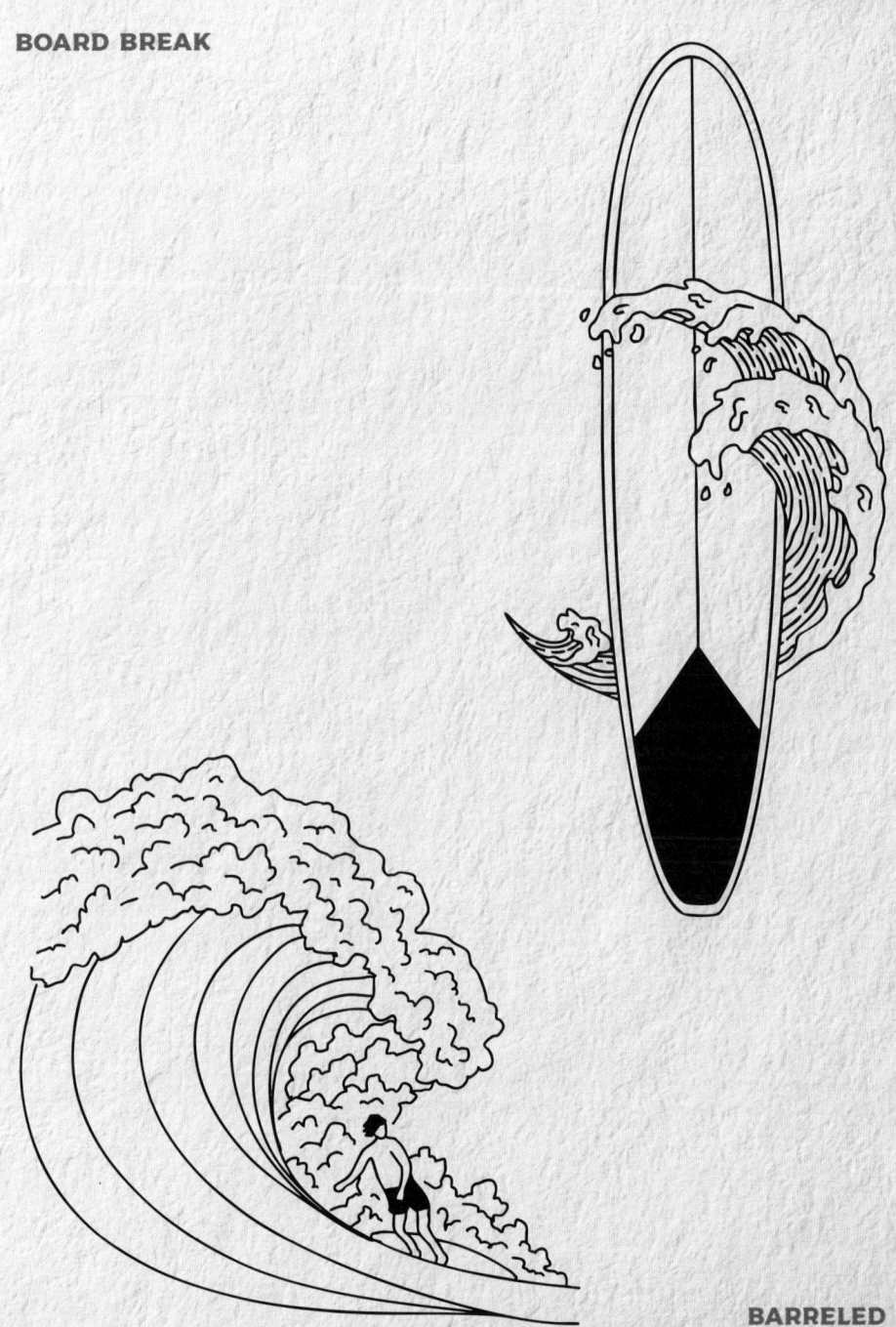

BARRELED

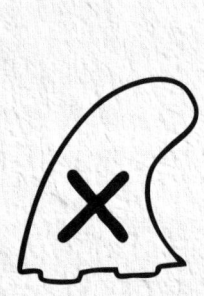

FIN FLOW

"BOUNDLESS, BLUE, AND BEAUTIFUL, RESTLESS, ROARING, RUSHING SEA!"
– GEORGE HENRY BOKER, "THE SEA"

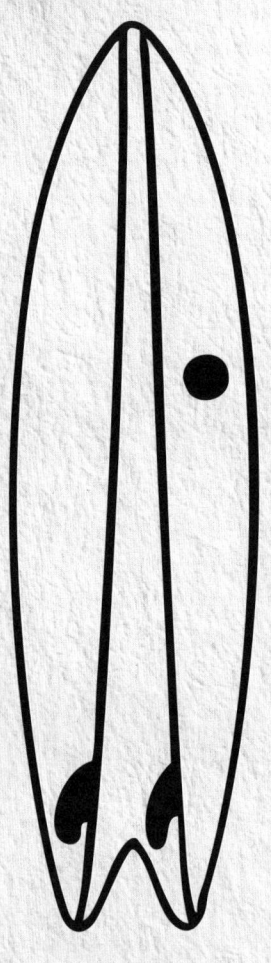

SOMETHING FISHY

A surfboard shaped like a fish,
complete with fins and a curious eye,
part ocean creature, part playful design.
It captures the humor and joy of surf
life. Sometimes it's enough just to ride,
laugh, and let the ocean carry you.

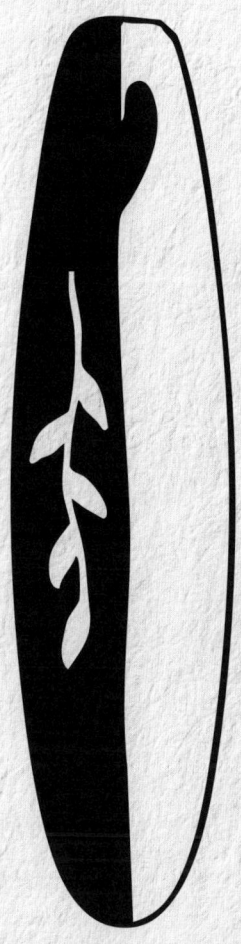

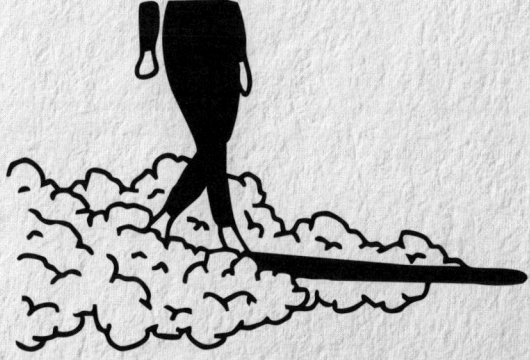

FOAM RIDER

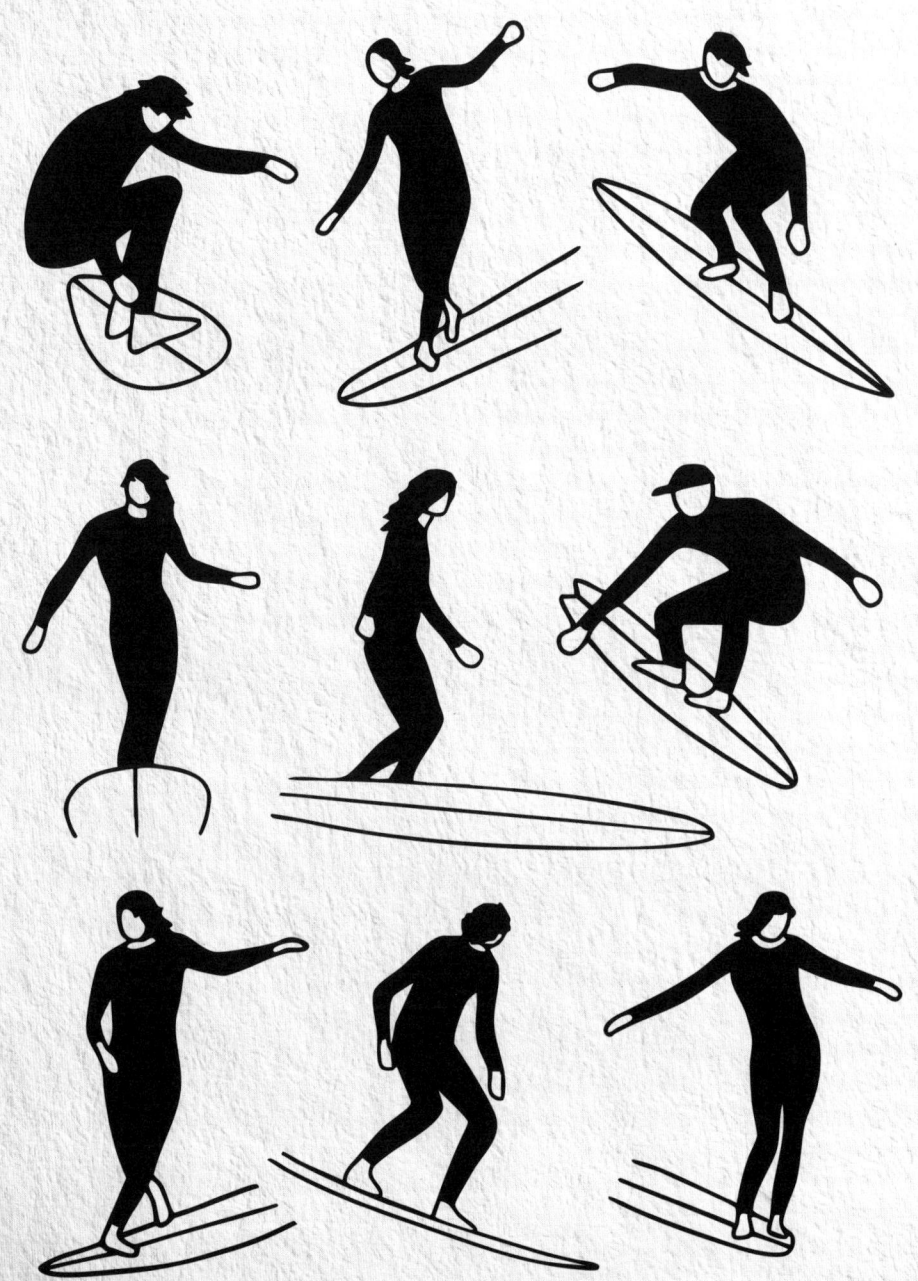

SURFER GIRL

She stands in profile, board resting
taller than she is, hair flowing. Calm
and unhurried, she feels at home
between sand and ocean. This
moment is all sunlight and salt, a quiet
portrait of strength.

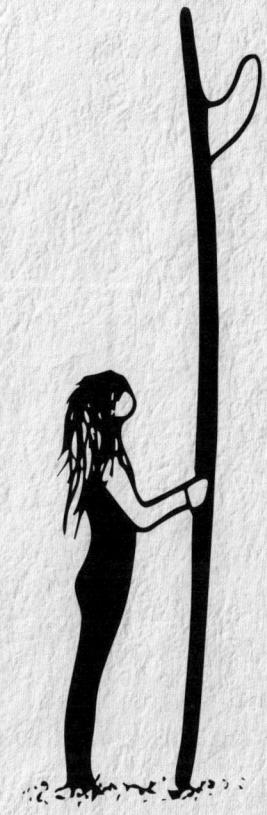

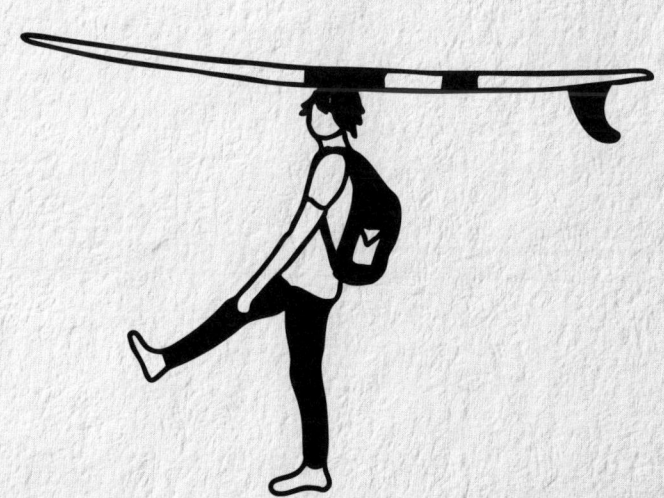

BOARD BALANCE

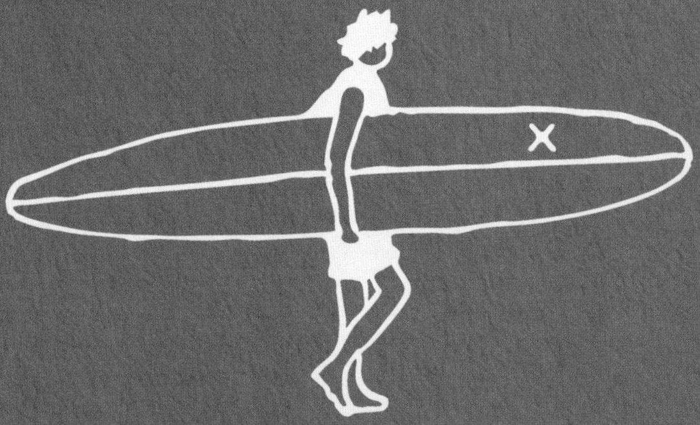

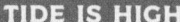

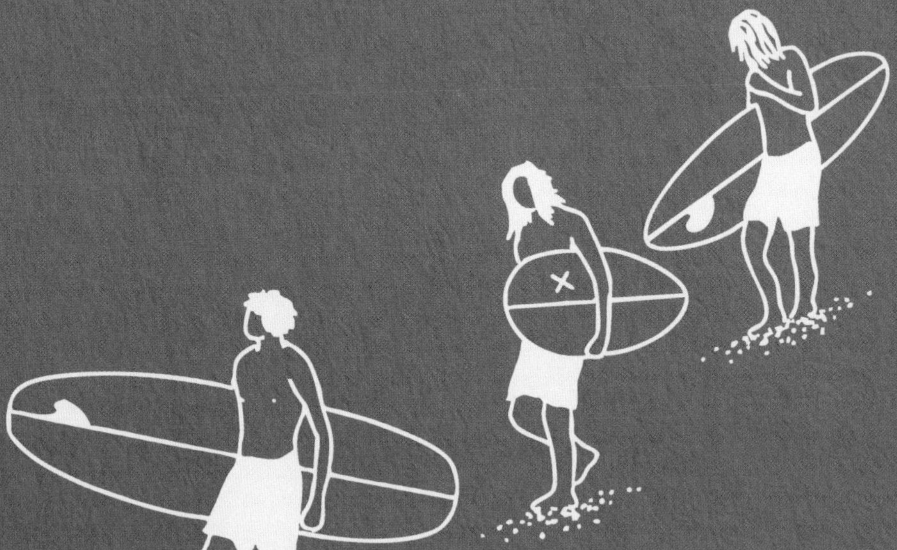

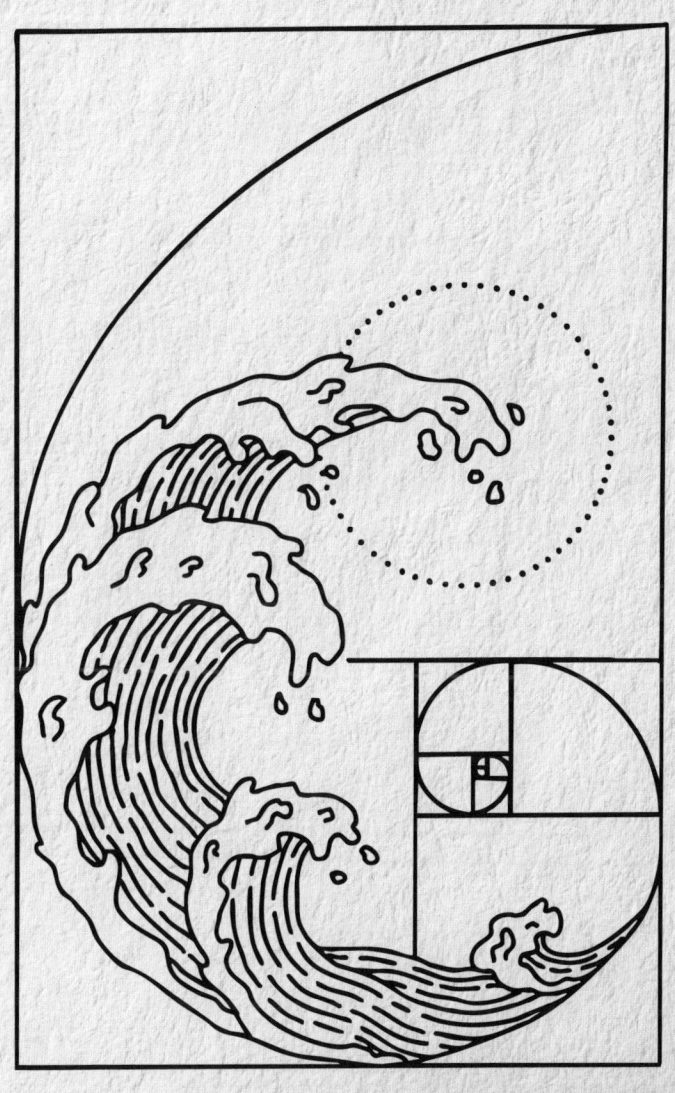

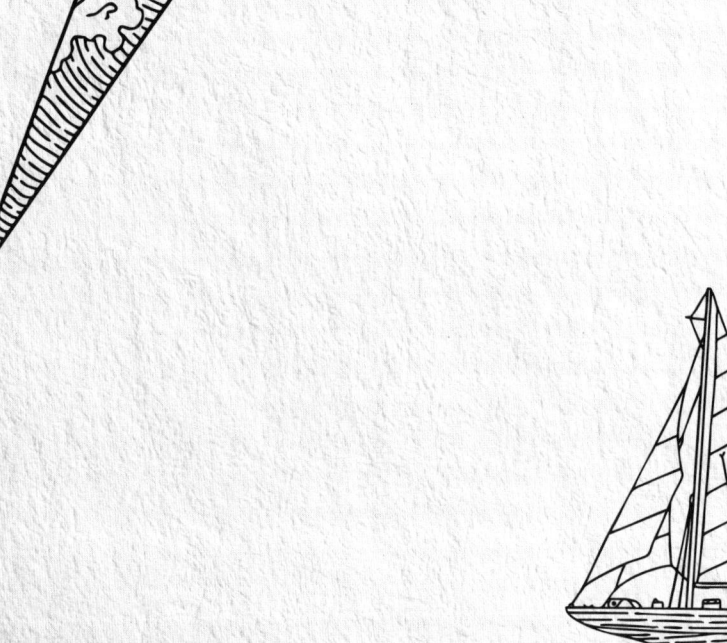

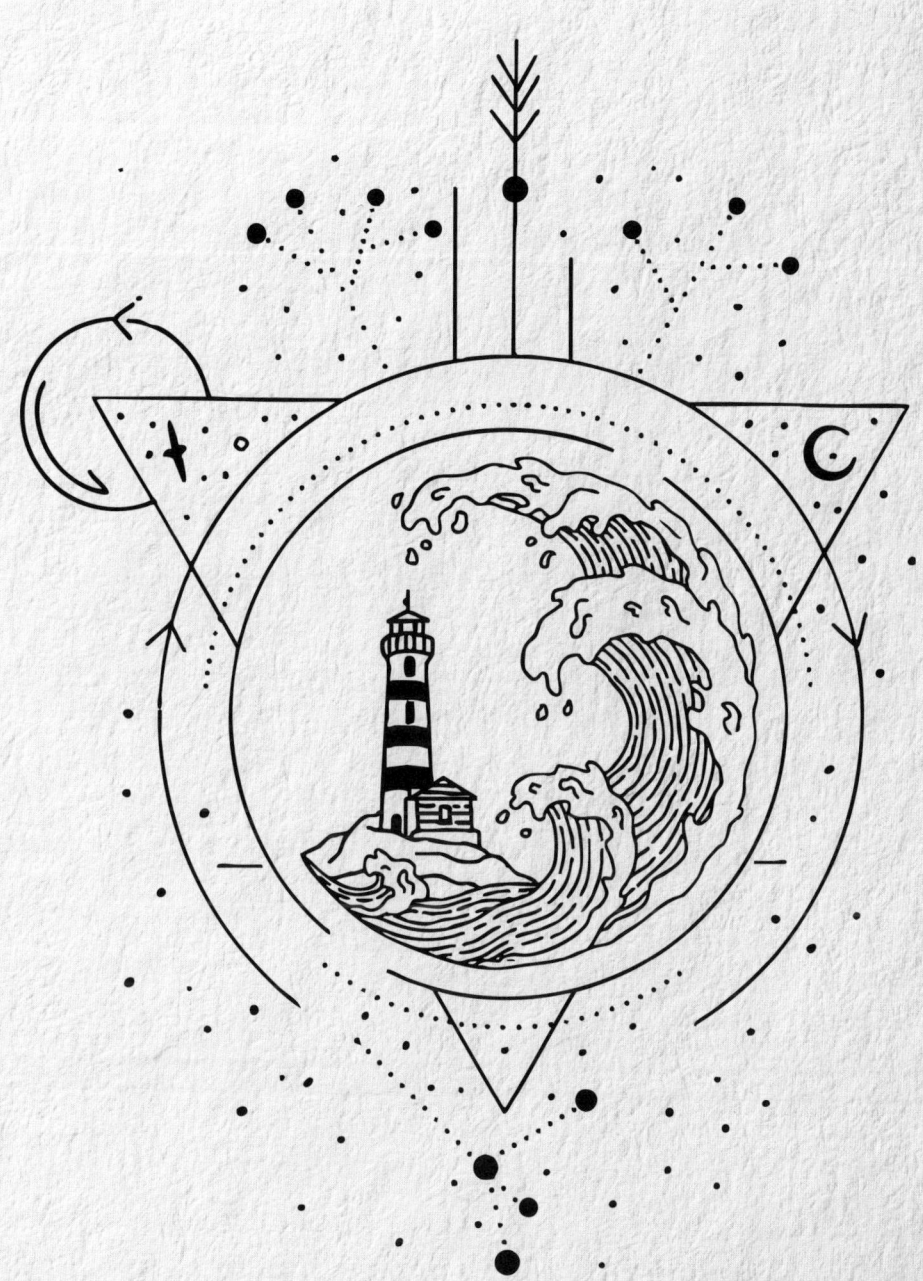

LIGHT THE WAY

"THE VOICE OF THE SEA SPEAKS TO THE SOUL."
– KATE CHOPIN

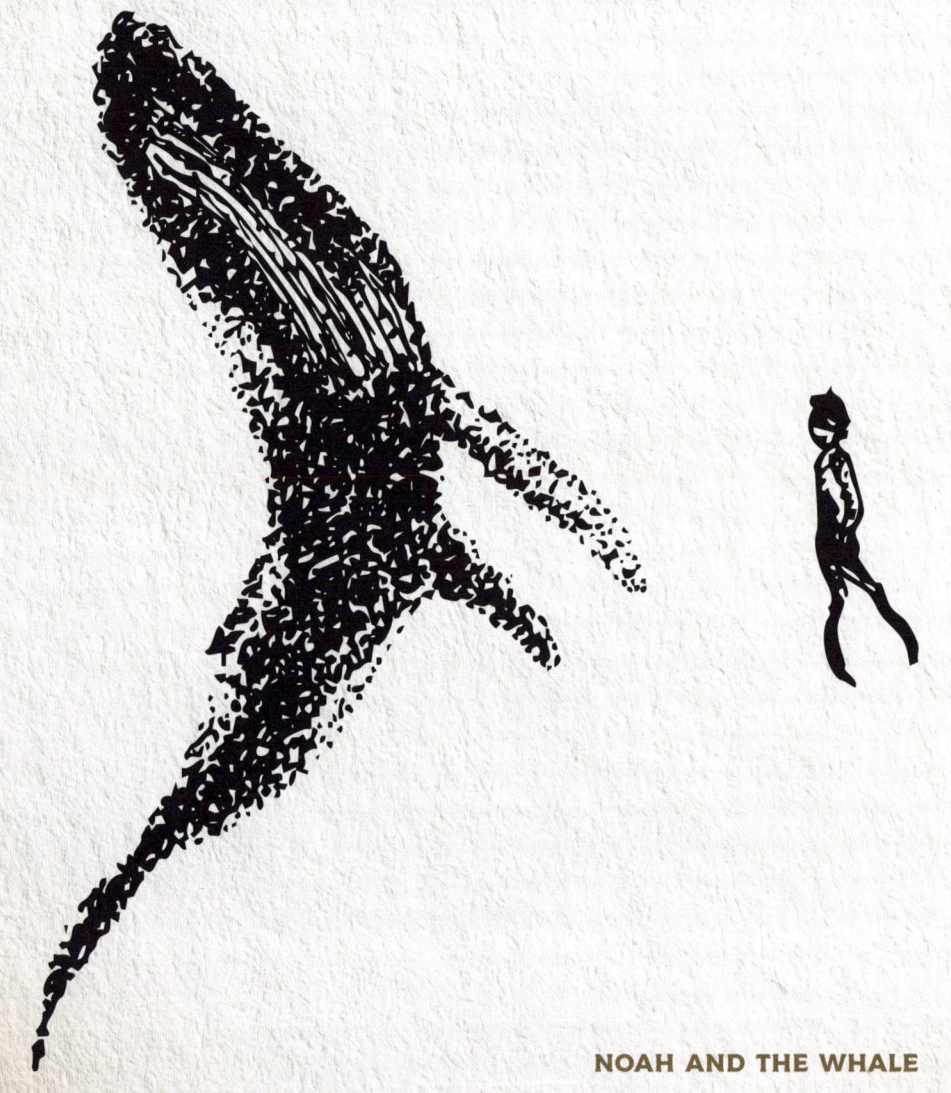

NOAH AND THE WHALE

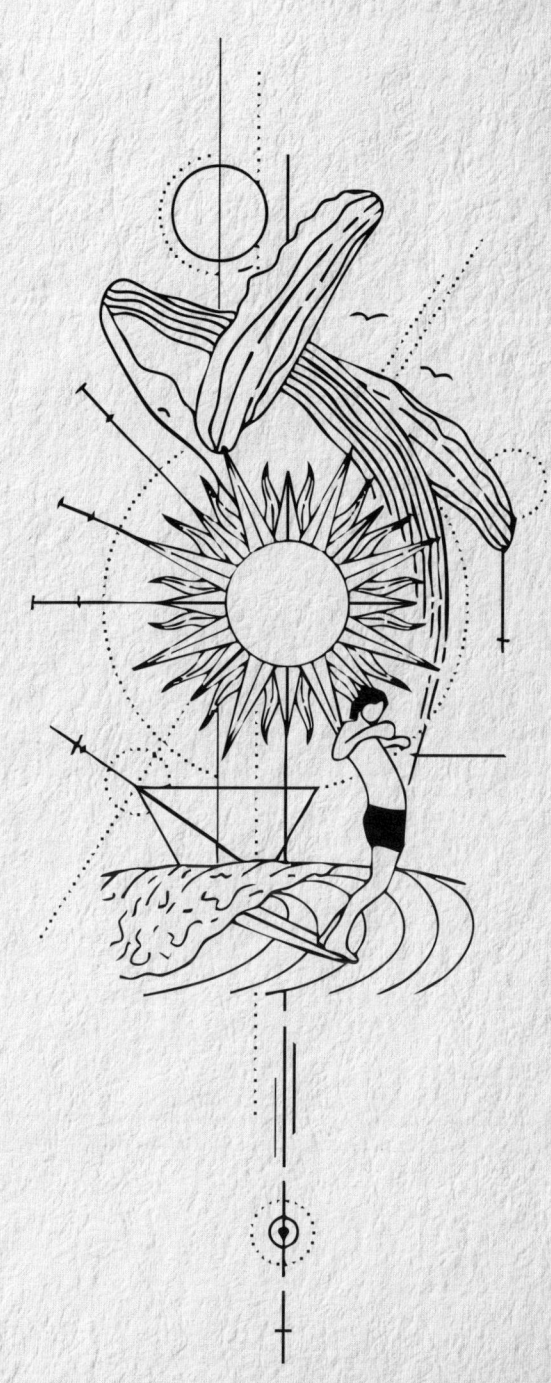

CURRENTS

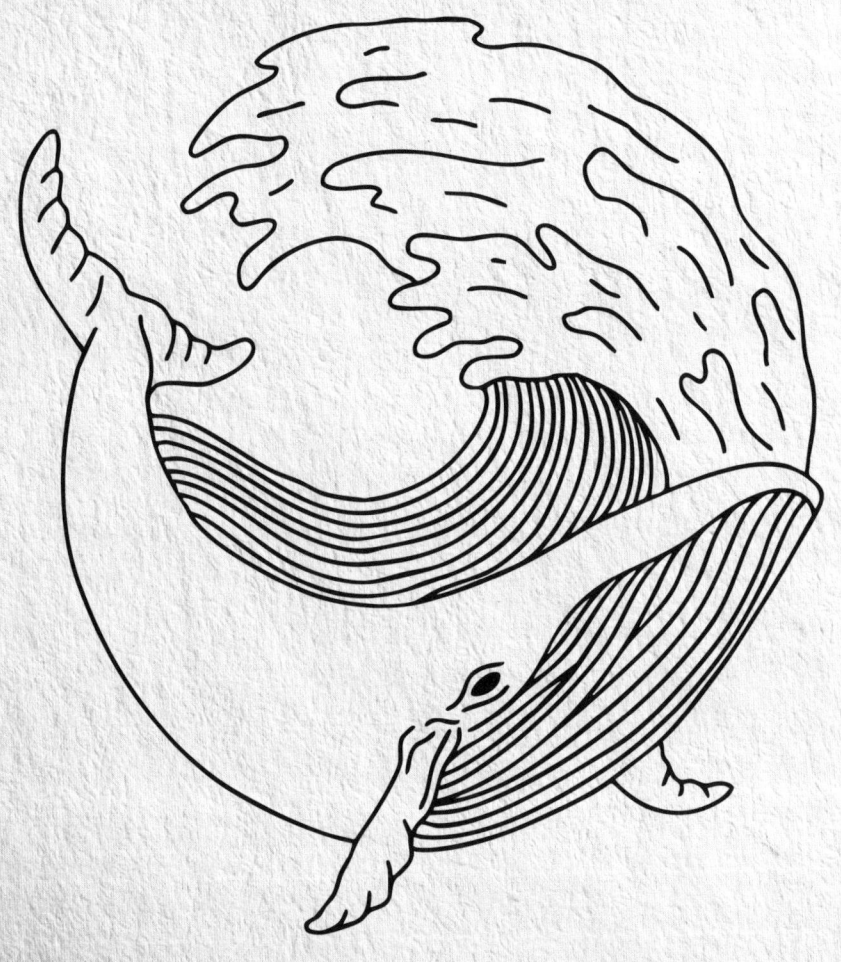

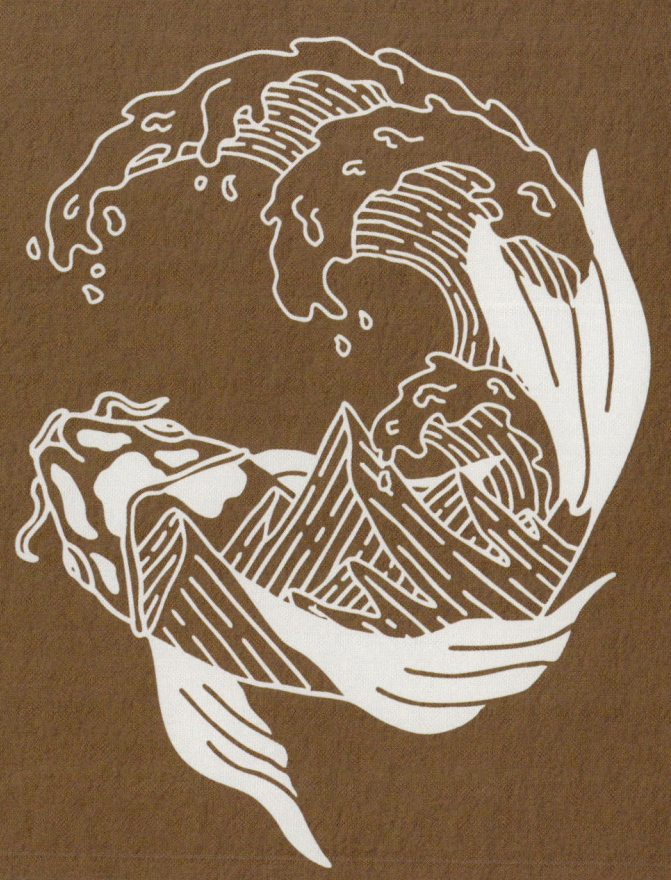

WILD KOI

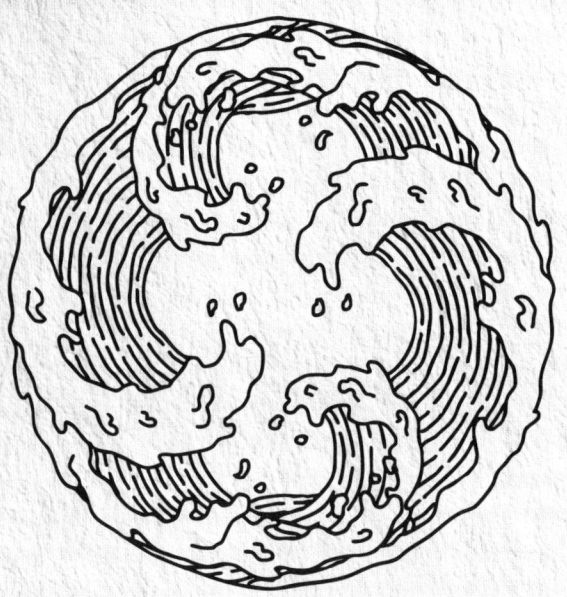

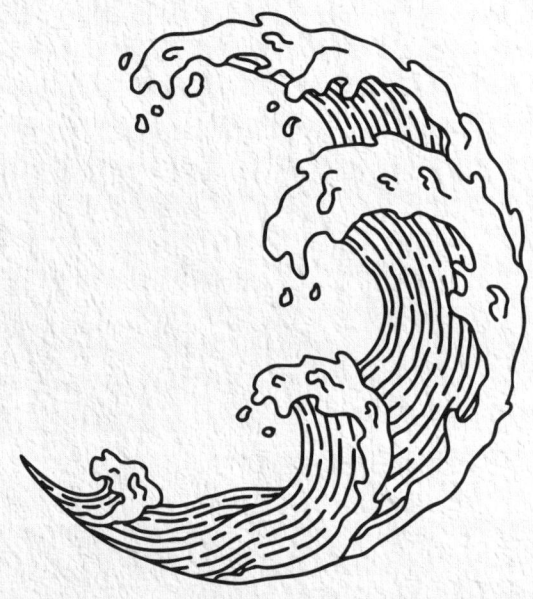

"MY SOUL IS FULL OF
LONGING FOR THE
SECRET OF THE SEA,
AND THE HEART OF THE
GREAT OCEAN SENDS
A THRILLING PULSE
THROUGH ME."

– HENRY WADSWORTH LONGFELLOW

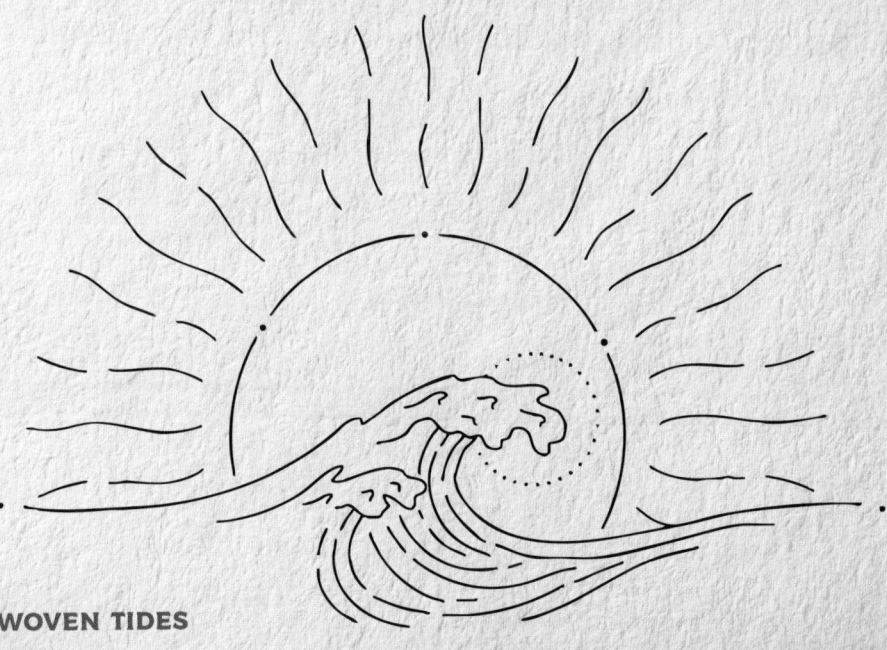

WOVEN TIDES

CHAPTER 12

INK BETWEEN US

Some marks, like these, are meant to be shared. These designs were drawn with connection and love in mind—symbols that people could treasure forever. They're for the people who are close, even when they're far apart. They're for love in all of its quiet forms. For anyone who shares a connection that doesn't need explaining.

Matching tattoos don't have to be bold or obvious. They can be twin lines, linked shapes, a memento of a shared moment or a small promise—a quiet symbol that says "I'm here too" without actually speaking the words.

These designs are a nod to the experiences shared with someone else and to the ways in which nature can bring us together.

NATURAL CYCLES

Two mirrored mountains rising, a sun lifting, a wave curling below. Each half belongs to one person, complete only together. A symbol of balance and belonging, it honors the natural rhythm shared between souls separate yet connected through the cycles of earth and time.

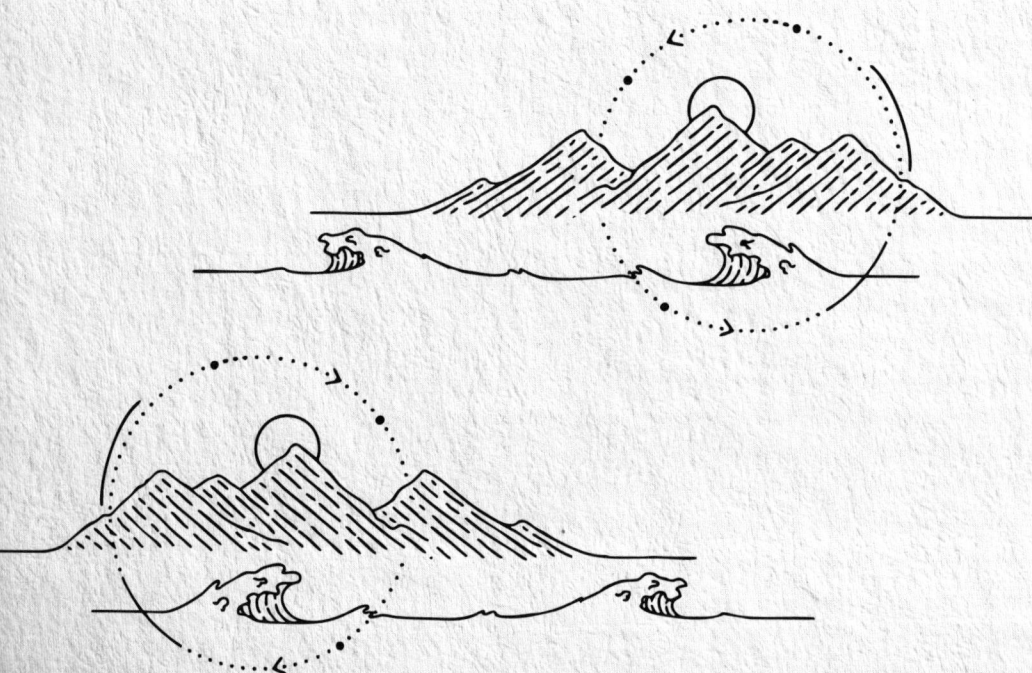

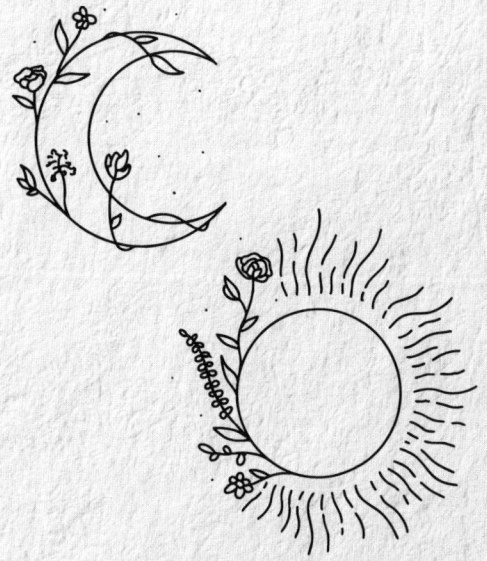

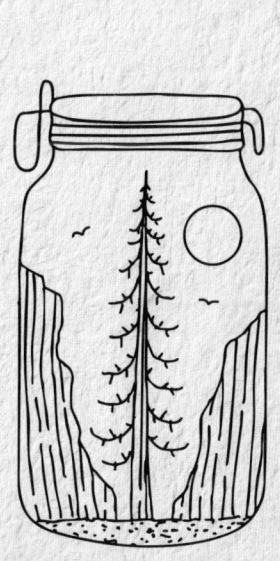

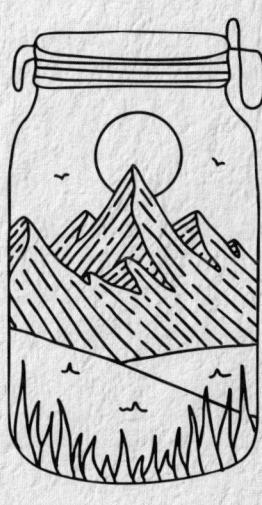

"WHATEVER OUR SOULS ARE MADE OF, HIS AND MINE ARE THE SAME."
– EMILY BRONTË, *WUTHERING HEIGHTS*

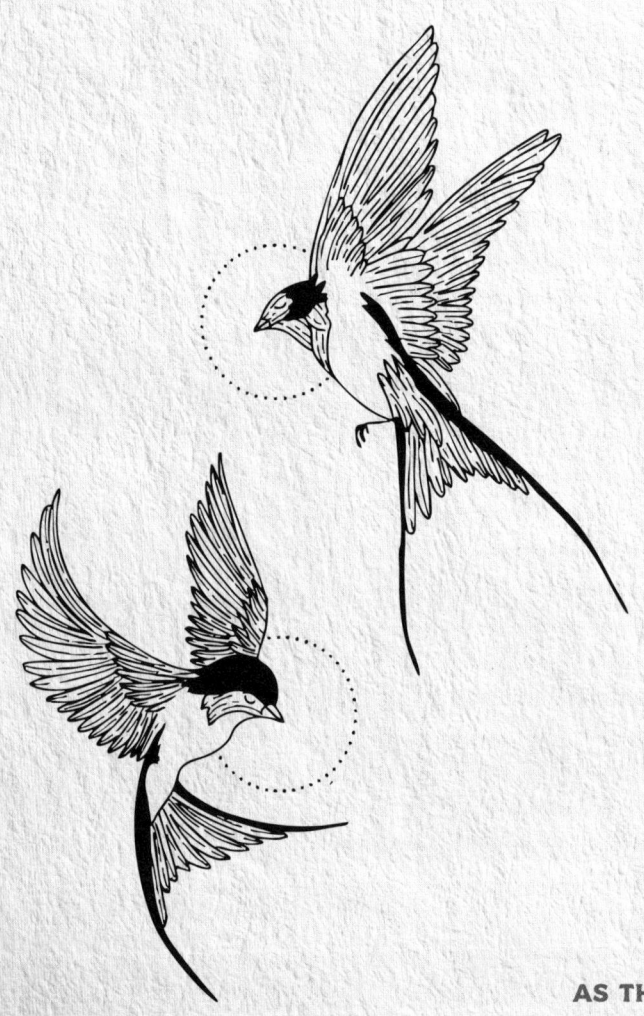

AS THE SWALLOW FLIES

SWALLOW DANCE

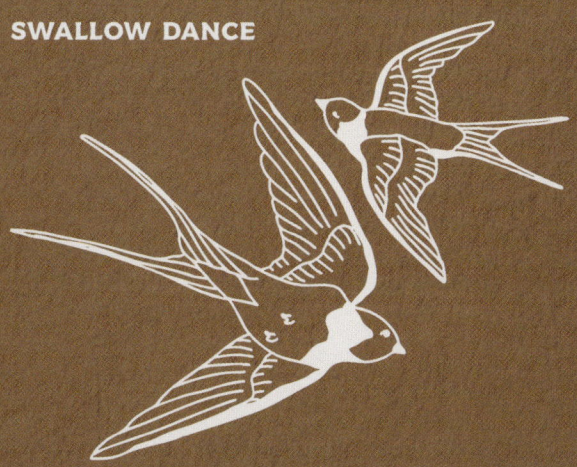

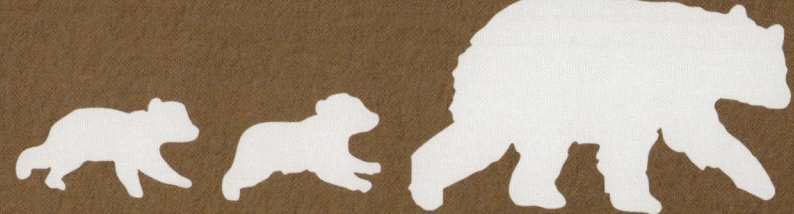

FOLLOW THE LEADER

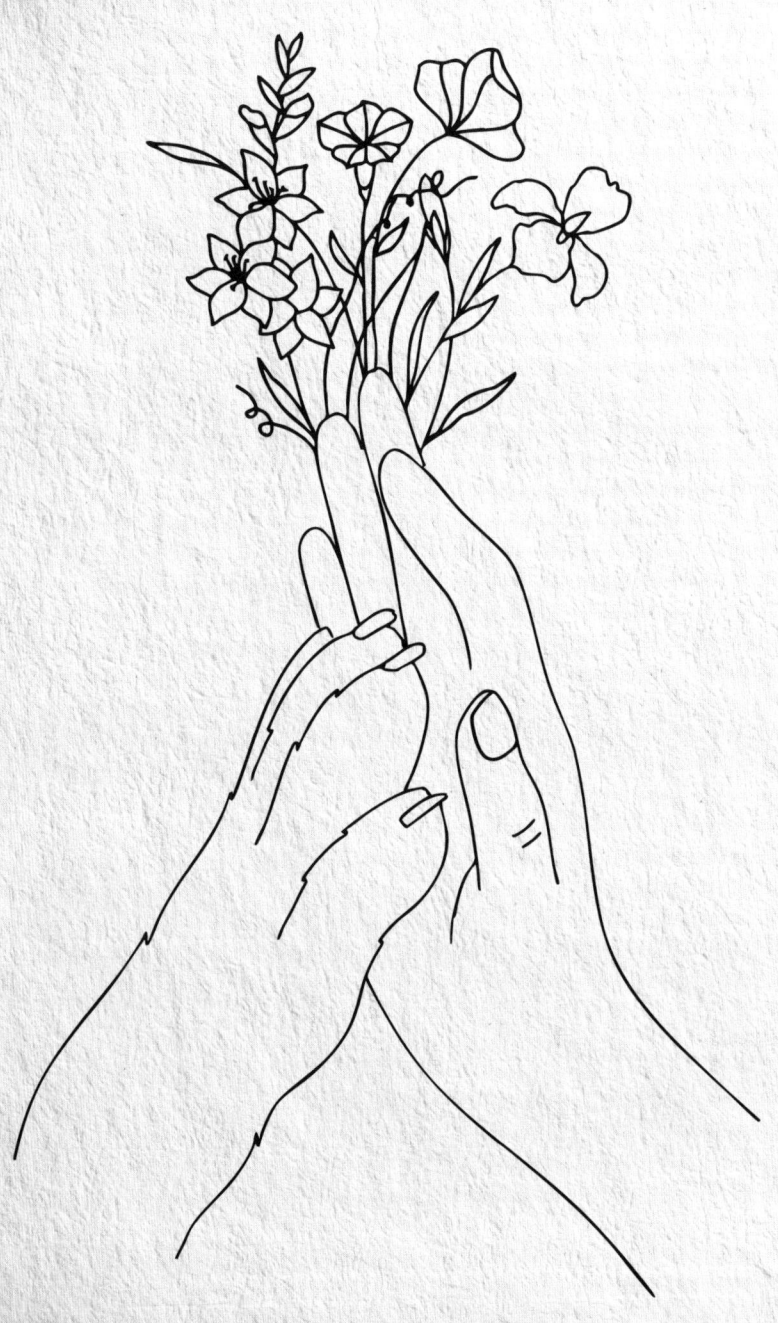

CREATURE COMFORT

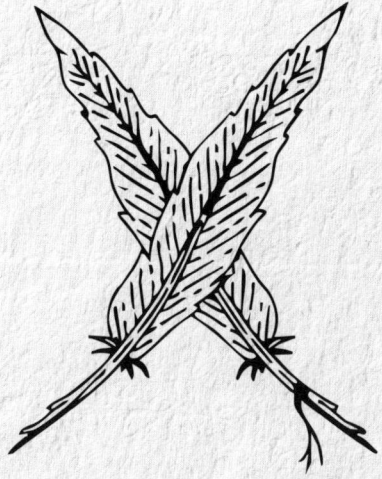

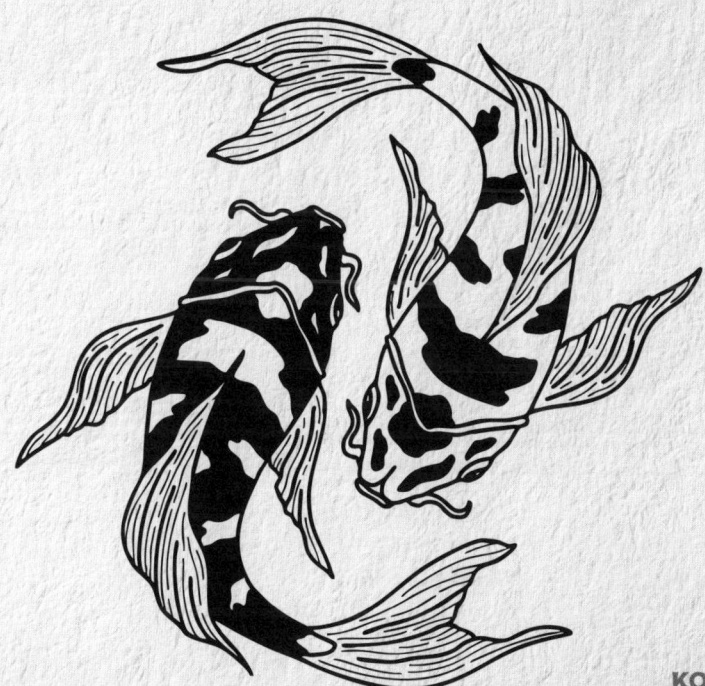

KOI CONNECTION

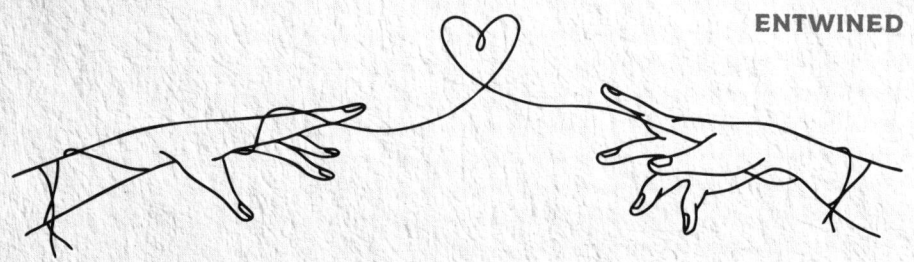

ENTWINED

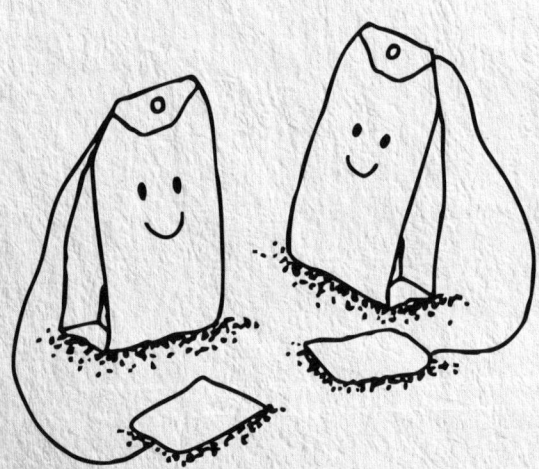

BREW CREW

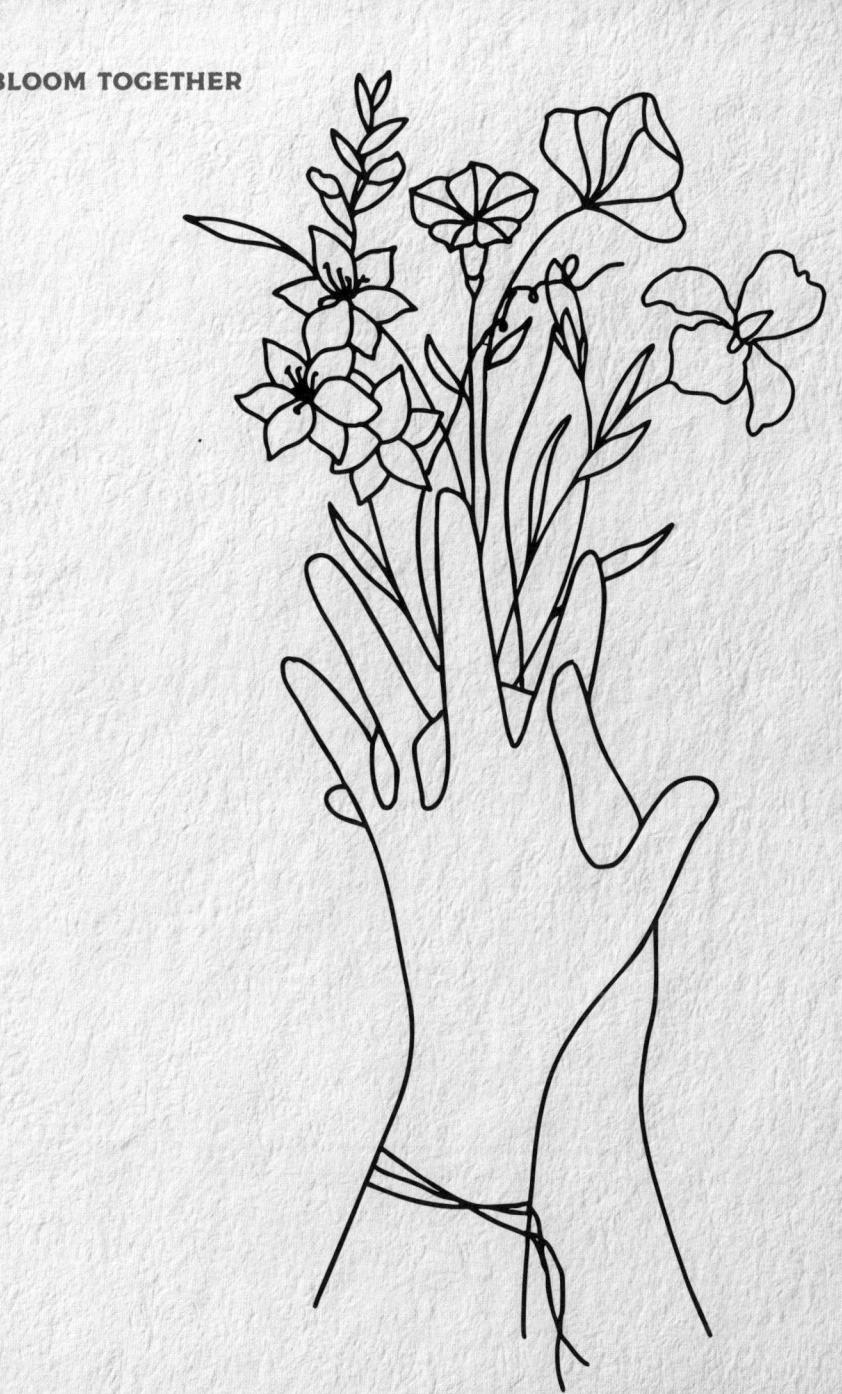

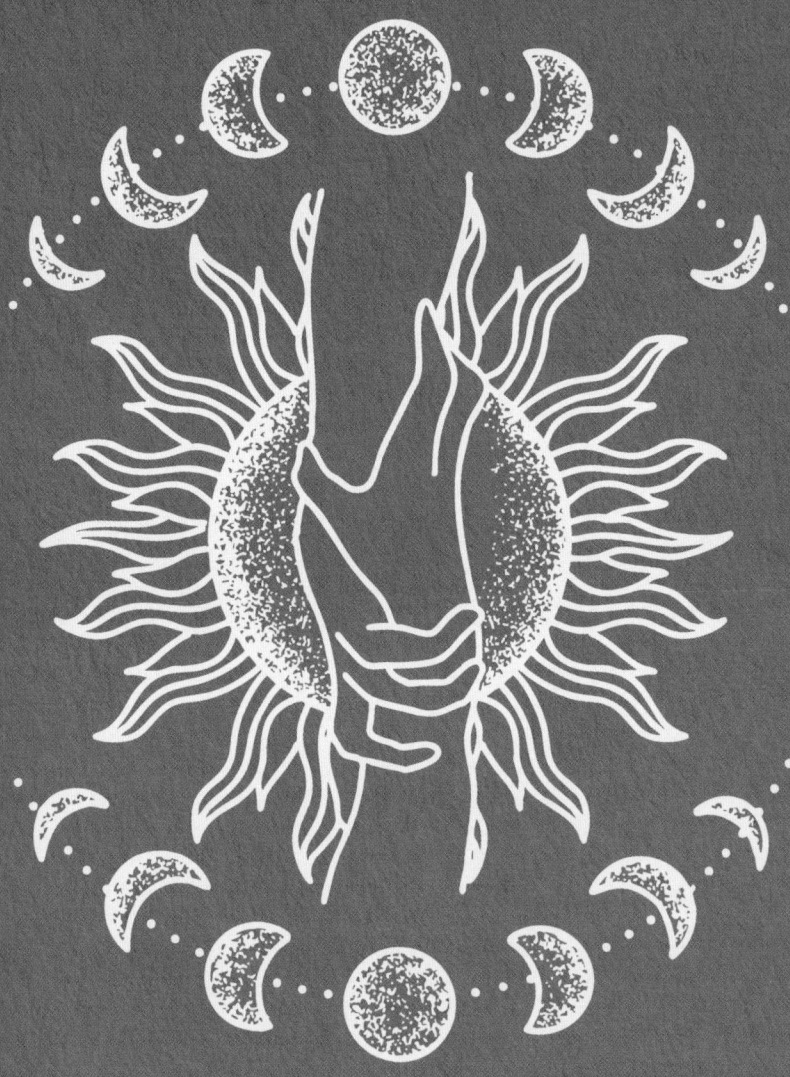

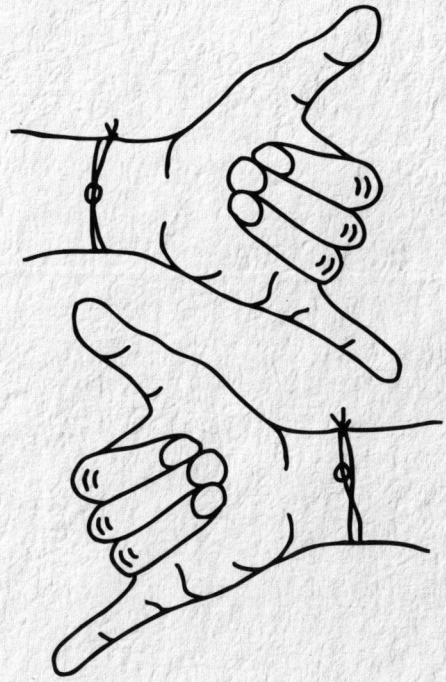

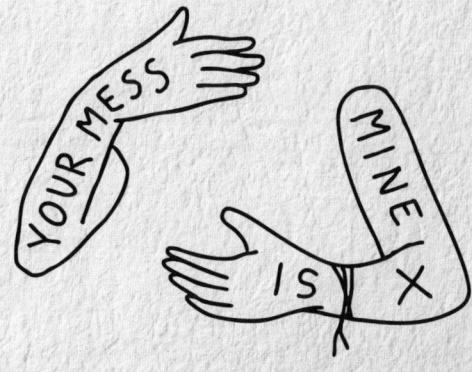

YOUR MESS IS MINE

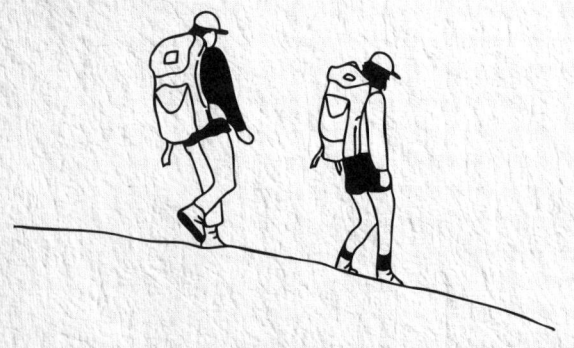

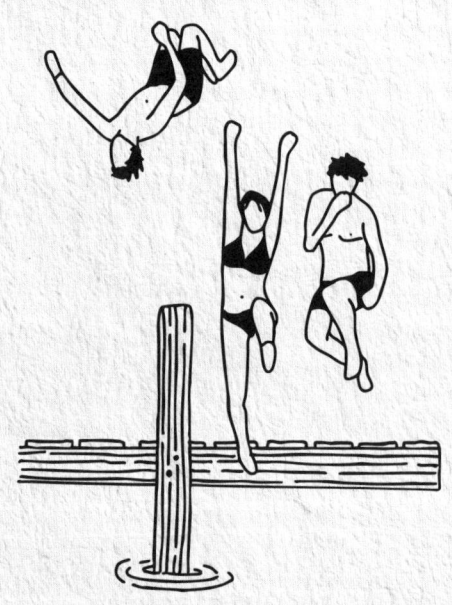

PLUNGE

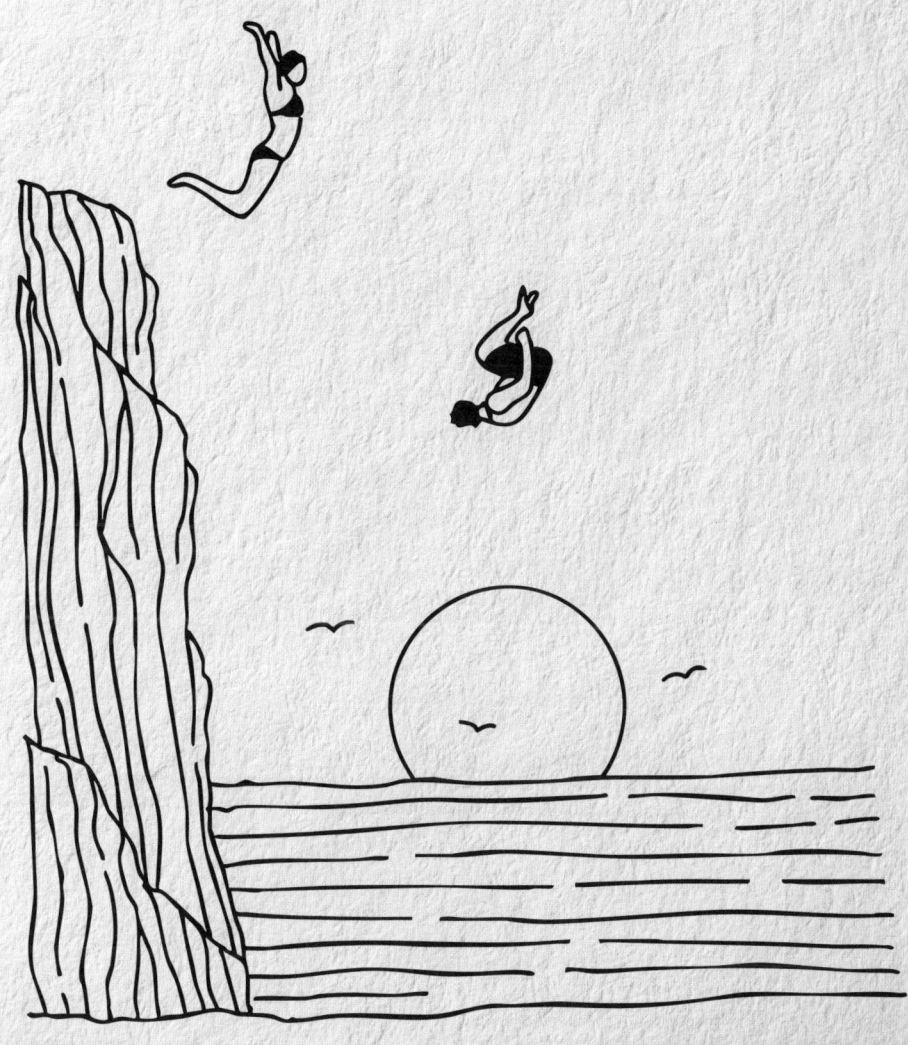

TAKE THE LEAP

Three figures jump from a mountain into still water, one waiting, one midair, one already floating. It's a moment of trust, freedom, and shared courage. A reminder that the best leaps in life are taken together, when someone beside you says, "Go on, I'm right behind you."

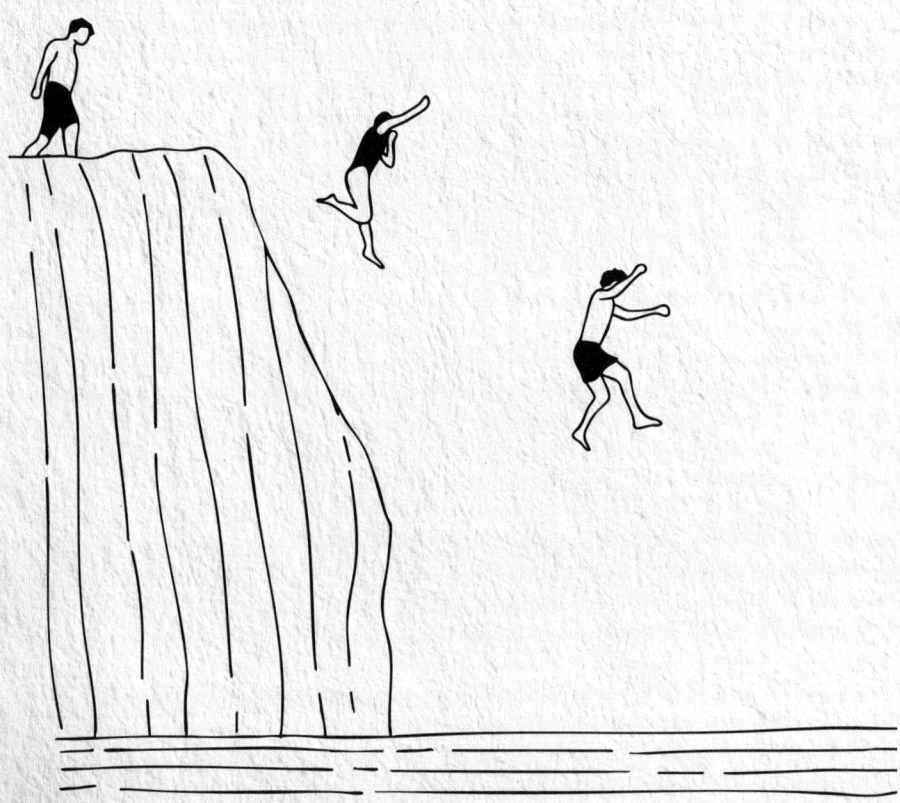

"THE HEART HAS ITS REASONS, WHICH REASON KNOWS NOTHING OF."

– BLAISE PASCAL

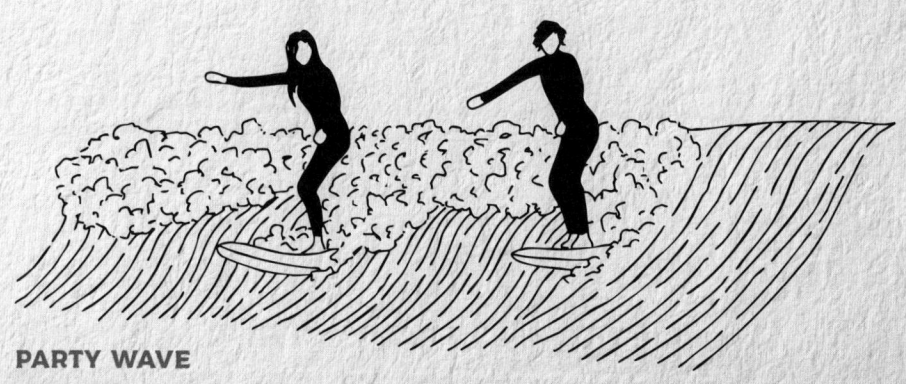

PARTY WAVE

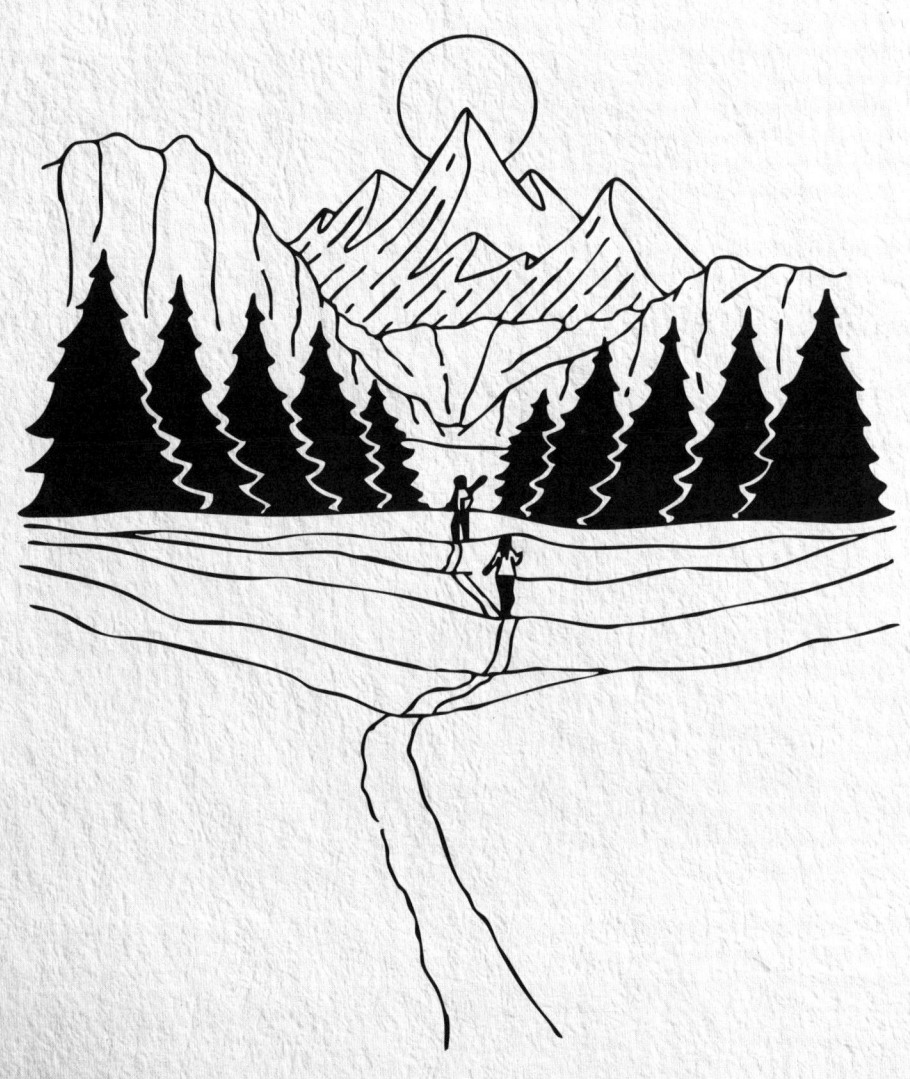

STARGAZING

Two people lie side by side, legs
outstretched, knees touching. Bare feet
against the earth, one points to the
stars as the sky opens above them. It's
quiet, simple, infinite.

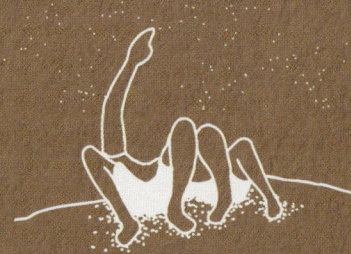

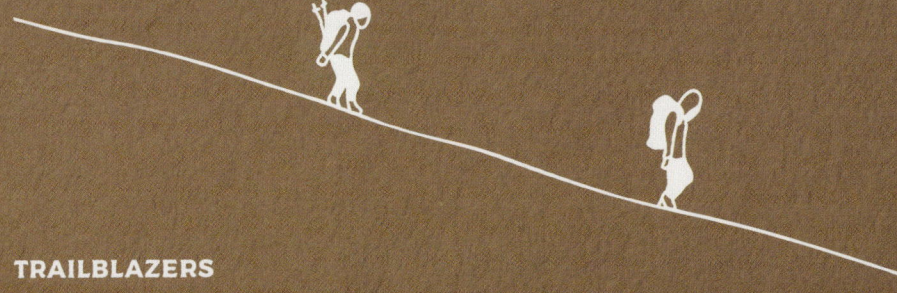

TRAILBLAZERS

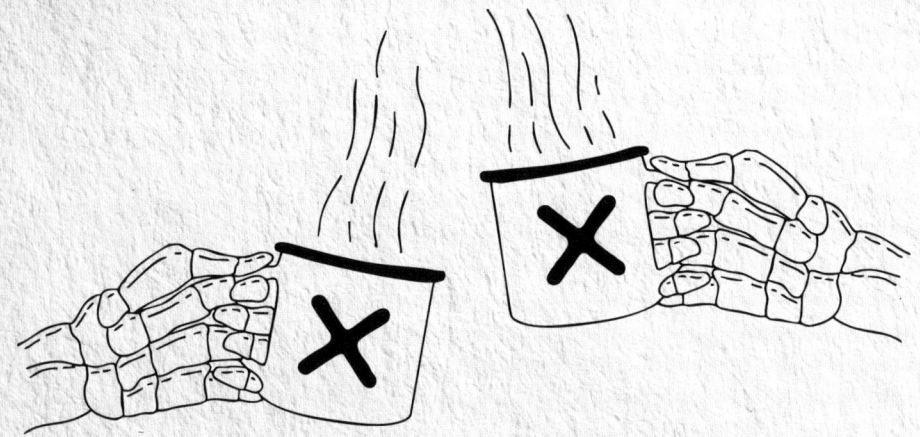

TILL THE END

Two skeletal hands lift steaming mugs marked with an X, a toast shared beyond time. It's a playful, eternal promise, warmth even in the afterlife, laughter through the bones. A reminder that loves, like coffee and connection, endure far longer than flesh and far past the final chapter.

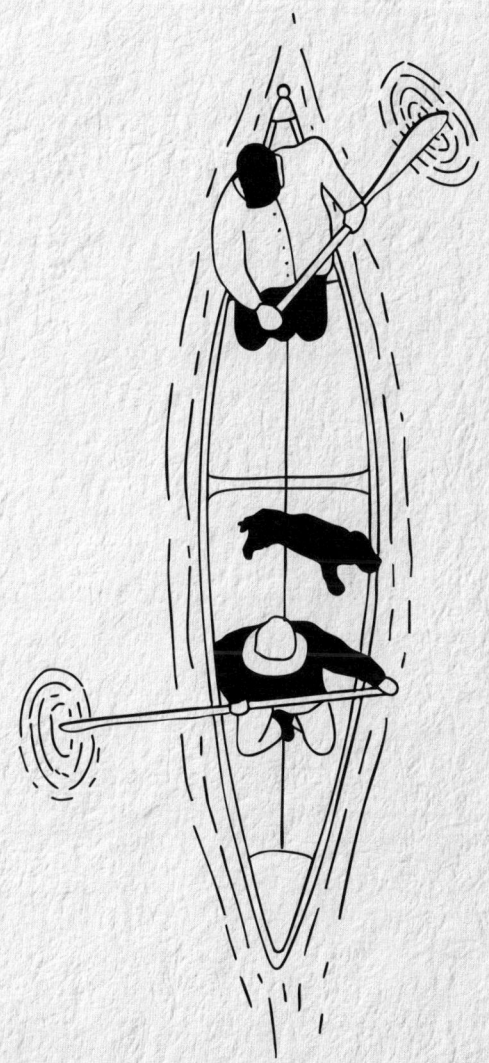

"LOVE CONQUERS ALL;
LET US, TOO, YIELD
TO LOVE."

– VIRGIL

UP THE CREEK

FINAL TRAILS
AND
REFLECTIONS

If you've made it to this page, thank you. I really appreciate the time you've taken to look at my work.

This book has been years in the making, not just in that it took a while to put it together, but in the way that it's full of so many memories and experiences, it's like my brain has been put on the page.

These designs were never intended to be collected this way; they're just little moments I recorded throughout my adventures. To see them now in this book is honestly mind-blowing, and it feels pretty special that you get to look through it.

I hope something in these pages stayed with you. Maybe a drawing reminded you of a trip, a person, or a place. Maybe it gave you an idea for your own creative project, or maybe it just made you pause and smile for a second. That's all I could ever hope for: to make something that connects, quietly and honestly.

And I hope this book has inspired you to get outside and head off on your own adventure—get on the road, hike mountains, or just walk around the park. There's so much inspiration out there. And I hope you carry a little bit of calm, wonder, and curiosity, knowing that these drawings were made with the same inspiration from the outdoors.

LET'S STAY CONNECTED

Instagram: @os.illustration

One of the best things about sharing my work is the people I get to meet along the way. If something in this book spoke to you, I'd love to hear about it.

You can find me most easily on Instagram @os.illustration. That's the best place to see more of any project or learn when new commissions, prints, T-shirts, or stickers are available.

If you want to go a step further, you can sign up to my mailing list, which has all of my updates—usually just the occasional alert when something exciting is happening. There's a link to my mailing list on my Instagram.

My shop is always open at www.osillustration.com. Supporting through the shop and its tattoo tokens helps me keep drawing, keep traveling, and keep making more of the work you see here.

If you ever feel like sharing this book with a friend, tagging me in a post, or leaving a kind word, it helps more than you know. Independent art lives and grows through people like you.

See you out there.

INDEX

ABOUT
THE
AUTHOR

Ollie Smither is a UK-based fine-line illustrator and tattoo designer whose work is inspired by the adventures he takes, experiences mainly grounded in the great outdoors.

Working under the name @os.illustration, Ollie has built a creative practice that blends traditional hand-drawn techniques with themes drawn from the natural world. From dense forests and open coastlines to mountain trails and woodland creatures, his artwork captures the feeling of being out in the wild and at peace.

Based in South Devon, Ollie spends his time between his cottage studio and the road, often traveling in his camper van with his dog, Tucker. Surfing, snowboarding, hiking, and van life all play a big role in shaping his ideas. Much of his work begins as quick sketches done on the move. These moments become the foundation for detailed illustrations that hold both simplicity and a story.

Ollie specializes in creating fine-line designs for tattoos, branding, and commissioned illustrations. His work is known for its clean, minimal aesthetic and a storytelling quality that resonates with clients around the world and helps people connect with nature.

Above all, Ollie's art is shaped by a love for honest connection: to places, people, and the natural experiences of life lived outside. Each piece is made with care, reflecting a sense of stillness, movement, and presence. Whether drawn for a personal tattoo or shared as part of a print or T-shirt collection, his designs are meant to be carried with you, to remind, to ground, and to inspire.

Ollie's growing community of followers and clients continues to support his journey as an independent artist. His hope is that through his work, others feel encouraged to slow down, get outside, and pay attention to the small details.

You can follow his work and journey on Instagram @os.illustration or explore available prints and tattoo tokens through his online shop at www.osillustration.com

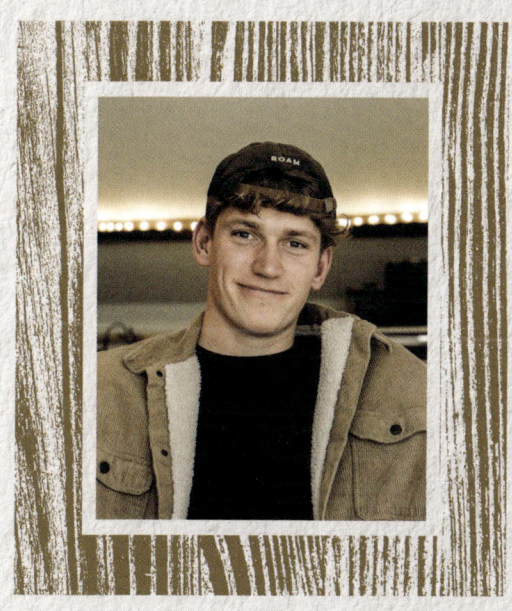

First published in 2026 by Epic Ink,
an imprint of The Quarto Group,
135 West 36th Street, 13th Floor,
New York, NY 10018, USA
(212) 779-4972
www.Quarto.com

EEA Representation, WTS Tax d.o.o.,
Žanova ulica 3, 4000 Kranj, Slovenia.
www.wts-tax.si

Epic Ink titles are also available at discount for retail, wholesale, promotional,
and bulk purchase. For details, contact the Special Sales Manager by
email at specialsales@quarto.com or by mail at The Quarto Group, Attn: Special
Sales Manager, 100 Cummings Center Suite 265D, Beverly, MA 01915 USA.

10 9 8 7 6 5 4 3 2 1

ISBN: 978-1-57715-849-3

Library of Congress Cataloging-in-Publication Data available upon request.

Group Publisher: Rage Kindelsperger
Creative Director: Laura Drew
Managing Editor: Cara Donaldson
Editor: Flannery Wiest
Interior Design: Scott Richardson
Cover Illustration: Ollie Smither

Printed in Huizhou City, Guangdong, China TT012026

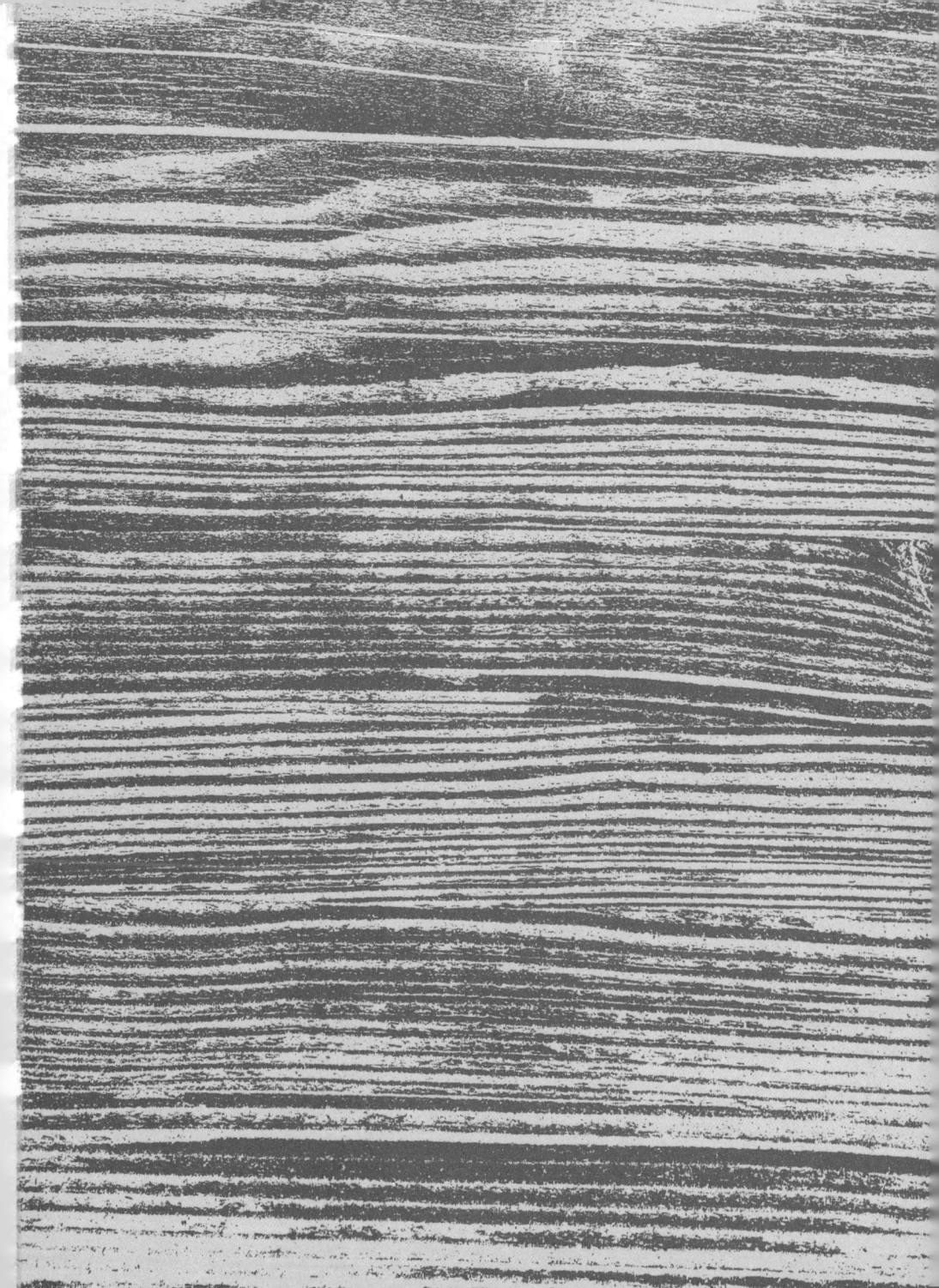